TinyML Cookbook

Combine artificial intelligence and ultra-low-power embedded devices to make the world smarter

Gian Marco Iodice

BIRMINGHAM—MUMBAI

TinyML Cookbook

Copyright © 2022 Packt Publishing

Publishing Product Manager: Devika Battike
Senior Editors: Roshan Kumar, Nathanya Dias
Content Development Editor: Tazeen Shaikh
Technical Editor: Rahul Limbachiya
Copy Editor: Safis Editing
Project Coordinator: Aparna Ravikumar Nair
Proofreader: Safis Editing
Indexer: Hemangini Bari
Production Designer: Shankar Kalbhor
Marketing Coordinator: Abeer Dawe

First published: April 2022

Production reference: 1040322

Published by Packt Publishing Ltd.
Livery Place
35 Livery Street
Birmingham
B3 2PB, UK.

ISBN 978-1-80181-497-3

www.packt.com

It is because of the source of support from my wife, Eleonora, during the long nights of writing that I managed to complete this unique journey. I dedicate this book to her, who believed in this project from the very beginning.

Foreword

Without a doubt, the tech industry continues to have an ever-increasing impact on our daily lives. The changes are as rapid as they are constant and are happening all around us – in our phones, cars, smart speakers, and the micro gadgets we use to improve efficiency, wellbeing, and connectivity. Machine learning is one of the most transformative technologies of our age. Businesses, academics, and engineering communities continue to understand, evolve, and explore the capabilities of this incredible technology, and are unlocking the greater potential to enable new use cases across many industries.

I am a product manager for machine learning at Arm. In this role, I am at the center of the ML revolution that is happening in smartphones, the automotive industry, gaming, AR, VR, and other devices. It is clear to me that there will be ML functionality in every single electronics device in the near future – from the world's largest supercomputers, down to the smallest, low-powered microcontrollers. Working in ML has introduced me to some of the most brilliant and brightest minds in tech – those who challenge the orthodoxies that exist in traditional industries, ask the tough questions, and unlock new value through the use of ML.

When I first met Gian Marco, I could barely spell "ML," yet at that time he was already a veteran in the space. I was astonished by the breadth and depth of his knowledge and his ability to solve difficult problems. Together with the team at Arm, he has worked to make **Arm Compute Library** (**ACL**) the most performant library available for ML on Arm. The success of ACL is unrivaled. It's deployed on billions of devices worldwide – from servers to flagship smartphones, to smart ovens.

When Gian Marco told me he was writing a book on ML, my immediate reaction was "Which part?" The ML ecosystem is so diverse, with many different technologies, platforms, and frameworks to consider. At the same time, I knew that he was the right person for the job due to his extensive knowledge of all aspects of ML. Additionally, Gian Marco has an amazing way of explaining things in a straightforward and logical manner.

Gian Marco's book demystifies the world of TinyML by guiding us through a series of practical, real-world examples. Each example is outlined like a recipe, with a clear and consistent format throughout, providing an easy-to-follow, step-by-step guide. Beginning with the first principles, he explains the basics of the electronics or software techniques that will be used in the recipe. The book then introduces the platforms and technologies used, followed by the ML – where neural network models are developed, trained, and deployed on the target device. This really is a "soup to nuts" guide. Each recipe is a little more challenging than the last, and there is a nice mix of established and nascent technologies. You don't just learn the "how," you also get an understanding of the "why." When it comes to edge devices, this book really does provide a panoramic view of the ML space.

Machine learning continues to disrupt all aspects of technology and getting started is a must for software developers. This book enables quick onboarding through the use of readily available and inexpensive technologies. Whether you are new to ML or have some experience, each recipe provides a steady ramp of knowledge and leaves enough scope for further self-development and experimentation. Whether you use this book as a guide or a reference, you will develop a strong foundation in ML for future development. It will empower your team to get new insights and to achieve new efficiencies, performance improvements, and even new functionality for your products.

– Ronan Naughton

Senior Product Manager for Machine Learning at Arm

Contributors

About the author

Gian Marco Iodice is team and tech lead in the Machine Learning Group at Arm, who co-created the Arm Compute Library in 2017. The Arm Compute Library is currently the most performant library for ML on Arm, and it's deployed on billions of devices worldwide – from servers to smartphones.

Gian Marco holds an MSc degree, with honors, in electronic engineering from the University of Pisa (Italy) and has several years of experience developing ML and computer vision algorithms on edge devices. Now, he's leading the ML performance optimization on Arm Mali GPUs.

In 2020, Gian Marco cofounded the TinyML UK meetup group to encourage knowledge-sharing, educate, and inspire the next generation of ML developers on tiny and power-efficient devices.

About the reviewer

Alessandro Grande is a physicist, an engineer, a community builder, and a communicator with a visceral passion for connecting and empowering humans to build more efficient and sustainable technology. Alessandro is the director of technology at Edge Impulse and cofounded TinyML meetups in the UK and in Italy. Prior to Edge Impulse, Alessandro worked at Arm as a developer evangelist and ecosystem manager with a focus on IoT and ML. While at Arm, Alessandro launched a weekly live stream – Innovation Coffee – with his colleague Robert Wolff. He holds a master's degree in nuclear and electronic physics from the University of Rome, La Sapienza.

Daksh Trehan began his career as a data analyst. His love for data and statistics is unimaginable. Various statistical techniques introduced him to the world of ML and data science. While his focus is on being a data analyst, he loves to forecast given data using ML techniques. He understands the power of data in today's world and constantly tries to change the world using various ML techniques and his concrete data visualization skills. He loves to write articles on ML and AI, and these have bagged him more than 100,000 views to date. He has also contributed as an ML consultant to 365 Days as a TikTok creator, written by Dr. Markus Rach, available publicly on the Amazon e-book store.

Table of Contents

3

Building a Weather Station with TensorFlow Lite for Microcontrollers

4

Voice Controlling LEDs with Edge Impulse

5

Indoor Scene Classification with TensorFlow Lite for Microcontrollers and the Arduino Nano

6

Building a Gesture-Based Interface for YouTube Playback

7

Running a Tiny CIFAR-10 Model on a Virtual Platform with the Zephyr OS

8

Toward the Next TinyML Generation with microNPU

Index

Other Books You May Enjoy

Preface

This book is about TinyML, a fast-growing field at the unique intersection of **machine learning** (**ML**) and embedded systems to make AI work with extremely low-powered devices, such as microcontrollers.

TinyML is an exciting field full of opportunities. With a small budget, we can give life to objects that interact with the world around us smartly and transform the way we live for the better. However, this field can be hard to approach if we come from an ML background with little familiarity with embedded systems, such as microcontrollers. Therefore, this book aims to dispel these barriers and make TinyML also accessible to developers with no embedded programming experience through practical examples. Each chapter will be a self-contained project to learn how to use some of the technologies at the heart of TinyML, interface with electronic components such as sensors, and deploy ML models on memory-constrained devices.

TinyML Cookbook starts with a practical introduction to this multidisciplinary field to get you up to speed with some of the fundamentals for deploying intelligent applications on Arduino Nano 33 BLE Sense and Raspberry Pi Pico. As you progress, you'll tackle various problems that you may encounter while prototyping microcontrollers, such as controlling the LED state with GPIO and a push-button and supplying power to microcontrollers with batteries. After that, you'll cover recipes relating to temperature, humidity, and the **three V** (**voice**, **vision**, and **vibration**) sensors to gain the necessary skills to implement end-to-end smart applications in different scenarios. Then, you'll learn best practices to build tiny models for memory-constrained microcontrollers. Finally, you'll explore two of the most recent technologies, microTVM and microNPU, which will help you step up your TinyML game.

By the end of this book, you'll be well versed in best practices and ML frameworks to develop ML apps easily on microcontrollers and have a clear understanding of the key aspects to consider during the development phase.

Who this book is for

This book is for ML developers/engineers interested in developing ML applications on microcontrollers through practical examples quickly. The book will help you expand your knowledge of the revolution of TinyML by building end-to-end smart projects with real-world data sensors on the Arduino Nano 33 BLE Sense and the Raspberry Pi Pico. Basic familiarity with C/C++, Python programming, and a **command-line interface** (**CLI**) is required. However, no prior knowledge of microcontrollers is necessary.

What this book covers

Chapter 1, Getting Started with TinyML, provides an overview of TinyML, presenting the opportunities and challenges to bring ML on extremely low-power microcontrollers. This chapter focuses on the fundamental elements behind ML, power consumption, and microcontrollers that make TinyML unique and different from conventional ML in the cloud, desktop, or even smartphones.

Chapter 2, Prototyping with Microcontrollers, presents concise and straightforward recipes to deal with the relevant microcontroller programming basics. We will deal with code debugging and how to transmit data to the Arduino serial monitor. After that, we will discover how to program GPIO peripherals with the ARM Mbed API and use the breadboard to connect external components, such as LEDs and push-buttons. In the end, we will see how to power the Arduino Nano 33 BLE Sense and the Raspberry Pi Pico with batteries.

Chapter 3, Building a Weather Station with TensorFlow Lite for Microcontrollers, guides you through all the development stages of a TensorFlow-based application for microcontrollers and teaches you how to acquire temperature and humidity sensor data. The application developed in the chapter is an ML-based weather station for snow forecasts.

In the first part, we will focus on dataset preparation by acquiring historical weather data from WorldWeatherOnline. After that, we will present the relevant basics to train and test a model with TensorFlow. In the end, we will deploy the model on the Arduino Nano 33 BLE Sense and the Raspberry Pi Pico with TensorFlow Lite for Microcontrollers.

Chapter 4, Voice Controlling LEDs with Edge Impulse, shows how to develop an end-to-end **keyword spotting** (**KWS**) application with Edge Impulse and get familiar with audio data acquisition and **analog-to-digital** (**ADC**) peripherals. The application considered for this chapter voice controls the LED emitting color (red, green, and blue) and the number of times to make it blink (one, two, and three).

In the first part, we will focus on the dataset preparation, showing how to acquire audio data with a mobile phone. After that, we will design a model using the **mel-frequency cepstral coefficient** (**MFCC**) features and optimize the performance with EON Tuner. In the end, we will finalize the KWS application on the Arduino Nano 33 BLE Sense and the Raspberry Pi Pico.

Chapter 5, Indoor Scene Classification with TensorFlow Lite for Microcontrollers and the Arduino Nano, aims to show you how to apply transfer learning with TensorFlow and get familiar with the best practices to use a camera module with a microcontroller. For the purpose of this chapter, we will develop an application to recognize indoor environments with the Arduino Nano 33 BLE Sense and the OV7670 camera module.

In the first part, we will see how to acquire images from the OV7670 camera module. After that, we will focus on the model design, applying transfer learning with Keras to recognize kitchen and bathroom rooms. In the end, we will deploy the quantized TensorFlow Lite model on the Arduino Nano 33 BLE Sense with the help of TensorFlow Lite for Microcontrollers.

Chapter 6, Building a Gesture-Based Interface for YouTube Playback, aims to develop an end-to-end gesture recognition application with Edge Impulse and the Raspberry Pi Pico to get acquainted with inertial sensors, teach you how to use I2C peripherals, and write a multithreading application in Arm Mbed OS.

In the first part, we will collect the accelerometer data through the Edge Impulse data forwarder to prepare the dataset. After that, we will design a model using features in the frequency domain to recognize three gestures. In the end, we will deploy the application on the Raspberry Pi Pico and implement a Python program with the PyAutoGUI library to build a touchless interface for YouTube video playback.

Chapter 7, Running a Tiny CIFAR-10 Model on a Virtual Platform with the Zephyr OS, provides best practices to build tiny models for memory-constrained microcontrollers. In this chapter, we will be designing a model for the CIFAR-10 image classification dataset on a virtual Arm Cortex-M3-based microcontroller.

In the first part, we will install Zephyr, the primary framework used in this chapter to accomplish our task. After that, we will design a tiny quantized CIFAR-10 model with TensorFlow. This model will fit on a microcontroller with only 256 KB of program memory and 64 KB of RAM. In the end, we will build an image classification application with TensorFlow Lite for Microcontrollers and the Zephyr OS and run it on a virtual platform using **Quick Emulator** (**QEMU**).

Chapter 8, Toward the Next TinyML Generation with microNPU, helps familiarize you with microNPU, a new class of processors for ML workloads on edge devices. In this chapter, we will be running a quantized CIFAR-10 model on a virtual Arm Ethos-U55 microNPU with the help of TVM.

In the first part, we will learn how the Arm Ethos-U55 microNPU works and install the software dependencies to build and run the model on the Arm Corstone-300 fixed virtual platform. After that, we will use the TVM compiler to convert a pretrained TensorFlow Lite model to C code. In the end, we will show how to compile and deploy the code generated by TVM into Arm Corstone-300 to perform inference with the Arm Ethos-U55 microNPU.

To get the most out of this book

You will need a computer (either a laptop or desktop) with an x86-64 architecture and at least one USB port for programming the Arduino Nano 33 BLE Sense and the Raspberry Pi Pico microcontroller boards. For the first six chapters, you can use Ubuntu 18.04 (or later) or Windows (for example, Windows 10) as an OS. However, you will need Ubuntu 18.04 (or later) for *Chapter 7, Running a Tiny CIFAR-10 Model on a Virtual Platform with the Zephyr OS*, and *Chapter 8, Toward the Next TinyML Generation with microNPU*.

The only software prerequisites for your computer are:

- Python (Python 3.7 recommended)

- Text editor (for example, gedit on Ubuntu)

- Media player (for example, VLC)

- Image viewer (for example, the default app in Ubuntu or Windows 10)

- Web browser (for example, Google Chrome)

During our TinyML journey, we will require different software tools to cover ML development and embedded programming. Thanks to Arduino, Edge Impulse, and Google, these tools will be in the cloud, browser-based, and with a free plan for our usage.

Arduino Nano 33 BLE Sense and Raspberry Pi Pico programs will be developed directly in the web browser with the Arduino Web Editor (`https://create.arduino.cc`). However, the Arduino Web Editor has a limit of 200 seconds of compilation time per day. Therefore, you may consider upgrading to any paid plan or using the free local Arduino IDE (`https://www.arduino.cc/en/software`) to get unlimited compilation time. If you are interested in the free local Arduino IDE, we have provided on GitHub (`https://github.com/PacktPublishing/TinyML-Cookbook/blob/main/Docs/setup_local_arduino_ide.md`) the instructions to set it up.

The following table summarizes the hardware devices and software tools covered in each chapter:

Chapter	Hardware devices	Software tools
1	Arduino Nano 33 BLE Sense Raspberry Pi Pico	Arduino Web Editor
2	Arduino Nano 33 BLE Sense Raspberry Pi Pico	Arduino Web Editor, Google Colaboratory
3	Arduino Nano 33 BLE Sense Raspberry Pi Pico	Arduino Web Editor, Google Colaboratory
4	Arduino Nano 33 BLE Sense Raspberry Pi Pico	Arduino Web Editor, Edge Impulse Python 3.6 (local)
5	Arduino Nano 33 BLE Sense	Arduino Web Editor, Google Colaboratory, Python 3.6 (local)
6	Raspberry Pi Pico	Arduino Web Editor, Edge Impulse Python 3.6 (local)
7	Virtual platform	Google Colaboratory, Python 3.6 (local), Zephyr SDK
8	Virtual platform	Arm Corstone-300, Python 3.6 (local), TVM/microTVM

The projects may require sensors and additional electronic components to build realistic TinyML prototypes and experience the complete development workflow. All the components are listed at the beginning of each chapter and in the README.md file on GitHub (https://github.com/PacktPublishing/TinyML-Cookbook). Since you will build real electronic circuits, we require an electronic components kit that includes at least a solderless breadboard, colored LEDs, resistors, push-buttons, and jumper wires. Don't worry if you are an electronics beginner. You will learn more about these components in the first two chapters of this book. Furthermore, we have prepared a beginner shopping list on GitHub so you know precisely what to buy: https://github.com/PacktPublishing/TinyML-Cookbook/blob/main/Docs/shopping_list.md.

If you are using the digital version of this book, we advise you to type the code yourself or access the code via the GitHub repository (link available in the next section). Doing so will help you avoid any potential errors related to the copying and pasting of code.

Download the example code files

You can download the example code files for this book from GitHub at `https://github.com/PacktPublishing/TinyML-Cookbook`. In case there's an update to the code, it will be updated on the existing GitHub repository.

We also have other code bundles from our rich catalog of books and videos available at `https://github.com/PacktPublishing/`. Check them out!

Download the color images

We also provide a PDF file that has color images of the screenshots/diagrams used in this book. You can download it here: `https://static.packt-cdn.com/downloads/9781801814973_ColorImages.pdf`.

Conventions used

There are a number of text conventions used throughout this book.

`Code in text`: Indicates code words in text, database table names, folder names, filenames, file extensions, pathnames, dummy URLs, user input, and Twitter handles. Here is an example: "Enter the `~/project_npu` folder and create three folders, named `binaries`, `src`, and `sw_libs`."

A block of code is set as follows:

```
export PATH=~/project_npu/binaries/FVP_Corstone_SSE-300/models/
Linux64_GCC-6.4:$PATH
```

When we wish to draw your attention to a particular part of a code block, the relevant lines or items are set in bold:

```
[default]
exten => s,1,Dial(Zap/1|30)
exten => s,2,Voicemail(u100)
exten => s,102,Voicemail(b100)
exten => i,1,Voicemail(s0)
```

Any command-line input or output is written as follows:

```
$ cd ~/project_npu
$ mkdir binaries
$ mkdir src
```

Bold: Indicates a new term, an important word, or words that you see onscreen. For example, words in menus or dialog boxes appear in the text like this. Here is an example: "Click on **Corstone-300 Ecosystem FVPs** and then click on the **Download Linux** button."

> **Tips or Important Notes**
> Appear like this.

Sections

In this book, you will find several headings that appear frequently (*Getting ready*, *How to do it...*, and *There's more...*).

To give clear instructions on how to complete a recipe, use these sections as follows:

Getting ready

This section tells you what to expect in the recipe and describes how to set up any software or any preliminary settings required for the recipe.

How to do it...

This section contains the steps required to follow the recipe.

There's more...

This section consists of additional information about the recipe in order to make you more knowledgeable about the recipe.

Get in touch

Feedback from our readers is always welcome.

General feedback: If you have questions about any aspect of this book, mention the book title in the subject of your message and email us at customercare@packtpub.com.

Errata: Although we have taken every care to ensure the accuracy of our content, mistakes do happen. If you have found a mistake in this book, we would be grateful if you would report this to us. Please visit www.packtpub.com/support/errata, selecting your book, clicking on the Errata Submission Form link, and entering the details.

Piracy: If you come across any illegal copies of our works in any form on the Internet, we would be grateful if you would provide us with the location address or website name. Please contact us at copyright@packt.com with a link to the material.

If you are interested in becoming an author: If there is a topic that you have expertise in and you are interested in either writing or contributing to a book, please visit authors.packtpub.com.

Share Your Thoughts

Once you've read *TinyML Cookbook*, we'd love to hear your thoughts! Please click here to go straight to the Amazon review page for this book and share your feedback.

Your review is important to us and the tech community and will help us make sure we're delivering excellent quality content.

1
Getting Started with TinyML

Here we are, with our first step into the world of **TinyML**.

This chapter starts with an overview of this emerging field, presenting the opportunities and challenges to bring **machine learning** (**ML**) to extremely low-power **microcontrollers**.

The body of this chapter focuses on the fundamental elements behind ML, power consumption, and microcontrollers that make TinyML unique and different from conventional ML in the cloud, desktops, or even smartphones. In particular, the *Programming microcontrollers* section will be crucial for those with little experience in embedded programming.

After introducing the TinyML building blocks, we shall set up the development environment for a simple LED application, which will officially mark the beginning of our practical TinyML journey.

In contrast to what we will find in the following chapters, this chapter has a more theoretical structure to get you familiar with the concepts and terminology of this fast-growing technology.

In this chapter, we're going to cover the following topics:

- Introducing TinyML
- Summary of deep learning
- Learning the difference between power and energy
- Programming microcontrollers
- Presenting Arduino Nano 33 BLE Sense and Raspberry Pi Pico
- Setting up Arduino Web Editor, TensorFlow, and Edge Impulse
- Running a sketch on Arduino Nano and Raspberry Pi Pico

Technical requirements

To complete the practical example in this chapter, we need the following:

- Arduino Nano 33 BLE Sense board
- Raspberry Pi Pico board
- Micro-USB cable
- Laptop/PC with either Ubuntu 18.04 or Windows 10 on x86-64

Introducing TinyML

Throughout all the recipes presented in this book, we will give practical solutions for **tiny machine learning**, or, as we will refer to it, **TinyML**. In this section, we will learn what TinyML is and the vast opportunities it brings.

What is TinyML?

TinyML is the set of technologies in ML and embedded systems to make use of smart applications on extremely low-power devices. Generally, these devices have limited memory and computational capabilities, but they can *sense* the physical environment through sensors and act based on the decisions taken by ML algorithms.

In TinyML, ML and the deployment platform are not just two independent entities but rather entities that need to know each other at best. In fact, designing an ML architecture without considering the target device characteristics will make it challenging to deploy effective and working TinyML applications.

On the other hand, it would be impossible to design power-efficient processors to expand the ML capabilities of these devices without knowing the software algorithms involved.

This book will consider microcontrollers as the target device for TinyML, and the following subsection will help motivate our choice.

Why ML on microcontrollers?

The first and foremost reason for choosing microcontrollers is their *popularity* in various fields, such as automotive, consumer electronics, kitchen appliances, healthcare, and telecommunications. Nowadays, microcontrollers are everywhere and also invisible in our day-to-day electronic devices.

With the rise of the **internet of things** (**IoT**), microcontrollers saw exponential market growth. In 2018, the market research company IDC (`https://www.idc.com`) reported 28.1 billion microcontrollers sold worldwide and forecasted growth to 38.2 billion by 2023 (`www.arm.com/blogs/blueprint/tinyML`). Those are impressive numbers considering that the smartphone and PC markets reported 1.5 billion and 67.2 million devices, respectively, sold in the same year.

Therefore, TinyML represents a significant step forward for IoT devices, driving the proliferation of tiny connected objects capable of performing ML tasks locally.

The second reason for choosing microcontrollers is that they are inexpensive, easy to program and are powerful enough to run sophisticated **deep learning** (**DL**) algorithms.

However, why can't we offload the computation to the cloud since it is much more performant? In other words, why do we need to run ML locally?

Why run ML locally?

There are three main answers to this question – latency, power consumption, and privacy:

- *Reducing latency:* Sending data back and forth to and from the cloud is not instant and could affect applications that must respond reliably within a time frame.

- *Reducing power consumption:* Sending and receiving data to and from the cloud is not power-efficient even when using low-power communication protocols such as Bluetooth.

In the following stacked bar chart, we report the power consumption breakdown for the onboard components on the Arduino Nano 33 BLE Sense board, one of the two microcontroller boards employed in this book:

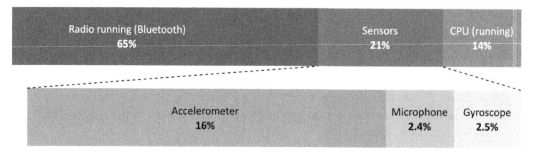

Figure 1.1 – Power consumption breakdown for the Arduino Nano 33 BLE Sense board

As we can see from the power consumption breakdown, the CPU computation is more power-efficient than Bluetooth communication (14% versus 65%), so it is preferable to compute more and transmit less to reduce the risk of rapid battery drain. Generally, radio is the component that consumes the most energy in typical embedded devices.

- *Privacy:* Local ML means preserving user privacy and avoiding sharing sensitive information.

Now that we know the benefits of running ML on these tiny devices, what are the practical opportunities and challenges of bringing ML to the very edge?

The opportunities and challenges for TinyML

TinyML finds its natural home wherever a power supply from the mains is impossible or complex to have, and the application must operate with a battery for as long as possible.

If we think about it, we are already surrounded by battery-powered devices that use ML under the hood. For example, wearable devices, such as smartwatches and fitness tracking bands, can recognize human activities to track our health goals or detect dangerous situations, such as a fall to the ground.

These everyday objects are TinyML applications for all intents and purposes because they are battery-powered and need on-device ML to give meaning to the data acquired by the sensors.

However, battery-powered solutions are not limited to wearable devices only. There are scenarios where we might need devices to monitor environments. For example, we may consider deploying battery-powered devices running ML in a forest to detect fires and prevent fires from spreading over a large area.

There are unlimited potential use cases for TinyML, and the ones we just briefly introduced are only a few of the likely application domains.

However, along with the opportunities, there are some critical challenges to face. The challenges are from the computational perspective because our devices are limited in memory and processing power. We work on systems with a few kilobytes of RAM and, in some cases, processors with no floating-point arithmetic acceleration.

On the other hand, the deployment environment could be unfriendly. Environmental factors, such as dust and extreme weather conditions, could get in the way and influence the correct execution of our applications.

In the following subsection, we will present the typical deployment environments for TinyML.

Deployment environments for TinyML

A TinyML application could live in both **centralized** and **distributed** systems.

In a **centralized** system, the application does not necessarily require communication with other devices.

A typical example is **keyword spotting**. Nowadays, we interact with our smartphones, cameras, drones, and kitchen appliances seamlessly with our voices. The magic words *OK Google*, *Alexa*, and so on that we use to wake up our smart assistants are a classic example of an ML model constantly running locally in the background. The application requires running on a low-power system without sending data to the cloud to be effective, instantly, and minimize power consumption.

Usually, centralized TinyML applications aim to trigger more power-hungry functionalities and benefit from being private by nature since they do not need to send any data to the cloud.

In a **distributed** system, the device (that is, the **node** or **sensor node**) still performs ML locally but also communicates with nearby devices or a host to achieve a common goal, as shown in the following figure:

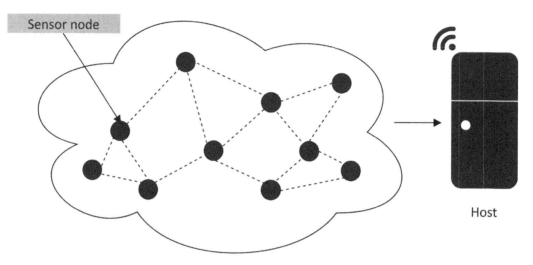

Figure 1.2 – Wireless sensor network

> **Important Note**
> Since the nodes are part of a network and typically communicate through wireless technologies, we commonly call the network a **wireless sensor network (WSN)**.

Although this scenario could be contrasted with the power consumption implications of transmitting data, the devices may need to cooperate to build meaningful and precise knowledge about the working environment. Knowing the temperature, humidity, soil moisture, or other physical quantities from a specific node could be irrelevant for some applications that need a global understanding of the diffusion of those quantities instead.

For example, consider an application to improve agriculture efficiency. In this case, a WSN might help identify what areas of the field require less or more water than others and make the irrigation more efficient and autonomous. As we can imagine, efficient communication protocols will be vital for the network lifetime, and also TinyML plays a role in achieving this goal. Since sending raw data consumes too much energy, ML could perform a partial computation to reduce the data to transmit and the frequency

of communications.

TinyML offers endless possibilities, and **tinyML Foundation** is the best place to find out the endless opportunities given by this fast-growing field of ML and embedded systems.

tinyML Foundation

tinyML Foundation (`www.tinyml.org`) is a non-profit professional organization supporting and connecting the TinyML world.

To do this, tinyML Foundation, supported by several companies, including Arm, Edge Impulse, Google, and Qualcomm, is growing a diverse community worldwide (such as the US, UK, Germany, Italy, Nigeria, India, Japan, Australia, Chile, and Singapore) between hardware, software, system engineers, scientists, designers, product managers, and businesspeople.

The foundation has been promoting different free initiatives online and in-person to engage experts and newcomers to encourage knowledge sharing, connect, and create a healthier and more sustainable world with TinyML.

Tip

With several Meetup (`https://www.meetup.com`) groups in different countries, you can join a TinyML one near you for free (`https://www.meetup.com/en-AU/pro/TinyML/`) to always be up to date with new TinyML technologies and upcoming events.

After introducing TinyML, it is now time to explore its ingredients in more detail. The following section will analyze the one that makes our devices capable of intelligent decisions: DL.

Summary of DL

ML is the ingredient to make our tiny devices capable of making intelligent decisions. These software algorithms heavily rely on the right data to learn patterns or actions based on experience. As we commonly say, data is everything for ML because it is what makes or breaks an application.

This book will refer to DL as a specific class of ML that can perform complex classification tasks directly on raw images, text, or sound. These algorithms have state-of-the-art accuracy and could also be better than humans in some classification problems. This technology makes voice-controlled virtual assistants, facial recognition systems, and autonomous driving possible, just to name a few.

A complete discussion of DL architectures and algorithms is beyond the scope of this book. However, this section will summarize some of its essential points that are relevant to understand the following chapters.

Deep neural networks

A deep neural network consists of several stacked layers aimed at learning patterns.

Each layer contains several **neurons**, the fundamental compute elements for **artificial neural networks (ANNs)** inspired by the human brain.

A neuron produces a single output through a linear transformation, defined as the weighted sum of the inputs plus a constant value called **bias**, as shown in the following diagram:

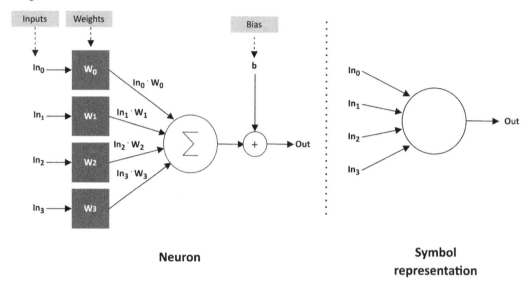

Figure 1.3 – Neuron representation

The coefficients of the weighted sum are called **weights**.

Weights and bias are obtained after an iterative training process to make the neuron capable of learning complex patterns.

However, neurons can only solve simple linear problems with linear transformations. Therefore, non-linear functions, called **activations**, generally follow the neuron's output to help the network learn complex patterns. Activation is a non-linear function performed on the neuron's output:

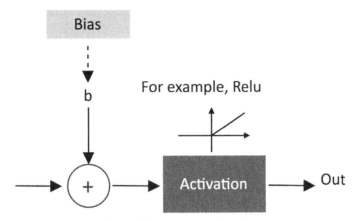

Figure 1.4 – Activation function

A widespread adopted activation function is the **rectified linear unit (ReLU)**, described in the following code block:

```
float relu(float input) {
    return max(input, 0);
}
```

Its computational simplicity makes it preferable to other non-linear functions, such as a hyperbolic tangent or logistic sigmoid, that require more computational resources.

In the following subsection, we will see how the neurons are connected to solve complex visual recognition tasks.

Convolutional neural networks

Convolutional neural networks (CNNs) are specialized deep neural networks predominantly applied to visual recognition tasks.

We can consider CNNs as the evolution of a regularized version of the classic **fully connected neural networks** with **dense layers** (that is, **fully connected layers**).

As we can see in the following diagram, a characteristic of fully connected networks is connecting every neuron to all the output neurons of the previous layer:

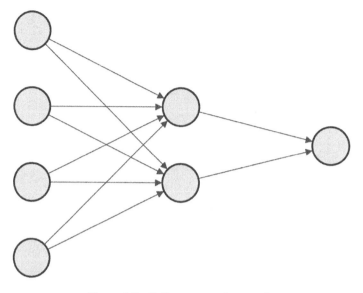

Figure 1.5 – Fully connected network

Unfortunately, this approach does not work well for training a model for image classification.

For instance, if we considered an RGB image of size 320x240 (width x height), we would need 230,400 (320*240*3) weights for just one neuron. Since our layers will undoubtedly need several neurons to discern complex problems, the model will likely **overfit** given the unmanageable number of trainable parameters.

In the past, data scientists adopted *feature engineering techniques* to extract a reduced set of good features from images. However, the approach suffered from being difficult to perform feature selection, which was time-consuming, and domain-specific.

With the rise of CNNs, visual recognition tasks saw improvement thanks to **convolution layers** that make feature extraction part of the learning problem.

Based on the assumption that we are dealing with images, and inspired by biological processes in the animal visual cortex, the convolution layer borrows the widely adopted convolution operator from image processing to create a set of learnable features.

The convolution operator is executed similarly to other image processing routines: sliding a window application (filter or kernel) on the entire input image and applying the dot product between its weights and the underlying pixels, as shown in the following figure:

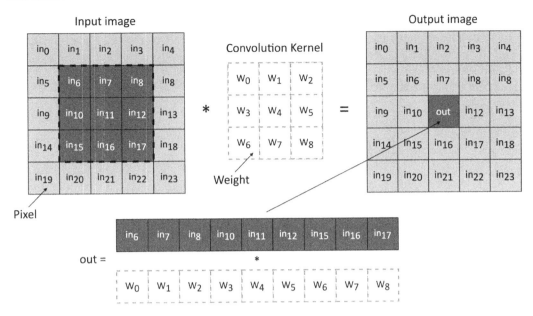

Figure 1.6 – Convolution operator

This approach brings two significant benefits:

- It extracts the relevant features automatically without human intervention.

- It reduces the number of input signals per neuron considerably.

For instance, applying a 3x3 filter on the preceding RGB image would only require 27 weights (3*3*3).

Like fully connected layers, convolution layers need several convolution kernels to learn as many features as possible. Therefore, the convolution layer's output generally produces a set of images (**feature maps**), commonly kept in a multidimensional memory object called a **tensor**.

When designing CNNs for visual recognition tasks, we usually place the fully connected layers at the network's end to carry out the prediction stage. Since the output of the convolution layers is a set of images, typically, we adopt subsampling strategies to reduce the information propagated through the network and then reduce the risk of overfitting when feeding the fully connected layers.

Typically, there are two ways to perform subsampling:

- Skipping the convolution operator for some input pixels. As a result, the output of the convolution layer will have fewer spatial dimensions than the input ones.

- Adopting subsampling functions such as **pooling layers**.

The following figure shows a generic CNN architecture, where the pooling layer reduces the spatial dimensionality and the fully connected layer performs the classification stage:

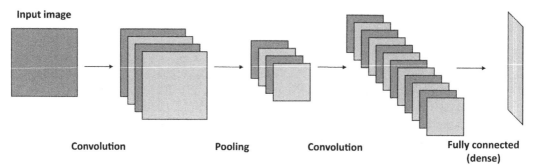

Figure 1.7 – Generic CNN with a pooling layer to reduce the spatial dimensionality

One of the most critical aspects to consider when deploying DL networks for TinyML is the model size, generally defined as the memory required for storing the weights.

Since our tiny platforms have limited physical memory, we require the model to be compact to fit the target device.

However, the memory constraint is not the only challenge we could encounter when deploying a model on microcontrollers. For example, although the trained model commonly employs arithmetic operations in floating-point precision, CPUs on microcontrollers could not have hardware acceleration for it.

Therefore, **quantization** is an indispensable technique to overcome the preceding limitations.

Quantization

Quantization is the process of performing neural network computations in lower bit precision. The widely adopted technique for microcontrollers applies the quantization post-training and converts the 32-bit floating-point weights to 8-bit integer values. This technique brings a 4x model size reduction and a significant latency improvement with very little or no accuracy drop.

DL is essential to building applications that make intelligent decisions. However, the key requirement for battery-powered applications is the adoption of a low-power device. So far, we have mentioned power and energy in general terms but let's see what they mean practically in the following section.

Learning the difference between power and energy

Power matters in TinyML, and the target we aim for is in the **milliwatt (mW)** range or below, which means thousands of times more efficient than a traditional desktop machine.

Although there are cases where we might consider using **energy** harvesting solutions, such as solar panels, those could not always be possible because of cost and physical dimensions.

However, what do we mean by power and energy? Let's discover these terms by giving a basic overview of the fundamental physical quantities governing electronic circuits.

Voltage versus current

Current is what makes an electronic circuit work, which is *the flow of electric charges across surface A of a conductor in a given time*, as described in the following diagram:

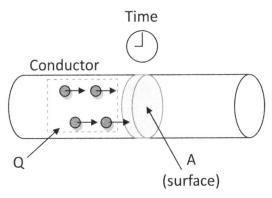

Figure 1.8 – Current is a flow of electric charges across surface A at a given time

The current is defined as follows:

$$I = \frac{Q}{t}$$

Here, we have the following:

- I: Current, measured in **amperes (A)**
- Q: The electric charges across surface A in a given time, measured in **coulombs (C)**
- t: Time, measured in **seconds (s)**

The current flows in a circuit in the following conditions:

- We have a *conductive material* (for example, copper wire) to allow the electric charge to flow.

- We have a *closed circuit*, so a circuit without interruption, providing a continuous path to the current flow.

- We have a *potential difference source*, called **voltage**, defined as follows:

$$V = V^+ - V^-$$

Voltage is measured with **volts** (**V**) and produces an electric field to allow the electric charge to flow in the circuit. Both the USB port and battery are potential difference sources.

The symbolic representation of a power source is given in the following figure:

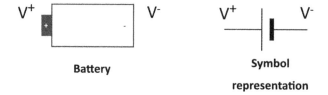

Battery   **Symbol representation**

Figure 1.9 – Battery symbol representation

To avoid constantly referring to V+ and V-, we define the battery's negative terminal as a reference by convention, assigning it **0 V** (**GND**).

Ohm's law relates voltage and current, which says through the following formula that the *current through a conductor is proportional to the voltage across a resistor*:

$$\frac{V}{R} = I$$

A **resistor** is an electrical component used to reduce the current flow. This component has a resistance measured with **Ohm** (**Ω**) and identified with the letter *R*.

The symbolic representation of a resistor is shown in the following figure:

Resistor   **Symbol representation**

Figure 1.10 – Resistor symbol representation
(https://openclipart.org/detail/276048/47k-ohm-resistor)

Resistors are essential components for any electronic circuit, and for the ones used in this book, their value is reported through colored bands on the elements. Standard resistors have four, five, or six bands. The color on the bands denotes the resistance value, as shown in the following example:

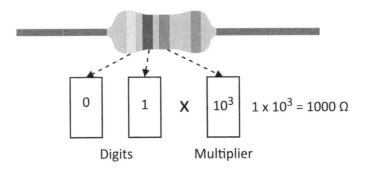

Figure 1.11 – Example of four-band resistor

To easily decode the color bands, we recommend using the online tool from Digi-Key (https://www.digikey.com/en/resources/conversion-calculators/conversion-calculator-resistor-color-code).

Now that we know the main physical quantities governing electronic circuits, we are ready to see the difference between power and energy.

Power versus energy

Sometimes we interchange the words *power* and *energy* because we think they're related, but actually, they refer to different physical quantities. In fact, energy is the capacity for doing work (for example, using force to move an object), while power is the rate of consuming energy.

In practical terms, *power tells us how fast we drain the battery*, so high power implies a faster battery discharge.

Power and energy are related to voltage and current through the following formulas:

$$P = V \cdot I$$
$$E = P \cdot T$$

The following table presents the physical quantities in the power and energy formulas:

Physical quantity	Unit	Meaning
P	Watt (W)	Power
E	Joule (J)	Energy
V	Volts (V)	Voltage supply
I	Ampere (A)	Current consumption
T	Seconds (s)	Operating time

Figure 1.12 – Table reporting the physical quantities in the power and energy formulas

On microcontrollers, the voltage supply is in the order of a few volts (for example, 3.3 V), while the current consumption is in the range of **micro-ampere (μA)** or **milli-ampere (mA)**. For this reason, we commonly adopt **microwatt (μW)** or **milliwatt (mW)** for power and **microjoule (μJ)** or **millijoule (mJ)** for energy.

Now, consider the following problem to get familiar with the power and energy concepts.

Suppose you have a processing task and you have the option to execute it on two different processors. These processors have the following power consumptions:

Processing unit	Power consumption
PU1	12
PU2	3

Figure 1.13 – Table reporting two processing units with different power consumptions

What processor would you use to execute the task?

Although PU1 has higher (4x) power consumption than PU2, this does not imply that PU1 is less energy-efficient. On the contrary, PU1 could be more computationally performant than PU2 (for example, 8x), making it the best choice from an energy perspective, as shown in the following formulas:

$$E_{PU1} = 12 \cdot T_1$$

$$E_{PU2} = 3 \cdot T_2 = 3 \cdot 8 \cdot T_1 = 24 \cdot T_1$$

From the preceding example, we can say that PU1 is our better choice because it requires less energy from the battery under the same workload.

Commonly, we adopt **OPS per Watt (arithmetic operations performed per Watt)** to bind the power consumption to the computational resources of our processors.

Programming microcontrollers

A **microcontroller**, often shortened to **MCU**, is a full-fledged computer because it has a processor (which can also be multicore nowadays), a memory system (for example, RAM or ROM), and some peripherals. Unlike a standard computer, a microcontroller fits entirely on an integrated chip, and it has incredibly low power and low price.

We often confuse microcontrollers with microprocessors, but they refer to different devices. In contrast to a microcontroller, a **microprocessor** integrates only the processor on a chip, requiring external connections to a memory system and other components to form a fully operating computer.

The following figure summarizes the main differences between a microprocessor and a microcontroller:

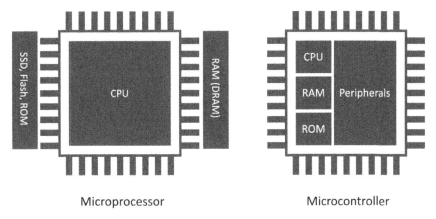

Figure 1.14 – Microprocessor versus microcontroller

As for all processing units, the target application influences their architectural design choice.

For example, a microprocessor tackles scenarios where the tasks are usually as follows:

- Dynamic (for example, can change with user interaction or time)
- General-purpose
- Compute intensive

A microcontroller addresses completely different scenarios, and in the following list, we shall highlight some of the critical ones:

- *The tasks are single-purpose and repetitive:*

  In contrast to microprocessor applications, the tasks are generally single-purpose and repetitive, so the microcontroller does not require strict re-programmability. Typically, the applications are less computationally intensive than the microprocessor ones and do not have frequent interactions with the user. However, they can interact with the environment or other devices.

  As an example, you could consider a thermostat. The device only requires monitoring the temperature at regular intervals and communicating with the heating system.

- *We could have time frame constraints:*

  Certain tasks must complete execution within a specific time frame. This requirement is the characteristic for **real-time applications** (**RTAs**), where the violation of the time constraint may affect the quality of service (*soft real time*) or be hazardous (*hard real time*).

  An **automobile safety system** (**ABS**) is an example of a hard RTA because the electronic system must respond within a time frame to prevent the wheels from locking when applying brake pedal pressure.

  We require a latency-predictable device to build an effective RTA, so all hardware components (CPU, memory, interrupt handler, and so on) must respond in a precise number of clock cycles. Hardware vendors commonly report the latency, expressed in clock cycles, in the datasheet.

  The time constraint poses some architectural design adaptations and limitations to a general-purpose microprocessor.

  An example is the **memory management unit** (**MMU**) that we primarily use to translate virtual memory addresses, and we do not usually have it in the CPU for microcontrollers.

- *Low-power constraints:*

  Applications could live in a battery-powered environment, so the microcontroller must be low-power to extend their lifetime.

  As per the time frame constraints, power consumption also poses some architectural design differences from a microprocessor.

  Without going deeper into the hardware details, all the off-chip components generally reduce power efficiency as a rule of thumb. That is the main reason why microcontrollers integrate both the RAM and a kind of hard drive (ROM) within the chip.

Typically, microcontrollers also have lower clock frequency than microprocessors to consume less energy.

*   *Physical size constraints:*

The device could live in products that are small in size. Since the microcontroller is a computer within a chip, it is perfect for these scenarios. The package size for a microcontroller can vary but typically is in the range of a few square millimeters.

In 2018, a team of engineers at the University of Michigan created the "world's smallest computer," which was 0.3 mm in size with a microcontroller powered by an Arm Cortex-M0+ processor and a battery-less sensor system for cellular temperature measurement (`https://news.umich.edu/u-m-researchers-create-worlds-smallest-computer/`).

*   *Cost constraints:*

All applications are cost-sensitive, and by designing a smaller chip that integrates a CPU, memory, and peripherals, we make microcontrollers economically more advantageous than microprocessors.

In the following table, we have summarized what we have just discussed for easy future reference:

Feature	Microprocessor	Microcontroller
Application	General-purpose	Single-purpose
CPU arithmetic	It can perform heavy mathematical calculations in floating-point or double precision	Mainly integer arithmetic
RAM	A few GB	A few hundred KB
ROM (or hard-drive)	GB or TB	KB or MB
Clock frequency	GHz	MHz
Power consumption	W	mW or below
Operating System (OS)	Required	Not strictly required
Cost	From ten to hundreds of dollars	From a few cents (low-end) to a few dollars (high-end)

Figure 1.15 – Table comparing a microprocessor with a microcontroller

In the next section, we will start going deeper into the architectural aspects of microcontrollers by analyzing the memory architecture and internal peripherals.

Memory architecture

Microcontrollers are CPU-based embedded systems, which means that the CPU is responsible for interacting with all its subcomponents.

All CPUs require at least memory to read the instructions and store/read variables during the program's execution.

In the microcontroller context, we physically dedicate two separate memories for the instructions and data:

- **Program memory (ROM)**

    This is non-volatile read-only memory reserved for the program to execute. Although its primary goal is to contain the program, it can also store constant data. Thus, program memory is similar to our everyday computers' hard drives.

- **Data memory (RAM)**

    This is volatile memory reserved to store/read temporary data. Since it is RAM, we lose its content when switching off the system.

Since program and data memory are functionally opposite, we usually employ different semiconductor technologies. In particular, we can find Flash technologies for the program memory and **static random-access memory** (**SRAM**) for the data memory.

Flash memories are non-volatile and offer low power consumption but are generally slower than SRAM. However, given the cost advantage over SRAM, we can find larger program memory than data memory.

Now that we know the difference between program and data memory, *where can we store the weights for our deep neural network model?*

The answer to this question depends on whether the model has constant weights. If the weights are constant, so do not change during inference, it is more efficient to store them in program memory for the following reasons:

- Program memory has more capacity than SRAM.
- It reduces memory pressure on the SRAM since other functions require storing variables or chunks of memory at runtime.

We want to remind you that microcontrollers have limited memory resources, so a decision like this can make a difference to memory efficiency.

Peripherals

Microcontrollers offer extra on-chip features to expand their capabilities and make these tiny computers different from each other. These features are the **peripherals** and are essential because they can interface with sensors or other external components.

Each peripheral has a dedicated functionality, and it is assigned to a metal leg (**pin**) of the integrated circuit.

We can refer to the *peripheral pin assignment* section in the microcontroller datasheet to find out each pin's functionalities. Hardware vendors typically number the pins anti-clockwise, starting from the top-left corner of the chip, marked with a dot for easy reference, as shown in the following figure:

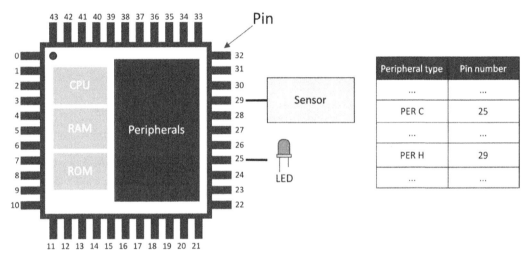

Figure 1.16 – Pin assignment. Pins are numbered anti-clockwise, starting from the top-left corner, marked with a dot

Since peripherals can be of various types, we can group them into four main categories for simplicity.

General-purpose input/output (GPIO or IO)

GPIOs do not have a predefined and fixed purpose. Their primary function is to provide or read binary signals that, by nature, can only live in two well-defined states: **HIGH (1)** or **LOW (0)**. The following figure shows an example of a binary signal:

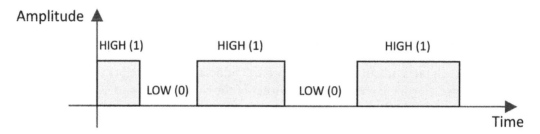

Figure 1.17 – A binary signal can only live in two states: HIGH (1) and LOW (0)

Typical GPIO usages are as follows:

- Turning on and off an LED
- Detecting whether a button is pressed
- Implementing complex digital interfaces/protocols such as VGA

GPIO peripherals are versatile and generally available in all microcontrollers.

Analog/digital converters

In TinyML, our applications will likely be dealing with time-varying physical quantities, such as images, audio, and temperature.

Whatever these quantities are, the **sensor** transforms them into a *continuous electrical signal* interpretable by the microcontrollers. This electrical signal, which can be either a voltage or current, is commonly called an **analog signal**.

The microcontroller, in turn, needs to convert the analog signal into a digital format so that the CPU can process the data.

Analog/digital converters act as *translators* between analog and digital worlds.

An **analog-to-digital converter** (**ADC**) samples the analog signal at fixed interval times and converts the electrical signal into a digital format.

A **digital-to-analog converter** (**DAC**) performs the opposite functionality: converting the internal digital format into an analog signal.

Serial communication

Communication peripherals integrate standard communication protocols to control external components. Typical serial communication peripherals available in microcontrollers are **I2C**, **SPI**, **UART**, and **USB**.

Timers

In contrast to all the peripherals we just described, the **timers** do not interface with external components since they are used to trigger or synchronize events.

With this section, we have completed the overview of the TinyML ingredients. Now that we are familiar with the terminology and general concepts, we can start presenting the development platforms used in this book.

Presenting Arduino Nano 33 BLE Sense and Raspberry Pi Pico

A **microcontroller board** is a **printed circuit board** (**PCB**) that combines the microcontroller with the necessary electronic circuit to make it ready to use. In some cases, the microcontroller board could integrate additional devices to target specific end applications.

Arduino Nano 33 BLE Sense (in short, Arduino Nano) and Raspberry Pico are the microcontroller boards used in this book.

Arduino Nano, designed by Arduino (`https://www.arduino.cc`), is a board that combines a microcontroller (**nRF52840**) powered by an Arm Cortex-M4 processor with several sensors and Bluetooth radio for an easy TinyML development experience. We will require just a few additional external components when developing on Arduino Nano since most are already available on-board.

Raspberry Pi Pico, designed by the Raspberry Pi Foundation (`https://www.raspberrypi.org`), does not provide sensors and the Bluetooth module on-board. Still, it has a microcontroller (**RP2040**) powered by a dual-core Arm Cortex-M0+ processor for unique and powerful TinyML applications. Therefore, this board will be ideal for learning how to interface with external sensors and build electronic circuits.

The following figure shows a side-by-side comparison to see the features that make our platforms different from each other:

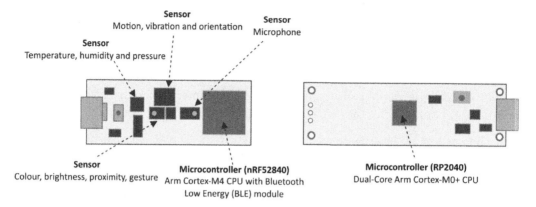

Arduino Nano 33 BLE sense board

CPU: Arm Cortex-M4 64MHz
Program memory: 1MB
Data memory: 256KB
Board size: 45x18mm
Cost: 31.10$

Raspberry Pi Pico

CPU: Dual core Arm Cortex-M0+ 133MHz
Program memory: 2MB
Data memory: 264KB
Board size: 51.3x21mm
Cost: 4$

Figure 1.18 – Arduino Nano 33 BLE Sense versus Raspberry Pi Pico

As we can see from the side-by-side comparison, they both have an incredibly small form-factor, a USB port for power/programming, and an Arm-based microcontroller. At the same time, they also have unique features that make the boards ideal for targeting different TinyML development scenarios.

Setting up Arduino Web Editor, TensorFlow, and Edge Impulse

For TinyML, we require different software tools to cover both ML development and embedded programming. Thanks to Arduino, Edge Impulse, and Google, most of the tools considered in this book are browser-based and require only a few configuration steps.

In this section, we will introduce these tools and prepare the Arduino development environment required for writing and uploading programs to Arduino Nano and Raspberry Pi Pico.

Getting ready with Arduino Web Editor

Arduino Integrated Development Environment (**Arduino IDE**) is a software application developed by Arduino (`https://www.arduino.cc/en/software`) for writing and uploading programs to Arduino-compatible boards. Programs are written in C++ and are commonly called **sketches** by Arduino programmers.

Arduino IDE makes software development accessible and straightforward to developers with no background in embedded programming. In fact, the tool hides all the complexities that we might have when dealing with embedded platforms, such as cross-compilation and device programming.

Arduino also offers a browser-based IDE (`https://create.arduino.cc/editor`). It is called **Arduino Web Editor** and makes programmability even more straightforward because programs can be written, compiled, and uploaded on microcontrollers directly from the web browser. All the Arduino projects presented in this book will be based on this cloud-based environment. However, since the free plan of Arduino Web Editor is limited to 200 seconds of compilation time per day, you may consider upgrading to a paid plan or using the free local Arduino IDE to get unlimited compilation time.

> **Note**
> In the following chapters of this book, we will use Arduino IDE and Arduino Web Editor interchangeably.

Getting ready with TensorFlow

TensorFlow (`https://www.tensorflow.org`) is an end-to-end free and open source software platform developed by Google for ML. *We will be using this software to develop and train our ML models using Python in Google Colaboratory.*

Colaboratory (`https://colab.research.google.com/notebooks`), in short, **Colab**, is a free Python development environment that runs in the browser using Google Cloud. It is like a **Jupyter** notebook but has some essential differences, such as the following:

- It does not need setting up.
- It is cloud-based and hosted by Google.
- There are numerous Python libraries pre-installed (including TensorFlow).
- It is integrated with Google Drive.

- It offers free access to GPU and TPU shared resources.

- It is easy to share (also on GitHub).

Therefore, TensorFlow does not require setting up because Colab comes with it.

In Colab, we recommend enabling the GPU acceleration on the **Runtime** tab to speed up the computation on TensorFlow. To do so, navigate to **Runtime | Change runtime type** and select **GPU** from the **Hardware accelerator** drop-down list, as shown in the following screenshot:

Notebook settings

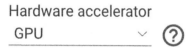

To get the most out of Colab Pro, avoid using a GPU unless you need one. Learn more

Figure 1.19 – You can enable the GPU acceleration from Runtime | Change runtime type

Since the GPU acceleration is a shared resource among other users, there is limited access to the free version of Colab.

> **Tip**
> You could subscribe to Colab Pro (`https://colab.research.google.com/`) to get priority access to the fastest GPUs.

TensorFlow is not the only tool from Google that we will use. In fact, once we have produced the ML model, we will need to run it on the microcontroller. For this, Google developed TensorFlow Lite for Microcontrollers.

TensorFlow Lite for Microcontrollers (`https://www.tensorflow.org/lite/microcontrollers`), in short, **TFLu**, is the key software library to unlock ML applications on low-power microcontrollers. The project is part of TensorFlow and allows running DL models on devices with a few kilobytes of memory. Written in C/C++, the library does not require an operating system and dynamic memory allocation.

TFLu does not need setting up because it is included in Arduino Web Editor.

Getting ready with Edge Impulse

Edge Impulse (`https://www.edgeimpulse.com`) is a software platform for end-to-end ML development. It is free for developers, and in a few minutes, we can have an ML model up and running on our microcontrollers. In fact, the platform integrates tools for the following:

- Data acquisition from sensor data
- Applying digital signal processing routines on input data
- Building and training ML models
- Testing ML models
- Deploying ML models on microcontrollers
- Finding the best signal processing block and ML model for your use case

> **Info**
> All these tools are also accessible through open APIs.

Developers just need to sign up on the website to access all these features directly within the UI.

How to do it...

The following subsections will show the steps for setting up Arduino Web Editor:

1. Sign up to Arduino at `https://auth.arduino.cc/register`.
2. Log in to Arduino Web Editor (`https://create.arduino.cc/editor`).
3. Install the Arduino agent following the step-by-step installation at `https://create.arduino.cc/getting-started/plugin/welcome`.
4. Install the Raspberry Pi Pico SDK:

   - *Windows*:

     i. Download the `pico-setup-windows` file from `https://github.com/ndabas/pico-setup-windows/releases`.

     ii. Install `pico-setup-installer`.

- *Linux*:

    i.   Open Terminal.

    ii. Create a temporary folder:

    ```
    $ mkdir tmp_pico
    ```

    iii. Change directory to your temporary folder:

    ```
    $ cd tmp_pico
    ```

    iv. Download the Pico setup script with `wget`:

    ```
    $ wget wget https://raw.githubusercontent.com/
    raspberrypi/pico-setup/master/pico_setup.sh
    ```

    v.   Make the file executable:

    ```
    $ chmod +x pico_setup.sh
    ```

    vi. Execute the script:

    ```
    $ ./pico_setup.sh
    ```

    vii. Add $USER to the `dialout` group:

    ```
    $ sudo usermod -a -G dialout $USER
    ```

5. Check whether Arduino Web Editor can communicate with Arduino Nano:

    i.   Open Arduino Web Editor in a web browser.

    ii. Connect the Arduino Nano board to a laptop/PC through a micro-USB cable.

    The editor should recognize the board in the device dropdown and report **Arduino Nano 33 BLE** and the port's name (for example, **/dev/ttyACM0**):

Figure 1.20 – Expected output when Arduino Web Editor can communicate with Arduino Nano

6. Check whether Arduino Web Editor can communicate with Raspberry Pi Pico:

    i.   Open Arduino Web Editor in a browser.

    ii. Connect the Raspberry Pi Pico board to a laptop/PC through a micro-USB cable.

The editor should recognize the board and report **Raspberry Pi Pico** and the port's name (for example, **/dev/ttyACM0**):

Figure 1.21 – Expected output when Arduino Web Editor can communicate with Raspberry Pi Pico

We have successfully set up the tools that will help us develop our future recipes. Before ending this chapter, we want to test a basic example on Arduino Nano and Raspberry Pi Pico to officially mark the beginning of our journey into the world of TinyML.

Running a sketch on Arduino Nano and Raspberry Pi Pico

In this recipe, we will blink the Arduino Nano and Raspberry Pi Pico LED using the **Blink** prebuilt example from Arduino Web Editor.

This "Hello World" program consists of a simple LED blinking through the GPIO peripheral; from there, we will be able to go anywhere.

This exercise aims to get you familiar with Arduino Web Editor and help you to understand how to develop a program with Arduino.

Getting ready

An Arduino sketch consists of two functions, `setup()` and `loop()`, as shown in the following code block:

```
void setup() {
}
void loop() {
}
```

`setup()` is the first function executed by the program when we press the reset button or power up the board. This function is executed only once and is generally responsible for initializing variables and peripherals.

After setup(), the program executes loop(), which runs iteratively and forever, as shown in the following figure:

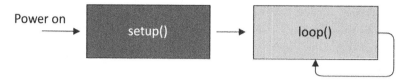

Figure 1.22 – Diagram of the structure

These two functions are required in all Arduino programs.

How to do it...

The steps reported in this section are valid for both Arduino Nano, Raspberry Pi Pico, and other compatible boards with Arduino Web Editor:

1. Connect the device to a laptop/PC through a micro-USB cable. Next, check that the Arduino IDE reports the name and port for the device.

2. Open the prebuilt **Blink** example by clicking on **Examples** from the left-hand side menu, **BUILT IN** from the new menu, and then **Blink**, as shown in the following screenshot:

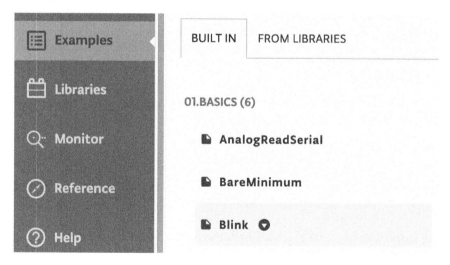

Figure 1.23 – Built-in LED blink example

Once you have clicked on the **Blink** sketch, the code will be visible in the editor area.

3. Click on the arrow near the board dropdown to compile and upload the program to the target device, as shown in the following figure:

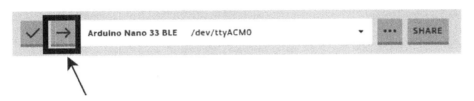

Figure 1.24 – The arrow near the board dropdown will compile and flash the program on the target device

The console output should return **Done** at the bottom of the page, and the on-board LED should start blinking.

2
Prototyping with Microcontrollers

Deploying **machine learning** (**ML**) applications on microcontrollers is cool because what we develop doesn't just live within our computer's brain. Instead, it can animate many things around us. Therefore, before diving into the ML world, let's take a glance at how to build basic applications on microcontrollers from a software and hardware perspective.

In this chapter, we will deal with code-debugging and present how to transmit data to the Arduino serial monitor. Next, we will discover how to program **GPIO** peripherals with the **Arm Mbed** API and use the solderless **breadboard** to connect external components such as **LEDs** and **push-buttons**. At the end of the chapter, we will see how to power the Arduino Nano and Raspberry Pi Pico with batteries.

The aim of this chapter is to cover the relevant microcontroller programming basics for the following topics in this book.

In this chapter, we're going to cover the following recipes:

- Code debugging 101

- Implementing an LED status indicator on the breadboard

- Controlling an external LED with the GPIO

- Turning an LED on and off with a ush-button

- Using interrupts to read the push-button state

- Powering microcontrollers with batteries

Technical requirements

To complete all the practical recipes of this chapter, we will need the following:

- An Arduino Nano 33 BLE Sense board

- A Raspberry Pi Pico board

- A micro-USB cable

- 1 x half-size solderless breadboard (30 rows and 10 columns)

- 1 x red LED

- 1 x 220 Ω resistor

- 1 x 3 AA battery holder (Raspberry Pi Pico only)

- 1 x 4 AA battery holder (Arduino Nano only)

- 4 x AA batteries

- 1 x push-button

- 5 x jumper wires

- Laptop/PC with either Ubuntu 18.04+ or Windows 10 on x86-64

The source code and additional material are available in the `Chapter02` folder on the GitHub repository (`https://github.com/PacktPublishing/TinyML-Cookbook/tree/main/Chapter02`).

Code debugging 101

Code debugging is a fundamental process of software development to uncover errors in code.

This recipe will show how to perform **print debugging** on an Arduino Nano and Raspberry Pi Pico by transmitting the following strings to the serial terminal:

- `Initialization completed`: Once we have completed the initialization of the serial port

- `Executed`: After every 2 seconds

The following Arduino sketch contains the code referred to in this recipe:

- `01_printf.ino`:

  `https://github.com/PacktPublishing/TinyML-Cookbook/blob/main/Chapter02/ArduinoSketches/01_printf.ino`

Getting ready

All programs are prone to bugs, and print debugging is a basic process that prints statements on the output terminal to give insight into the program execution, as shown in the following example:

```
int func (int func_type, int a) {
  int ret_val = 0;
  switch(func_type){
    case 0:
      printf("FUNC0\n");
      ret_val = func0(a)
      break;
    default:
      printf("FUNC1\n");
      ret_val = func1(a);
  }
  return ret_val;
}
```

To get ready with this first recipe, we only need to know how the microcontroller can send messages on the serial terminal.

The Arduino programming language offers a similar function to `printf()`, the `Serial.print()` function.

This function can send characters, numbers, or even binary data from the microcontroller board to our computer through the serial port, commonly called **UART** or **USART**. You can refer to `https://www.arduino.cc/reference/en/language/functions/communication/serial/print/` for the complete list of input arguments.

How to do it...

> **Note**
>
> The code reported in this recipe is valid for both the Arduino Nano and Raspberry Pi Pico. The Arduino IDE, in fact, will compile the code accordingly with the selected platform in the device drop-down menu.

Open the Arduino IDE and create a new empty project by clicking on **Sketchbook** from the leftmost menu (**EDITOR**) and then click on **NEW SKETCH**, as shown in the following figure:

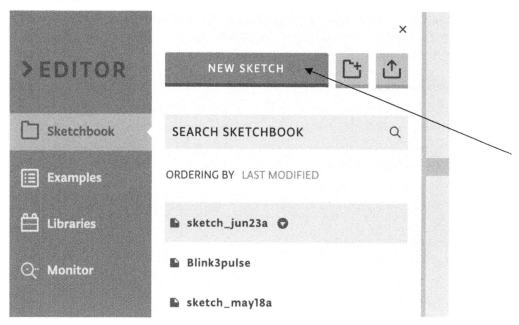

Figure 2.1 – Click on the NEW SKETCH button to create a new project

As we saw in *Chapter 1, Getting Started with TinyML*, all sketches require a file containing the `setup()` and `loop()` functions.

The following steps will show what to write in these functions to implement our print debugging recipe:

1. Initialize the UART baud rate in the `setup()` function and wait until the peripheral is open:

    ```
    void setup() {
      Serial.begin(9600);
      while (!Serial);
    ```

    In contrast to the standard C library `printf` function, the `Serial.print()` function requires initialization before transmitting data. Therefore, we initialize the peripheral with the Arduino `Serial.begin()` function, which only requires the **baud rate** as an input argument. The baud rate is the data transmission rate in bits per second, and it is set to `9600` bps.

    However, we can't use the peripheral immediately after the initialization because we should wait until it is ready to transmit. So, we use `while(!Serial)` to wait until the serial communication is open.

2. Print `Initialization completed` after `Serial.begin()` in the `setup()` function:

    ```
          Serial.print("Initialization completed\n");
        }
    ```

    We transmit the string `Initialization completed` with `Serial.print("Initialization completed\n")` to report the completion of the initialization.

3. Print `Executed` every 2 seconds in the `loop()` function:

    ```
    void loop() {
      delay(2000);
      Serial.print("Executed\n");
    }
    ```

    Since the `loop()` function is called iteratively, we use the Arduino's `delay()` function to pause the program execution for 2 seconds. `delay()` accepts the amount of time in milliseconds (1 s = 1000 ms) as an input argument.

Now, make sure the device is plugged into your computer through the micro-USB cable.

If the device is recognized, we can open the serial monitor by clicking on **Monitor** from the **Editor** menu. From there, we will see any data transmitted by the microcontroller through the UART peripheral. However, before any communication starts, ensure the serial monitor uses the same baud rate as the microcontroller peripheral (9600), as shown in the following figure:

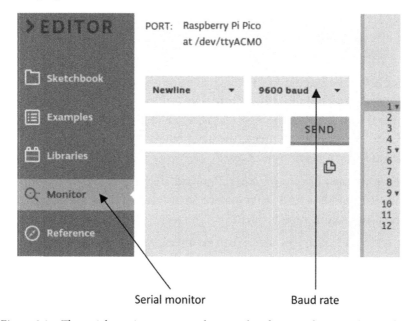

Figure 2.2 – The serial monitor must use the same baud rate as the UART's peripheral

With the serial monitor open, we can click on the arrow near the device drop-down menu to compile and upload the program to the target platform. Once the sketch has been uploaded, the serial monitor will receive the **Initialization completed** and **Executed** messages, as shown in the following screenshot:

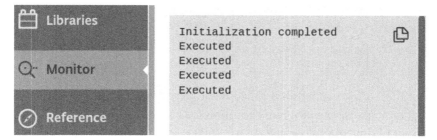

Figure 2.3 – Expected output on the serial monitor

As we can see from the serial monitor output, **Initialization completed** is printed once because the setup() function is just called when starting the program.

There's more

Print debugging is a simple debugging approach, but it has significant disadvantages with the increase of software complexity, such as the following:

- Needing to re-compile and flash the board every time we add or move `Serial.print()`.

- `Serial.print()` costs in terms of program memory footprint.

- We could make mistakes reporting the information (for example, using `print` to report an unsigned `int` variable that is actually signed).

We will not cover more advanced debugging in this book, but we recommend looking at **serial wire debug** (**SWD**) debuggers (`https://developer.arm.com/architectures/cpu-architecture/debug-visibility-and-trace/coresight-architecture/serial-wire-debug`) to make this process less painful. SWD is an Arm debug protocol for almost all Arm Cortex processors that you can use to flash the microcontroller, step through the code, add breakpoints, and so on with only two wires.

Implementing an LED status indicator on the breadboard

We have the chance to interact with the world around us with microcontrollers. For example, we can get data from sensors or perform physical actions, such as turning on and off an LED or moving an actuator.

In this recipe, we will learn how to connect external components with the microcontroller by building the following electronic circuit on the breadboard:

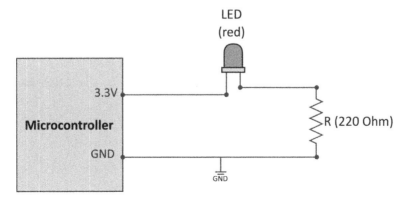

Figure 2.4 – LED power status indicator circuit

The preceding circuit uses a *red* LED to indicate whether the microcontroller is plugged into the power.

Getting ready

When connecting external components to the microcontroller, we mean physically joining two or more metal connectors together. Although we could solder these connectors, it is not usual for prototyping because it is not quick and straightforward.

Therefore, this *Getting ready* section aims to present a solderless alternative to connect our components effortlessly.

Making contacts directly with the microcontroller's pins can be extremely hard for the tiny space between each pin. For example, considering the RP2040 microcontroller, the pin space is roughly 0.5 mm since the chip size is 7x7 mm. Therefore, it would be practically impossible to connect any of our components safely since most terminals have a wire diameter of ~1 mm.

For this reason, our platforms provide alternative points of contact with wider spacing on the board. These contact points on the Arduino Nano and Raspberry Pi Pico are the two rows of pre-drilled holes located at the platform's edge.

The simplest way to know the correspondence between these contacts and the microcontroller pins is to refer to the datasheet of the microcontroller boards. Hardware vendors usually provide the pinout diagram to note the pins' arrangement and functionality.

For example, the following list reports the links to the Arduino Nano and Raspberry Pi Pico pinout diagrams:

- **Arduino Nano**:

  ```
  https://content.arduino.cc/assets/Pinout-NANOsense_latest.
  pdf
  ```

- **Rasberry Pi Pico**:

  ```
  https://datasheets.raspberrypi.org/pico/Pico-R3-A4-Pinout.
  pdf
  ```

On top of these pre-drilled holes, which often come with a 2.54 mm spacing, we can solder a **header** to insert and connect the electronic components easily.

The header can be either a male (pin header) or a female connector (socket header), as shown in the following figure:

Male header (pin header)   Female header (socket header)

Figure 2.5 – Male header versus female header
(image from https://en.wikipedia.org/wiki/Pin_header)

Important Note

We recommend buying devices with pre-soldered male headers if you are not familiar with soldering or just want a ready-to-go solution.

As we have seen, the boards provide a way to connect the external components with the microcontroller. However, how can we attach other electrical elements to build a complete electronic circuit?

Prototyping on a breadboard

The **breadboard** is a solderless prototyping platform to build circuits by pushing the device's pins in a rectangular grid of metal holes:

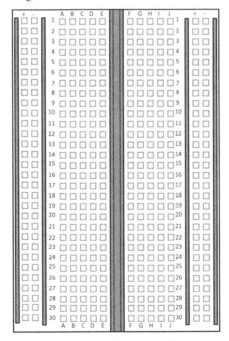

Figure 2.6 – Solderless breadboard

As shown in the previous figure, breadboards provide two connecting areas for our components:

- **Bus rails** are usually located on both sides of the breadboard and consist of two columns of holes identified with the symbols + and – as shown in the following diagram:

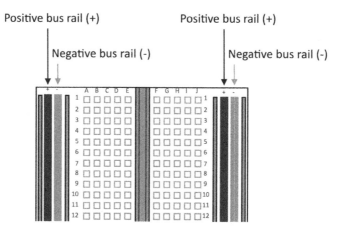

Figure 2.7 – Bus rails labeled with + and - on both sides of the breadboard

All the holes of the same column are internally connected. Therefore, we will have the same voltage through all its columns when applying a voltage to whatever hole.

Since bus rails are beneficial for having reference voltages for our circuits, we should never apply different voltages on the same bus column.

- **Terminal strips** are located in the central area of the breadboard and join only the holes of the same row so that the following occurs:

  - Holes on the same row have the same voltage.

  - Holes on the same column might have a different voltage.

However, since we typically have a notch running parallel in the middle of the breadboard, we have two different terminal strips per row, as shown in the following figure:

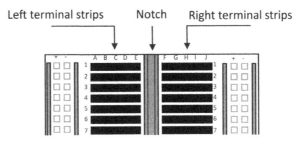

Figure 2.8 – Terminal strips are located in the central area of the breadboard

We can place several devices on the breadboard and connect them through **jumper wires**.

> **Note**
>
> The size of a breadboard is defined by the number of rows and columns in the terminal area. In our case, we will always refer to a half-sized breadboard with 30 rows and 10 columns.

How to do it...

Before building any circuits, unplug the micro-USB cable from the microcontroller board to remove the possibility of unintentionally damaging any components.

Once we have disconnected the board from the power, follow the following steps to build the circuit to turn the LED on when the platform is plugged into the power:

1. Put the microcontroller board on the breadboard:

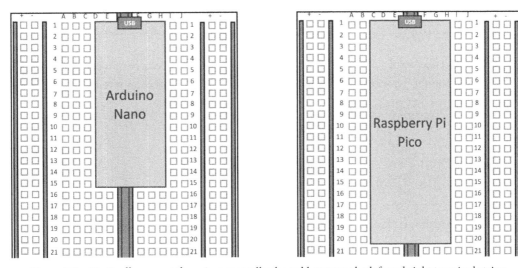

Figure 2.9 – Vertically mount the microcontroller board between the left and right terminal strips

Since we have a notch running parallel, it is safe to put the platforms in this way because the left and right pin headers touch two different terminal strips.

2. Use two jumper wires to connect the 3.3 V and GND pins of the microcontroller board with the + and - bus rails:

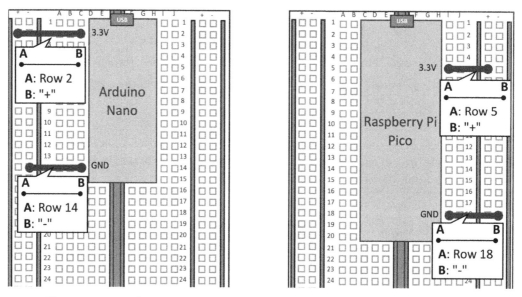

Figure 2.10 – Use the jumper wires to connect the 3.3 V and GND to the + and - bus rails

It is important to note that all holes of the bus rails will have 3.3 V and GND, respectively, only when the microcontroller is connected to the power.

3. Insert the LED pins on two terminal strips:

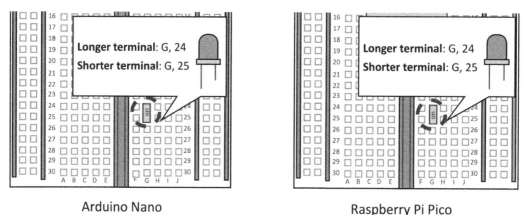

Figure 2.11 – Insert the LED on the breadboard

In the preceding figure, we insert the longer LED terminal in **(H, 24)** and the shorter one in **(H, 25)**. Do not invert the longer and shorter terminals because then the LED won't turn on.

4. Place the 220 Ω resistor in series with the LED:

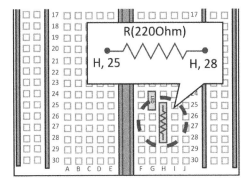
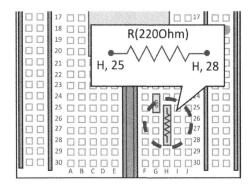

Arduino Nano   Raspberry Pi Pico

Figure 2.12 – Place the resistor in series with the LED

The color bands of the resistor can be determined through the *Digikey* web tool (`https://www.digikey.com/en/resources/conversion-calculators/conversion-calculator-resistor-color-code`). For example, a 220Ω resistor with five or six bands is encoded with the following colors:

*   First band: red (2)
*   Second band: red (2)
*   Third band: black (0)
*   Fourth band: black (1)

As reported in the circuit presented at the beginning of this recipe, one terminal of the resistor should touch the shorter LED pin. In our case, we insert one terminal in **(H, 25)**. The remaining terminal of the resistor goes in whichever unused terminal strip. In our case, we insert this terminal in **(H, 28)**.

5. Close the circuit by connecting the + bus rail (3.3 V) to the longer LED pin and the - bus rail (GND) to the resistor terminal:

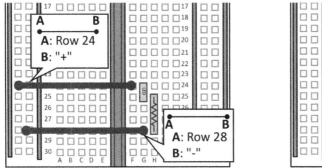 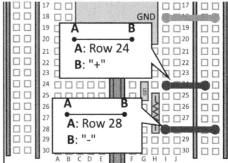

Arduino Nano   Raspberry Pi Pico

Figure 2.13 – Close the circuit by connecting 3.3 V and GND

The previous figure shows how to connect the two remaining jumper wires used to close the circuit. One jumper wire connects the + bus rail with the longer LED terminal **(H, 24)** while the other one connects the - bus rail with the resistor **(H, 28)**.

Now, the LED should emit light whenever you plug the microcontroller into the power with the micro-USB cable.

Controlling an external LED with the GPIO

Nowadays, LEDs are everywhere, particularly in our houses, because they use less energy than older lights for the same luminous intensity. However, the LEDs considered for our experiments are not light bulbs but through-hole LEDs for rapid prototyping on the breadboard.

In this recipe, we will discover how to build a basic circuit with an external LED and program the GPIO peripheral to control its light.

The following Arduino sketch contains the code referred to in this recipe:

*   `03_gpio_out.ino`:

    `https://github.com/PacktPublishing/TinyML-Cookbook/blob/main/Chapter02/ArduinoSketches/03_gpio_out.ino`

Getting ready

To implement this recipe, we need to know how the LED works and how to program the microcontroller GPIO peripheral in output mode.

LED stands for **Light-Emitting Diode** and is a semiconductor component that emits light when the current flows through it.

A through-hole LED is made of the following:

- A **head** of transparent material from where the light comes. The head can be of different diameters, but typically comes in 3mm, 5mm, and 10mm sizes.

- Two legs (**leads**) of different lengths to identify the positive (**anode**) from the negative (**cathode**) terminal. The anode is the longer lead.

The following diagram shows the basic structure of a through-hole LED and its symbolic representation in an electronic circuit.

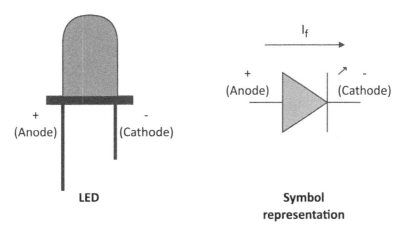

Figure 2.14 – LED with symbolic representation

As mentioned, the LED emits light when the current flows through it. However, in contrast to the resistors, the current flows only in one direction, specifically from the anode to the cathode. This current is commonly called **forward current** (*If*).

The brightness of the LED is proportional to *If*, so the higher it is, the brighter it will appear.

The LED has a maximum operating current that we must not exceed to avoid breaking it instantly. For standard through-hole 5 mm LEDs, the maximum current is typically 20 mA, so values between 4 mA and 15 mA should be enough to see the LED emitting the light.

To allow the current to flow, we need to apply a specific voltage to the terminals' LED, called **forward voltage** (*Vf*). We define the *Vf* as:

$$V_f = V_{anode} - V_{cathode}$$

We report the typical *Vf* range for some LED colors in the following table:

LED color	Forward voltage (V)
Red	1.8 – 2.1
Orange	1.9 - 2.2
Yellow	1.9 – 2.2
Green	2 – 3.1
Blue	3 – 3.7
White	3 – 3.4

Figure 2.15 – Typical LED forward voltage

From the preceding table, we can observe the following about the forward voltage range:

- It depends on the color.

- It is narrow and less than the typical 3.3 V required to power a microcontroller in most cases.

From these observations, three questions come into mind:

- First, how can we apply the forward voltage on the LED terminals since we typically only have 3.3 V from the microcontroller?

- What happens if we apply a voltage lower than the minimum *Vf*?

- What happens if we apply a voltage higher than the maximum *Vf*?

The answers rely on the following physical relationship between the voltage and current of the LED:

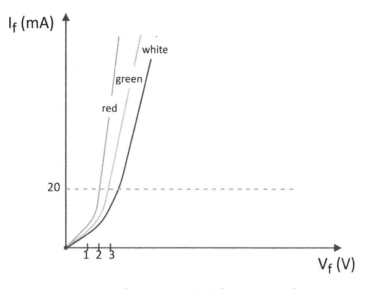

Figure 2.16 – Voltage-current (VI) characteristic of LED

From the previous chart where the x and y axes report the voltage and current, we can deduce the following:

- If we applied a voltage much lower than Vf to the LED, the LED would not turn on because the current would be low.

- If we applied a voltage much higher than Vf on the LED, the LED would be damaged because the current would exceed the 20 mA limit.

Therefore, fixing the voltage at the required operating Vf is crucial to ensure that the device works and is not damaged.

The solution is simple and only requires a resistor in series with the LED, as shown in the following figure:

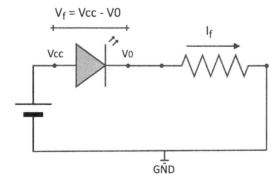

Figure 2.17 – The resistor in series with the LED limits the current

At this point, it should be clear why we included the resistor in the circuit of the previous recipe. Since the LED has a fixed voltage drop when it emits the light (*Vf*), the resistor limits the current at the value we want, such as 4 mA–15 mA. Therefore, having the LED current in the acceptable range means that the *Vf* does not fall out of the expected operating range.

We can calculate the resistor's value using the following formula:

$$R = \frac{Vcc - V_f}{I_f}$$

Where:

- *Vf* is the forward voltage.
- *If* is the forward current.
- *R* is the resistance.

The forward voltage/current and LED brightness information is generally available in the LED datasheet.

Now, let's see how we can control the status of this device with the GPIO peripheral.

Introducing the GPIO peripheral

General-purpose input/output (GPIO) is the most common and versatile peripheral on microcontrollers.

As the name suggests, GPIO does not have a fixed functionality. Instead, its primary function is to provide (output) or read (input) digital signals (*1* or *0*) through the external pins, commonly called either *GPIO*, *IO*, or *GP*.

A microcontroller can integrate several GPIO peripherals, where each one can control a dedicated pin of the integrated chip.

GPIO has similar behavior to `std::cout` and `std::cin` of the C++ `iostream` library but with the difference that it writes and reads fixed voltages rather than characters.

The commonly applied voltages for the logical *1* and *0* levels are as follows:

Logical level	Voltage (V)
1 or HIGH	Vcc, microcontroller supply voltage (e.g., 3.3 V, 5V)
0 or LOW	GND

Figure 2.18 – Relation between logical levels and voltages

The LED blinking is a typical example of configuring the GPIO peripheral in output mode to supply either 3.3 V (*1*) or 0 V (*0*) programmatically.

There are two ways to connect the LED with the GPIO pin, and the direction of the current makes them different. The first way is **current sourcing**, where the current flows out of the microcontroller board. To do so, we need to do the following:

- Connect the LED anode to the GPIO pin.
- Connect the LED cathode to the resistor in the series.
- Connect the remaining resistor terminal to GND.

The following circuit shows how to drive an LED with a current sourcing circuit:

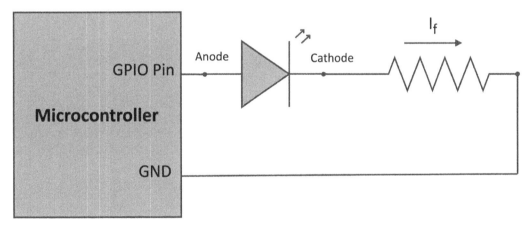

Figure 2.19 – Current sourcing. The current goes out of the microcontroller board

From the preceding circuit, we can observe that the GPIO pin should supply the logical level *1* to turn on the LED.

The second and opposite way is **current sinking**, where the current flows into the microcontroller board. In this case, we need to do the following:

- Connect the LED cathode to the GPIO pin.
- Connect the LED anode to the resistor in series.
- Connect the remaining resistor terminal to 3.3 V.

As we can observe from the following circuit, the GPIO pin should supply the logical level *0* to turn on the LED:

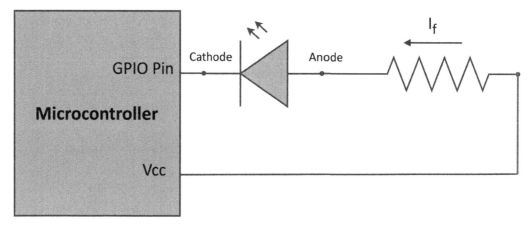

Figure 2.20 – Current sinking. The current goes into the microcontroller board

Whatever solution we adopt, it is essential to keep in mind that the pin has limits on the maximum current, which can be different depending on its direction. For example, the Arduino Nano has a maximum output current of 15 mA and a maximum input current of 5 mA. So, when designing the circuit to drive the LED, we should always consider these limitations for correctly operating and not damaging the device.

How to do it...

Disconnect the microcontroller boards from the power and keep the LED and resistor on the breadboard as in the previous recipe. However, unplug all the jumper wires except the one connected to the - bus rail (GND). The following diagram shows what you should have on the breadboard:

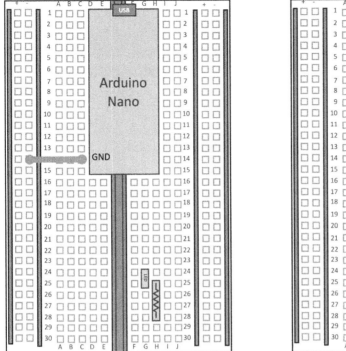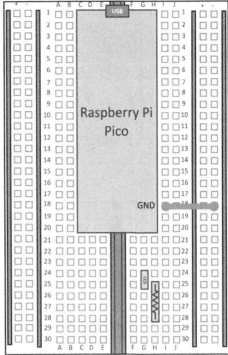

Figure 2.21 – We keep the microcontroller board, LED, and resistor from the Implementing an LED status indicator on the breadboard recipe

Since the LED cathode is connected to the terminal resistor, the LED will be driven by a current sourcing circuit.

The following steps will show how to control the LED light through the GPIO peripheral:

1. Choose the GPIO pin to drive the LED. The following table reports our choice:

Platform	GPIO Pin
Arduino Nano	P0.23
Raspberry Pi Pico	GP22

Figure 2.22 – GPIO pin selected for driving the LED

2. Connect the LED anode to the GPIO pin with a jumper wire:

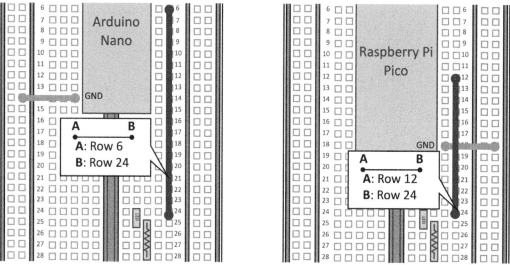

Figure 2.23 – Connect the LED anode to the GPIO pin

On the Arduino Nano, we use a jumper wire to connect (**J, 6**) with (**J, 24**). On the Raspberry Pi Pico, we use a jumper wire to connect (**J, 12**) with (**J, 24**).

3. Connect the terminal resistor to GND:

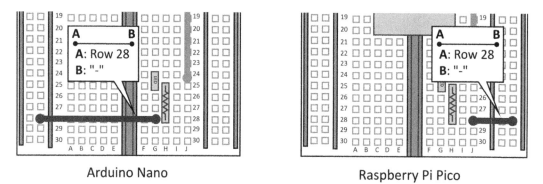

Figure 2.24 – Connect the resistor to GND

On both the Arduino Nano and Raspberry Pi Pico, we connect (**J, 28**) with the - bus rail.

The 220Ω resistor imposes an LED current of ~5 mA, which is below the maximum 20 mA LED current and below the maximum output GPIO current, as reported in the following table:

Platform	Max GPIO current (sourcing) – mA
Arduino Nano	12
Raspberry Pi Pico	10

Figure 2.25 – Max GPIO current (sourcing) on the Arduino Nano and Raspberry Pi Pico

Once the circuit is ready, we can focus on the GPIO programming.

4. Open the Arduino IDE and create a new sketch. Declare and initialize a global `mbed::DigitalOut` object with the pin name used for driving the LED.

    For the Arduino Nano, we have the following:

    ```
    mbed::DigitalOut led(p23);
    ```

    And this for the Raspberry Pi Pico:

    ```
    mbed::DigitalOut led(p22);
    ```

    Mbed, or rather **Mbed OS** (`https://os.mbed.com/`), is a **real-time operating system** (**RTOS**) specifically for Arm Cortex-M processors, which offers functionalities typical of a canonical OS and drivers to control microcontroller peripherals. All programs on the Arduino Nano 33 BLE Sense board and Raspberry Pi Pico are built on top of this tiny operating system. In this recipe, we use the `mbed::DigitalOutput` object (`https://os.mbed.com/docs/mbed-os/v6.15/apis/digitalout.html`) from Mbed OS to interface with the GPIO peripheral in output mode. The peripheral initialization requires the GPIO pin (`PinName`) connected to the LED. `PinName` always starts with the letter p, followed by the pin number.

    On the Arduino Nano, the pin number is obtained from the y number reported in the pin label `P<x>.<y>`. Therefore, `PinName` is p23.

    On the Raspberry Pi Pico, the pin number is obtained from the y number reported in the label `GPy`. Therefore, `PinName` is p22.

5. Set `led` to 1 for turning on the LED in the `loop()` function:

    ```
    void loop() {
        led = 1;
    }
    ```

Compile the sketch and upload the program to the microcontroller.

Turning an LED on and off with a push-button

In contrast to a PC where the keyboard, mouse, or even a touchscreen facilitates human interactions with the software applications, a physical button represents the easiest way for a user to interact with a microcontroller.

This recipe will teach us how to program the GPIO to read the status of a push-button (*pushed* or *released*) to control the LED light.

The following Arduino sketch contains the code referred to in this recipe:

- `04_gpio_in_out.ino`:

  `https://github.com/PacktPublishing/TinyML-Cookbook/blob/main/Chapter02/ArduinoSketches/04_gpio_in_out.ino`

Getting ready

To get ready for this recipe, we need to know how this device works and program the GPIO peripheral in input mode.

The **push-button** is a type of button used with microcontrollers, and it has *boolean* behavior since its state can either be *pushed* (*true*) or *released* (*false*).

From an electronics point of view, a push-button is a device that makes (a.k.a. short) or breaks (a.k.a. open) the connection between two wires. When we press the button, we connect the wires through a mechanical system, allowing the current to flow. However, it is not like a standard light switch that keeps the wires connected when released. When we don't apply pressure to the button, the wires disconnect, and the current stops flowing.

Although this device has four metal legs, it is a two-terminal device because the contacts on the opposite side (1, 4 and 2, 3) are connected, as shown in the following figure:

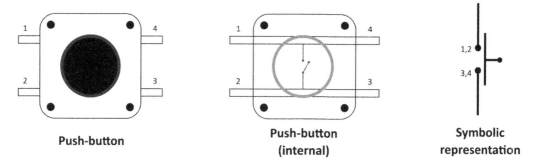

Push-button   **Push-button (internal)**   **Symbolic representation**

Figure 2.26 – Push-button representation

When building a circuit with this component, the legs on the same side (1,2 or 4,3 in the preceding figure) are responsible for connecting two points. These two points will have the same voltage when the push-button is pressed.

The state of a push-button can be read with the GPIO peripheral in input mode. When configuring the GPIO in input mode, the peripheral reads the applied voltage on the pin to infer the logical level. From this value, we can guess whether the button is pressed.

In the following diagram, the voltage on the GPIO pin is GND when we press the button. However, what is the voltage when the button is released?

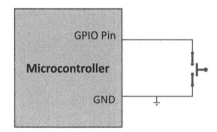

Figure 2.27 – What is the voltage on the GPIO pin when we release the push-button?

Although the pin could only assume two logical levels, this could not be true in some input mode circumstances. A third logical level called **floating** (or **high impedance**) could occur if we do not take circuit precautions. When the floating state occurs, the pin's logical level is undefined because the voltage fluctuates between 3.3 V and GND. Since the voltage is not constant, we cannot know whether the push-button is pressed. To prevent this problem, we must include a resistor in our circuit to always have a well-defined logical level under all conditions.

Depending on what logical level we want in the *pushed* state, the resistor can be as follows:

- **Pull-up**: The resistor connects the GPIO pin to the 3.3 V. Thus, the GPIO pin reads *LOW* in the pushed state and *HIGH* in the released state.

- **Pull-down**: The resistor connects the GPIO pin to GND in contrast to the pull-up configuration. Thus, the GPIO pin reads the logical level *HIGH* in the pushed state and *LOW* in the released state.

The following diagram shows the difference between the pull-up and pull-down configurations:

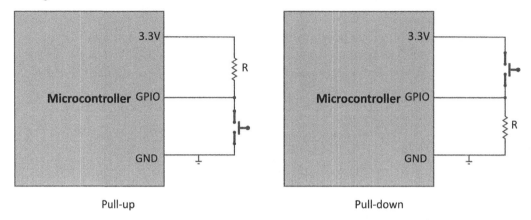

Figure 2.28 – Pull-up versus pull-down configurations

Typically, a 10 K resistor should be okay for both cases. However, most microcontrollers offer an internal and programmable pull-up resistor so the external one is often not needed.

How to do it...

Keep all the components on the breadboard. The following steps will show what to change in the previous sketch to control the LED status with the push-button:

1. Choose the GPIO pin for reading the push-button state. The following table reports our choice.

Platform	GPIO Pin INPUT
Arduino Nano	P0.30
Raspberry Pi Pico	GP10

Figure 2.29 – GPIO pin used to read the push-button state

2. Mount the push-button between the breadboard's left and right terminal strips:

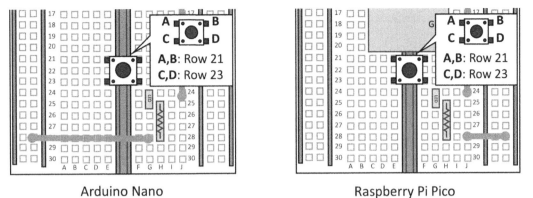

Arduino Nano   Raspberry Pi Pico

Figure 2.30 – The push-button is mounted between the terminal strips 21 and 23

As we can observe from the preceding diagram, we use terminal strips not employed by other devices.

3.   Connect the push-button to the GPIO pin and GND:

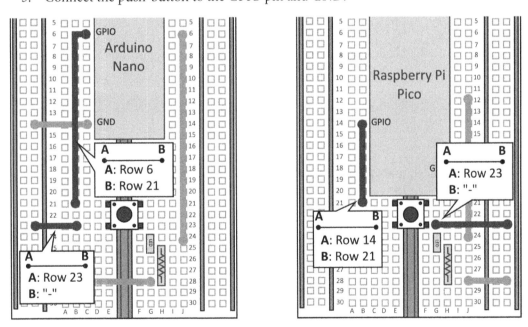

Figure 2.31 – The push-button is only connected to the GPIO pin and GND

The floating state will not occur because we use the microcontroller pull-up resistor.

4. Open the sketch developed in the previous recipe. Declare and initialize a global `mbed::DigitalIn` object with the pin name used for the push-button.

For the Arduino Nano:

```
mbed::DigitalIn button(p30);
```

And this for the Raspberry Pi Pico:

```
mbed::DigitalIn button(p10);
```

`mbed::DigitalIn`(https://os.mbed.com/docs/mbed-os/v6.15/apis/digitalin.html) is used to interface with the GPIO peripheral in input mode. The initialization only requires the GPIO pin (`PinName`) connected to the push-button.

5. Set the button mode to `PullUp` in the `setup()` function:

```
void setup() {
    button.mode(PullUp);
}
```

The preceding code enables the microcontroller's internal pull-up resistor.

6. Turn on the LED when the push-button is *LOW (0)* in the `loop()` function:

```
void loop() {
    led = !button;
}
```

We just need to set the `led` object to the opposite value returned by `button` to light up the LED when the push-button is pressed.

Compile the sketch and upload the program to the microcontroller.

Tip

When the push-button is pressed, the switch could generate spurious logical-level transitions due to the mechanical nature of the component. This issue is called **button bouncing** because the switch response bounces between *HIGH* and *LOW* for a short time. You may consider adopting a **switch debouncing** algorithm (for example, `https://os.mbed.com/teams/ TVZ-Mechatronics-Team/wiki/Timers-interrupts-and- tasks`) to prevent the generation of multiple transitions.

Using interrupts to read the push-button state

The previous recipe explained how to read digital signals with the GPIO peripheral. However, the proposed solution is inefficient because the CPU wastes cycles waiting for the button to be pressed while it could do something else in the meantime. Furthermore, this could be a scenario where we would keep the CPU in low-power mode when there is nothing else to do.

This recipe will teach us how to read the push-button state efficiently by using the interrupts on the Arduino Nano.

The following Arduino sketch contains the code referred to in this recipe:

- `05_gpio_interrupt.ino`:

  `https://github.com/PacktPublishing/TinyML-Cookbook/blob/main/Chapter02/ArduinoSketches/05_gpio_interrupt.ino`

Getting ready

Let's prepare this recipe by learning what an interrupt is and what Mbed OS API we can use to read the push-button efficiently.

An **interrupt** is a signal that temporarily pauses the main program to respond to an event with a dedicated function, called an **interrupt handler** or **interrupt service routine (ISR)**. Once the ISR ends the execution, the processor resumes the main program from the point it was left at, as shown in the following diagram:

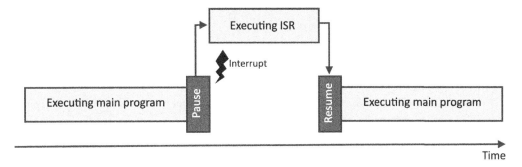

Figure 2.32 – Interrupt pauses the main program temporarily

The interrupt is a powerful mechanism to save energy because the CPU could enter the sleep state and wait for an event before starting the computation.

A microcontroller has several interrupt sources, and for each one, we can program a dedicated ISR.

Although the ISR is a function, there are limitations to its implementation:

- It does not have input arguments.

- It does not return a value. Therefore, we need to use global values to report status changes.

- It must be short to not steal too much time from the main program. We want to remind you that *the ISR is not a thread* since the processor can only resume the computation when the ISR finishes.

For GPIO peripherals in input mode, we can use the mbed::InterruptIn (https://os.mbed.com/docs/mbed-os/v6.15/apis/interruptin.html) object to trigger an event whenever the logical level on the pin changes:

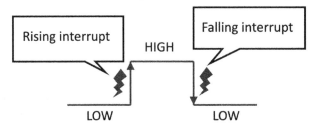

Figure 2.33 – Rising interrupt versus falling interrupt

As we can observe from the preceding diagram, mbed::InterruptIn can trigger interrupts when the logical level on the pin goes from *LOW* to *HIGH* (*rising interrupts*) or *HIGH* to *LOW* (*falling interrupt*).

How to do it...

Open the sketch built in the previous recipe and follow these steps to turn on and off the LED with the GPIO interrupt:

1. Define and initialize the mbed::InterruptIn object with the PinName of the GPIO pin connected to the push-button.

    For the Arduino Nano:

    ```
    mbed::InterruptIn button(p30);
    ```

    For the Raspberry Pi Pico:

    ```
    mbed::InterruptIn button(p10);
    ```

    The mbed::DigitalIn object is not required anymore since mbed::InterruptIn also controls the interface with the GPIO peripheral in input mode.

2. Write an ISR for handling the interrupt request on the rising edge (*LOW* to *HIGH*) of the input signal:

```
void rise_ISR() {
  led = 0;
}
```

The LED is turned off when the preceding ISR is called (`led = 0`).

Next, write an ISR for handling the interrupt request on the falling edge (*HIGH* to *LOW*) of the input signal:

```
void fall_ISR() {
  led = 1;
}
```

The LED switches on when the preceding ISR is called (`led = 1`).

3. Initialize `button` in the `setup()` function:

```
void setup() {
  button.mode(PullUp);
  button.rise(&rise_ISR);
  button.fall(&fall_ISR);
}
```

We configure the `mbed::InterruptIn` object by doing the following:

*   Enabling the internal pull-up resistor (`button.mode(PullUp)`)

*   Attaching the ISR function to call when the rising interrupt occurs (`button.rise(&rise_ISR)`)

*   Attaching the ISR function to call when the falling interrupt occurs (`button.fall(&fall_ISR)`)

4. Replace the code in the `loop()` function with `delay(4000)`:

```
void loop() {
  delay(4000);
}
```

In theory, we could leave the `loop()` function empty. However, we recommend calling `delay()` when nothing has to be done because it can put the system in low-power mode.

Compile the sketch and upload the program to the microcontroller.

Powering microcontrollers with batteries

For many TinyML applications, batteries could be the only power source for our microcontrollers.

In this final recipe, we will learn how to power microcontrollers with AA batteries.

The following Colab notebook contains the code referred to in this recipe:

- `06_estimate_battery_life.ipynb`:

  `https://github.com/PacktPublishing/TinyML-Cookbook/blob/main/Chapter02/ColabNotebooks/06_estimate_battery_life.ipynb`

Getting started

Microcontrollers don't have a built-in **battery**, so we need to supply an external one to make the device work when it is not connected through the micro-USB cable.

To get ready for this recipe, we need to know what types of batteries we need and how we can use them correctly to supply power.

Batteries are sources of electric power and have a limited energy capacity. The energy capacity (or battery capacity) quantifies the energy stored and is measured in **milli-ampere-hour (mAh)**. Therefore, a higher mAh implies a longer battery life.

The following table reports some commercial batteries that find applicability with microcontrollers:

Battery type	Voltage (V)	Energy capacity (mAh)
AAA	1.5	~1000
AA	1.5	~2400 (Alkaline)
CR2032	3.6	~240
CR2016	3.6	~90

Figure 2.34 – Suitable commercial batteries for microcontrollers

The battery selection depends on the required microcontroller voltage and other factors such as energy capacity, form factor, and operating temperature.

As we can observe from the preceding table, the AA battery provides a higher capacity, but it supplies 1.5 V, typically insufficient for microcontrollers.

Therefore, how can we power microcontrollers with AA batteries?

In the following subsections, we will show standard techniques to either increase the supplied voltage or the energy capacity.

Increasing the output voltage by connecting batteries in series

When connecting *batteries in series*, the positive terminal of one battery is connected to the negative terminal of the other one, as shown in the following figure:

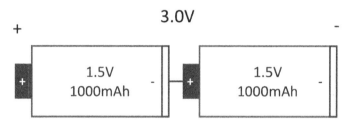

Figure 2.35 – Batteries in series

> **Important Note**
> This approach will not extend the battery capacity but just the supplied voltage.

The new supplied voltage (V_{new}) is as follows:

$$V_{new} = V_{battery} \cdot N$$

Where N is the number of connected batteries in series.

For example, since one AA battery supplies 1.5 V for 2400 mAh, we could connect two AA batteries in series to produce 3.0 V for the same energy capacity.

However, if the battery capacity is not enough for our application, how can we increase it?

Increasing the energy capacity by connecting batteries in parallel

When connecting *batteries in parallel*, the positive terminals of the batteries are tied together with one wire. The same applies to the negative terminals, which are joined together as shown in the following figure:

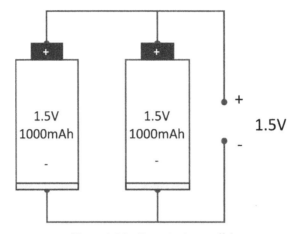

Figure 2.36 – Batteries in parallel

> **Important Note**
> This approach will not increase the output voltage but just the battery capacity.

The new battery capacity (BC_{new}) is as follows:

$$BC_{new} = BC_{battery} \cdot N$$

Where N is the number of connected batteries in parallel.

For example, since one AA battery has a battery capacity of 2400 mAh, we could connect two AA batteries in parallel to increase the battery capacity by two times.

Now that we know how to connect multiple batteries together to get the desired output voltage and energy capacity, let's see how we can use them to power the microcontrollers.

Connecting batteries to the microcontroller board

Microcontrollers have dedicated pins for supplying power through external energy sources, such as batteries. These pins have voltage limits, commonly reported in the datasheet.

On the Arduino Nano, the external power source is supplied through the **Vin** pin. The **Vin** input voltage can range from 5 V–21 V.

On the Raspberry Pi Pico, the external power source is supplied through the **VSYS** pin. The **VSYS** input voltage can range from 1.8 V – 5.5 V.

On both platforms, the onboard voltage regulator will convert the supplied voltage to 3.3 V.

How to do it...

Disconnect the Arduino Nano and Raspberry Pi Pico from the micro-USB and keep all the components on the breadboard.

The battery holder considered for this recipe connects the AA batteries in series. We recommend not inserting the batteries in the battery holder yet. The batteries should only be inserted when the electric circuit is completed.

The following steps will show how to power the Arduino Nano and Raspberry Pi Pico with batteries:

1. Connect the positive (red) and negative (black) wires of the battery holder to the + and – bus rails respectively:

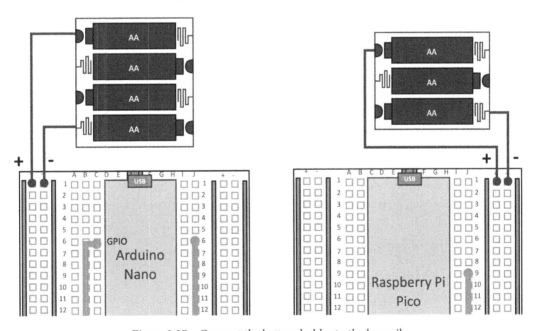

Figure 2.37 – Connect the battery holder to the bus rails

2. The Arduino Nano and Raspberry Pi Pico have different voltage limits for the external power source. Therefore, we cannot use the same number of AA batteries on both platforms. In fact, three AA batteries are enough for the Raspberry Pi Pico but not for the Arduino Nano. In contrast, four AA batteries are enough for the Arduino Nano but beyond the voltage limit on the Raspberry Pi Pico. For this reason, we use a 4 x AA battery holder for the Arduino Nano to supply 6 V and a 3 x AA battery holder for the Raspberry Pi Pico to supply 4.5 V.

3. Connect the external power source to the microcontroller board, as shown in the following diagram:

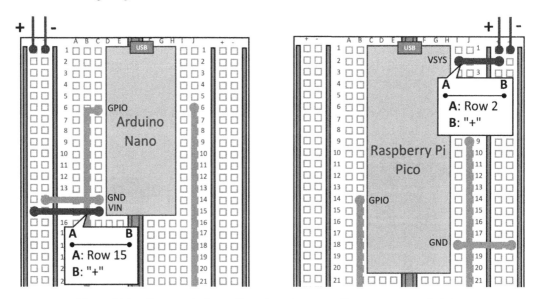

Figure 2.38 – Connect the bus rails to the microcontroller power pin and GND

As you can observe from the preceding figure, **VIN** (Arduino Nano) and **VSYS** (Raspberry Pi Pico) are connected to the positive battery holder terminal through the + bus rail.

4. Insert the batteries in the battery holder:

    ◆ 4 x AA batteries for the Arduino Nano

    ◆ 3 x AA batteries for the Raspberry Pi Pico

The LED application should now work again.

However, one thing we might be curious about is how can we evaluate the lifetime of a battery-powered application?

There's more

Once we have chosen the battery for the microcontroller, we can estimate its lifetime with the following formula:

$$BL = \frac{BC}{IL}$$

Where:

Quantity	Unit	Meaning
BL	Hours (h)	Battery life
BC	mAh	Battery capacity
IL	mA	Load current consumption required by the microcontroller

Figure 2.39 – Physical quantities of the battery lifetime estimate formula

The following Python code calculates the battery life in hours and days:

```
battery_cap_mah = 2400
i_load_ma = 1.5

battery_life_hours = battery_cap_mah / i_load_ma
battery_life_days = battery_life_hours / 24

print("Battery life:", battery_life_hours,"hours,", battery_
life_days, "days")
```

The preceding code estimates the battery life for the case when the battery capacity (battery_cap_mah) is *2400 mAh,* and the load current (i_load_ma) is 1.5 mA.

The expected output is as follows:

```
Battery life: 1600.0 hours, 66.66666666666667 days
```

Figure 2.40 – Expected output from the battery life estimator

Although the formula above is an estimation and valid under ideal conditions, it is enough to understand how long the system could last. A better model could include other factors such as battery self-discharge and temperature.

3
Building a Weather Station with TensorFlow Lite for Microcontrollers

Nowadays, it is straightforward to get the weather forecast with our smartphones, laptops, and tablets, thanks to internet connectivity. However, have you ever thought of what you would do if you had to track the weather in a remote region with no internet access?

This chapter will teach us how to implement a weather station with **machine learning (ML)** using the temperature and humidity of the last three hours.

In this chapter, we will focus on dataset preparation and show how to acquire historical weather data from **WorldWeatherOnline**. After that, we will explain how to train and test a model with **TensorFlow (TF)**. In the last part, we will deploy the model on an Arduino Nano and a Raspberry Pi Pico with **TensorFlow Lite for Microcontrollers (TFLu)** and build an application to predict whether it will snow.

The goal of this chapter is to guide you through all the development stages of a TF-based application for microcontrollers and explain how to acquire temperature and humidity sensor data.

In this chapter, we're going to implement the following recipes:

- Importing weather data from WorldWeatherOnline
- Preparing the dataset
- Training the model with TF
- Evaluating the model's effectiveness
- Quantizing the model with TFLite converter
- Using the built-in temperature and humidity sensor on an Arduino Nano
- Using the DHT22 sensor with a Raspberry Pi Pico
- Preparing the input features for the model inference
- On-device inference with TFLu

Technical requirements

To complete all the practical recipes of this chapter, we will need the following:

- An Arduino Nano 33 Sense board
- A Raspberry Pi Pico board
- A micro-USB cable
- 1 x half-size solderless breadboard (Raspberry Pi Pico only)
- 1 x AM2302 module with the DHT22 sensor (Raspberry Pi Pico only)
- 5 x jumper wires (Raspberry Pi Pico only)
- Laptop/PC with either Ubuntu 18.04+ or Windows 10 on x86-64

The source code and additional material are available in the `Chapter03` folder of the repository for this book (`https://github.com/PacktPublishing/TinyML-Cookbook/tree/main/Chapter03`).

Importing weather data from WorldWeatherOnline

The effectiveness of ML algorithms depends heavily on the data used for training. Hence, as we commonly say, *the ML model is only good as the dataset*. The essential requirement for a good dataset is that the input data must represent the problem we want to solve. Considering our context, we know from physics that temperature and humidity affect snow formation.

Hence, in this recipe, we will show how to gather historical hourly temperature, humidity, and snowfall data to build a dataset for forecasting snow.

The following Colab file (see the *Importing weather data from WorldWeatherOnline* section in the following repository) contains the code referred to in this recipe:

- `preparing_model.ipynb`:

  `https://github.com/PacktPublishing/TinyML-Cookbook/blob/main/Chapter03/ColabNotebooks/preparing_model.ipynb`

Getting ready

On the internet, there are various sources from which we can gather hourly weather data, but most of them are not free or have limited usage.

For this recipe, **WorldWeatherOnline** (`https://www.worldweatheronline.com/developer/`) has been our choice, which has a free trial period for 30 days and provides the following:

- Simple API through HTTP requests to acquire the data

- Historical worldwide weather data

- 250 weather data requests per day

> **Important Note**
> The limit on the weather data requests per day has no impact on this recipe.

You only need to sign up on the website to start fetching the data.

WorldWeatherOnline has an API called the *Past Historical Weather API* (`https://www.worldweatheronline.com/developer/premium-api-explorer.aspx`) that allows us to gather historical weather conditions from July 1, 2008.

However, we will not directly deal with its native API but use the Python package `wwo-hist` (`https://github.com/ekapope/WorldWeatherOnline`) to export the data directly to a pandas DataFrame.

How to do it...

Open Colab and create a new notebook. In the coding area, do the following:

1. Install the `wwo-hist` package:

```
!pip install wwo-hist
```

2. Import the `retrieve_hist_data` function from `wwo-hist`:

```
from wwo_hist import retrieve_hist_data
```

`retrieve_hist_data` is the only function required to acquire data from WorldWeatherOnline and can export to either pandas DataFrames or CSV files.

3. Acquire data for ten years (`01-JAN-2011` to `31-DEC-2020`) with an hourly frequency from Canazei:

```
frequency=1
api_key = 'YOUR_API_KEY'
location_list = [canazei]
df_weather = retrieve_hist_data(api_key,
                                location_list,
                                '01-JAN-2011',
                                '31-DEC-2020',
                                frequency,
                                location_label = False,
                                export_csv = False,
                                store_df = True)
```

`www-hist` will export the data to `df_weather`, a list of pandas DataFrames.

In this step, we set the input arguments for `retrieve_hist_data`. Let's unpack all of them:

- **API key**: The API key is reported in the WorldWeatherOnline subscription dashboard, and it should replace the `YOUR_API_KEY` string.

- **Location**: This is the list of locations from which to acquire the weather data. Since we are building a dataset to forecast the snow, we should consider places where it snows periodically. For example, you can consider *Canazei* (`https://en.wikipedia.org/wiki/Canazei`), located in the north of Italy, where snowfall can occur at any point between December and March. We could also add other locations to make the ML model more generic.

- **Start date/End date**: The start and end dates define the temporal interval in which to gather the data. The date format is *dd-mmm-yyyy*. Since we want a large representative dataset, we query 10 years of weather data. Therefore, the interval time is set to `01-JAN-2011 – 31-DEC-2020`.

- **Frequency**: This defines the hourly frequency. For example, *1* stands for every hour, *3* for every three hours, *6* for every six hours, and so on. We opt for an *hourly frequency* since we need the temperature and humidity of the last three hours to forecast snow.

- **Location label**: Since we might need to acquire data from different locations, this flag binds the acquired weather data to the place. We set this option to `False` because we are only using a single location.

- **export_csv**: This is the flag to export the weather data to a CSV file. We set it to `False` because we do not need to export the data to a CSV file.

- **store_df**: This is the flag to export the weather data to a pandas DataFrame. We set it to `True`.

Once the weather data is retrieved, the console output will report **export to canazei completed!**.

4. Export temperature, humidity, and output snowfall to lists:

```
t_list = df_weather[0].tempC.astype(float).to_list()
h_list = df_weather[0].humidity.astype(float).to_list()
s_list = df_weather[0].totalSnow_cm.astype(float).to_
         list()
```

The generated `df_weather[]` dataset includes several weather conditions for each requested date and time. For example, we can find the pressure in millibars, cloud coverage in percentage, visibility in kilometers, and, of course, the physical quantities that we're interested in:

- `tempC`: The temperature in degrees Celsius (°C)

- `humidity`: The relative air humidity in percentage (%)

- `totalSnow_cm`: Total snowfall in centimeters (cm)

In this final step, we export the hourly temperature, humidity, and snowfall in cm to three lists using the `to_list()` method.

Now, we have all we need to prepare the dataset for forecasting the snow.

Preparing the dataset

Preparing a dataset is a crucial phase in any ML project because it has implications for the effectiveness of the trained model.

In this recipe, we will put into action two techniques to make the dataset more suitable to get a more accurate model. These two techniques will balance the dataset with standardization and bring the **input features** into the same numerical range.

The following Colab file (see the *Preparing the dataset* section in the following repository) contains the code referred to in this recipe:

- `preparing_model.ipynb`:

  `https://github.com/PacktPublishing/TinyML-Cookbook/blob/main/Chapter03/ColabNotebooks/preparing_model.ipynb`

Getting ready

The temperature and humidity of the last three hours are our input features. If you wonder why we use the last three hours' weather conditions, it is just so we have more input features and Increase the chance of higher classification accuracy.

To get ready for the dataset preparation, we need to know why the dataset needs to be balanced and why the raw input features should not be used for training. These two aspects will be examined in the following subsections.

Preparing a balanced dataset

An **unbalanced dataset** is a dataset where one of the classes has considerably more samples than the others. Training with an unbalanced dataset could produce a model with high accuracy but that's incapable of solving our problem. For example, consider a dataset where one of the two classes has 99% of the samples. If the network miss-classified the minority class, we would still have 99% accuracy, but the model would be ineffective.

Therefore, we require a **balanced dataset** with roughly the same input samples for each output category.

Balancing a dataset can be done with the following techniques:

- **Acquiring more input samples for the minority class**: This should be the first thing we do to ensure we have correctly generated the dataset. However, it is not always possible to collect more data, particularly when dealing with infrequent events.

- **Oversampling the minority class**: We could randomly duplicate samples from the under-represented class. However, this approach may increase the risk of overfitting the minority class if we duplicate many instances.

- **Undersampling the majority class**: We could randomly delete samples from the over-represented class. Since this approach reduces the dataset's size, we could lose valuable training information.

- **Generating synthetic samples for the minority class**: We could develop artificially manufactured samples. The most common algorithm for this is **Synthetic Minority Over-sampling Technique (SMOTE)**. SMOTE is an oversampling technique that creates new samples instead of duplicating under-represented instances. Although this technique reduces the risk of overfitting caused by oversampling, the generated synthetic samples could be incorrect near the class separation border, adding undesirable noise to the dataset.

As we can see, despite the variety of techniques, there is not an overall best solution to fix an unbalanced dataset. The method or methods to adopt will depend on the problem to solve.

Feature scaling with Z-score

Our input features exist in different numerical ranges. For example, humidity is always between 0 and 100, while the temperature on the Celsius scale can be negative and has a smaller positive numerical range than humidity.

This is a typical scenario when dealing with various physical quantities and could impact the effectiveness of the training.

Generally, if the input features have different numerical ranges, the ML model may not generalize properly because it will be influenced more by the features with more significant values. Therefore, the input features need to be rescaled to ensure that each input feature contributes equally during training. Furthermore, another benefit of feature scaling in neural networks is that it helps converge the gradient descent faster toward the minima.

Z-score is a common scaling technique adopted in neural networks, and it is defined with the following formula:

$$value_{new} = \frac{value_{old} - \mu}{\sigma}$$

Let's break down this formula:

- μ: the mean of the input features
- σ: the standard deviation of the input features

Z-score can bring the input features to a similar numerical range, but not necessarily between zero and one.

How to do it...

Continue working on the Colab file and follow the following steps to discover how to balance the dataset and rescale the input features with Z-score:

1. Visualize the extracted physical measurements (temperature, humidity, and snow) in a 2D scatter chart. To do so, consider the snow formation only when the snowfall (`totalSnow_cm`) is above 0.5 cm:

```
def binarize(snow, threshold):
  if snow > threshold:
    return 1
  else:
    return 0
s_bin_list = [binarize(snow, 0.5) for snow in s_list]
cm = plt.cm.get_cmap('gray_r')
sc = plt.scatter(t_list, h_list, c=s_bin_list, cmap=cm,
label="Snow")
plt.figure(dpi=150)
plt.colorbar(sc)
plt.legend()
plt.grid(True)
plt.title("Snow(T, H)")
plt.xlabel("Temperature - °C")
plt.ylabel("Humidity - %")
plt.show()
```

The preceding code generates the following scatter plot:

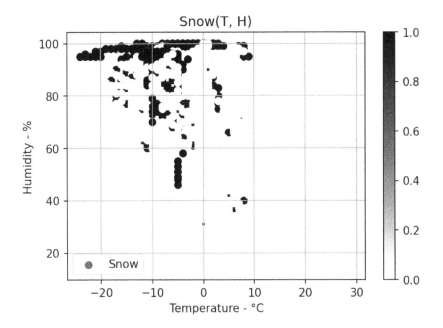

Figure 3.1 – Visualization of the temperature, humidity, and snow in a 2D chart.
Data provided by WorldWeatherOnline.com

In the preceding chart, the x-axis is the temperature, the y-axis is the humidity, and the black dot is the snow formation.

As you can observe from the distribution of the black dots, there are cases where the snow formation is reported for temperatures well above 0°C.

To simplify the recipe, we can ignore these cases and consider 2° C as the maximum temperature for the snow formation.

2. Generate the output labels (Yes and No):

```
def gen_label(snow, temperature):
  if snow > 0.5 and temperature < 2:
    return "Yes"
  else:
    return "No"
snow_labels = [gen_label(snow, temp) for snow, temp in
zip(s_list, t_list)]
```

Since we are only forecasting snow, only two classes are needed: *Yes, it snows*, or *No, it does not snow*. At this scope, we convert `totalSnow_cm` to the corresponding class (`Yes` or `No`) through the `gen_label()` function. The mapping function assigns `Yes` when `totalSnow_cm` exceeds 0.5 cm and the temperature is below 2° C.

3. Build the dataset:

```
csv_header = ["Temp0", "Temp1", "Temp2", "Humi0",
"Humi1", "Humi2", "Snow"]
```

```
df_dataset = pd.DataFrame(list(zip(t_list[:-2], t_
list[1:-1], t_list[2:], h_list[:-2], h_list[1:-1], h_
list[2:], snow_labels[2:])), columns = csv_header)
```

If *t0* is the current time, the values stored in the dataset are as follows:

- `Temp0`/`Humi0`: Temperature and humidity at time *t* = *t0* - *2*

- `Temp1`/`Humi1`: Temperature and humidity at time *t* = *t0* - *1*

- `Temp2`/`Humi2`: Temperature and humidity at time *t* = *t0*

- `Snow`: Label reporting whether it will snow at time *t* = *t0*

Therefore, we just need a `zip` and a few indices calculations to build the dataset.

4. Balance the dataset by undersampling the majority class:

```
df0 = df_dataset[df_dataset['Snow'] == "No"]
df1 = df_dataset[df_dataset['Snow'] == "Yes"]
```

```
if len(df1.index) < len(df0.index):
  df0_sub = df0.sample(len(df1.index))
  df_dataset = pd.concat([df0_sub, df1])
else:
  df1_sub = df1.sample(len(df0.index))
  df_dataset = pd.concat([df1_sub, df0])
```

The original dataset is unbalanced because, in the selected location, it typically snows during the winter season, which lasts from December to March. The following bar chart shows that the `No` class represents 87 % of all cases, so we need to apply one of the techniques shown in the *Getting ready* section to balance the dataset.

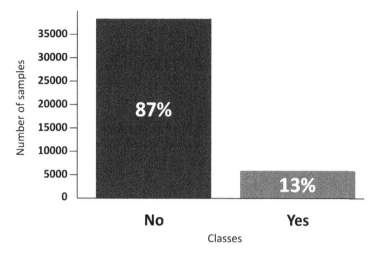

Figure 3.2 – Distribution of the dataset samples

Since the minority class has many samples (~5000), we can randomly undersample the majority class so the two categories have the same number of observations.

5. Scale the input features with Z-score independently. To do so, extract all the temperature and humidity values:

```
t_list = df_dataset['Temp0'].tolist()
h_list = df_dataset['Humi0'].tolist()
t_list = t_list + df_dataset['Temp2'].tail(2).tolist()
h_list = h_list + df_dataset['Humi2'].tail(2).tolist()
```

You can get all the temperature (or humidity) values from the Temp0 (or Humi0) column and the last two records of the Temp2 (or Humi2) column.

Next, calculate the mean and standard deviation of the temperature and humidity input features:

```
t_avg = mean(t_list)
h_avg = mean(h_list)
t_std = std(t_list)
h_std = std(h_list)
print("COPY ME!")
print("Temperature - [MEAN, STD]  ", round(t_avg, 5),
round(t_std, 5))
print("Humidity - [MEAN, STD]      ", round(h_avg, 5),
round(h_std, 5))
```

The expected output is as follows:

```
COPY ME!
Temperature - [MEAN, STD]   2.05179 7.33084
Humidity - [MEAN, STD]      82.30551 14.55707
```

Figure 3.3 – Expected mean and standard deviation values

Copy the mean and standard deviation values printed in the output log because they will be required when deploying the application on the Arduino Nano and Raspberry Pi Pico.

Finally, scale the input features with Z-score:

```
def scaling(val, avg, std):
    return (val - avg) / (std)


df_dataset['Temp0']=df_dataset['Temp0'].apply(lambda x:
scaling(x, t_avg, t_std))

df_dataset['Temp1']=df_dataset['Temp1'].apply(lambda x:
scaling(x, t_avg, t_std))

df_dataset['Temp2']=df_dataset['Temp2'].apply(lambda x:
scaling(x, t_avg, t_std))

df_dataset['Humi0']=df_dataset['Humi0'].apply(lambda x:
scaling(x, h_avg, h_std))

df_dataset['Humi1']=df_dataset['Humi1'].apply(lambda x:
scaling(x, h_avg, h_std))

df_dataset['Humi2']=df_dataset['Humi2'].apply(lambda x:
scaling(x, h_avg, h_std))
```

The following charts compare the raw and scaled input feature distributions:

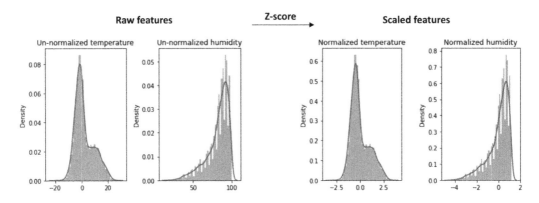

Figure 3.4 – Raw (left charts) and scaled (right charts) input feature distributions

As you can observe from the charts, Z-score provides roughly the same value range (the *x* axis) for both features.

Now, the dataset is ready to be used for training our snow forecast model!

Training the ML model with TF

The model designed for forecasting the snow is a **binary** classifier, and it is illustrated in the following diagram:

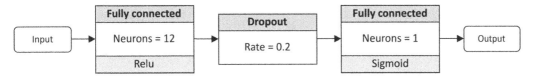

Figure 3.5 – Neural network model for forecasting the snow

The network consists of the following layers:

- 1 x **fully connected layers** with 12 neurons and followed by a ReLU activation function

- 1 x **dropout layer** with a 20% rate (0.2) to prevent **overfitting**

- 1 x **fully connected layer** with one output neuron and followed by a sigmoid activation function

In this recipe, we will train the preceding model with TF.

The following Colab file (see the *Training the ML model with TF* section in the following repository) contains the code referred to in this recipe:

- `preparing_model.ipynb:`

  `https://github.com/PacktPublishing/TinyML-Cookbook/blob/main/Chapter03/ColabNotebooks/preparing_model.ipynb`

Getting ready

The model designed in this recipe has one input and output node. The input node provides the six input features to the network: the temperature and humidity for each of the last three hours.

The model consumes the input features and returns the probability of the class in the output node. Since the sigmoid function produces the output, the result is between zero and one and considered *No* when it is below 0.5; otherwise, it's *Yes*.

In general, we consider the following four sequential steps when training a neural network:

1. Encoding the output labels
2. Splitting the dataset into training, test, and validation datasets
3. Creating the model
4. Training the model

In this recipe, we will use TF and scikit-learn to implement them.

Scikit-Learn (`https://scikit-learn.org/stable/`) is a higher-level Python library for implementing generic ML algorithms, such as SVMs, random forests, and logistic regression. It is not a DNN-specific framework but rather a software library for a wide range of ML algorithms.

How to do it...

The following steps show how to train the model presented in the *Getting ready* section with TF:

1. Extract the input features (x) and output labels (y) from the `df_dataset` pandas DataFrame:

```
f_names = df_dataset.columns.values[0:6]
l_name  = df_dataset.columns.values[6:7]
x = df_dataset[f_names]
y = df_dataset[l_name]
```

2. Encode the labels to numerical values:

```
labelencoder = LabelEncoder()
labelencoder.fit(y.Snow)
y_encoded = labelencoder.transform(y.Snow)
```

This step converts the output labels (*Yes* and *No*) to numerical values since neural networks can only deal with numbers. We use scikit-learn to transform the target labels to integer values (zero and one). The conversion requires calling the following three functions:

A. `LabelEncoder()` to initialize the `LabelEncoder` module
B. `fit()` to identify the target integer values by parsing the output labels
C. `transform()` to translate the output labels to numerical values

After `transform()`, the encoded labels are available in `y_encoded`.

3. Split the dataset into train, validation, and test datasets:

```
# Split 1 (85% vs 15%)
x_train, x_validate_test, y_train, y_validate_test =
train_test_split(x, y_encoded, test_size=0.15, random_
state = 1)
# Split 2 (50% vs 50%)
x_test, x_validate, y_test, y_validate = train_test_
split(x_validate_test, y_validate_test, test_size=0.50,
random_state = 3)
```

The following diagram shows how we split the *train*, *validation*, and *test* datasets:

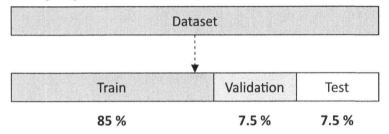

Figure 3.6 – The dataset is split into the train, validation, and test datasets

These three datasets are as follows:

*   **Training dataset**: This dataset contains the samples to train the model. The weights and biases are learned with these data.

*   **Validation dataset**: This dataset contains the samples to evaluate the model's accuracy on unseen data. The dataset is used during the training process to indicate how well the model generalizes because it includes instances not included in the training dataset. However, since this dataset is still used during training, we could indirectly influence the output model by fine-tuning some training hyperparameters.

*   **Test dataset**: This dataset contains the samples for testing the model after training. Since the test dataset is not employed during training, it evaluates the final model without bias.

From the original dataset, we assign 85% to the training dataset, 7.5% to the validation dataset, and 7.5% to the test dataset. With this split, the validation and test dataset will have roughly 1,000 samples each, enough to see if the model works properly.

The dataset splitting is done with the `train_test_split()` function from scikit-learn which splits the dataset into training and test datasets. The split proportion is defined with the `test_size` (or `train_size`) input argument, representing the input dataset's percentage to include in the test (or train) split.

We call this function twice to generate the three different datasets. The first split generates the 85% training dataset by providing `test_size=0.15`. The second split produces the validation and test datasets by halving the 15% dataset from the first split.

4. Create the model with the Keras API:

```
model = tf.keras.Sequential()
model.add(layers.Dense(12, activation='relu', input_
shape=(len(f_names),)))
model.add(layers.Dropout(0.2))
model.add(layers.Dense(1, activation='sigmoid'))
model.summary()
```

The preceding code generates the following output:

```
Model: "sequential"
```

Layer (type)	Output Shape	Param #
dense (Dense)	(None, 12)	84
dropout (Dropout)	(None, 12)	0
dense_1 (Dense)	(None, 1)	13

```
Total params: 97
Trainable params: 97
Non-trainable params: 0
```

Figure 3.7 – Model summary returned by model.summary()

The summary reports useful architecture information about the neural network model, such as the layer types, the output shapes, and the number of trainable weights required.

> **Important Note**
>
> In TinyML, it is important to keep an eye on the number of weights because it is related to the program's memory utilization.

5. Compile the model:

```
model.compile(loss='binary_crossentropy',
optimizer='adam', metrics=['accuracy'])
```

In this step, we initialize the training parameters, such as the following:

- **Loss function**: Training aims to find weights and biases to minimize a loss function. The loss indicates how far the predicted output is from the expected result, so the lower the loss, the better the model. **Cross-entropy** is the standard loss function for classification problems because it produces faster training with a better model generalization. For a binary classifier, we should use `binary_crossentropy`.

- **Performance metrics**: Performance metrics evaluate how well the model predicts the output classes. We use **accuracy**, defined as the ratio between the number of correct predictions and the total number of tests:

$$accuracy = \frac{number\ of\ correct\ predictions}{total\ number\ of\ tests}$$

- **Optimizer**: The optimizer is the algorithm used to update the weights of the network during training. The optimizer mainly affects the training time. In our example, we use the widely adopted **Adam** optimizer.

Once we have initialized the training parameters, we can train the model.

6. Train the model:

```
NUM_EPOCHS=20

BATCH_SIZE=64

history = model.fit(x_train, y_train, epochs=NUM_EPOCHS,
batch_size=BATCH_SIZE, validation_data=(x_validate, y_
validate))
```

During training, TF reports the loss and accuracy after each epoch on both the train and validation datasets, as shown in the following screenshot:

```
loss: 0.3118 - accuracy: 0.8668 - val_loss: 0.3261 - val_accuracy: 0.8479
```

Figure 3.8 – Accuracy and loss are reported on both the train and validation datasets

`accuracy` and `loss` are the accuracy and loss on the train data, while `val_accuracy` and `val_loss` are the accuracy and loss on the validation data.

It is best to rely on the accuracy and loss of the validation data to prevent **overfitting** and to see how the model behaves on unseen data.

7. Plot the accuracy and loss over training epochs:

```
loss_train = history.history['loss']
loss_val   = history.history['val_loss']
acc_train  = history.history['accuracy']
acc_val    = history.history['val_accuracy']
epochs     = range(1, NUM_EPOCHS + 1)

def plot_train_val_history(x, y_train, y_val, type_txt):
    plt.figure(figsize = (10,7))
    plt.plot(x, y_train, 'g', label='Training'+type_txt)
    plt.plot(x, y_val, 'b', label='Validation'+type_txt)
    plt.title('Training and Validation'+type_txt)
    plt.xlabel('Epochs')
    plt.ylabel(type_txt)
    plt.legend()
    plt.show()

plot_train_val_history(epochs, loss_train, loss_val,
"Loss")
plot_train_val_history(epochs, acc_train, acc_val,
"Accuracy")
```

The preceding code plots the following two charts:

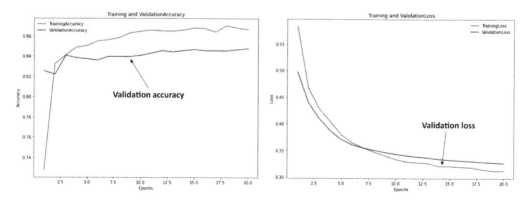

Figure 3.9 – Plot of the accuracy (left chart) and loss (right chart) over training epochs

From the plots of the accuracy and loss during training, we can see the trend of the model's performance. The trend tells us whether we should train less to avoid overfitting or more to prevent underfitting. The validation accuracy and loss are at their best around ten epochs in our case. Therefore, we should consider terminating the training earlier to prevent overfitting. To do so, you can either re-train the network for ten epochs or use the `EarlyStopping` Keras function to stop training when a monitored performance metric has stopped improving. You can discover more about `EarlyStopping` at the following link: `https://www.tensorflow.org/api_docs/python/tf/keras/callbacks/EarlyStopping`.

8. Save the entire TF model as a `SavedModel`:

```
model.save("snow_forecast")
```

`SavedModel` is a directory containing the following:

*   The TF model as a protobuf binary (with the `.pb` file extension)

*   A TF checkpoint (`https://www.tensorflow.org/guide/checkpoint`)

*   Training parameters such as optimizer, loss, and performance metrics

Therefore, the preceding command creates the `snow_forecast` folder, which you can explore using the file explorer pane on the left of Colab.

We have finally in our hands a model to forecast the snow!

Evaluating the model's effectiveness

Accuracy and loss are not enough to judge the model's effectiveness. In general, *accuracy is a good performance indicator if the dataset is balanced,* but it does not tell us the strengths and weaknesses of our model. For instance, what classes do we recognize with high confidence? What frequent mistakes does the model make?

This recipe will judge the model's effectiveness by visualizing the confusion matrix and evaluating the **recall**, **precision**, and **F1-score** performance metrics.

The following Colab file (see the *Evaluating the model's effectiveness* section in the following repository) contains the code referred to in this recipe:

*   `preparing_model.ipynb`:

    `https://github.com/PacktPublishing/TinyML-Cookbook/blob/main/Chapter03/ColabNotebooks/preparing_model.ipynb`

Getting ready

To complete this recipe, we need to know what a confusion matrix is and which performance metrics we can use to understand whether the model works fine.

The following subsections will examine these performance indicators.

Visualizing the performance with the confusion matrix

A **confusion matrix** is an *NxN* matrix reporting the number of correct and incorrect predictions on the test dataset.

For our binary classification model, we have a 2x2 matrix like the one in the following diagram:

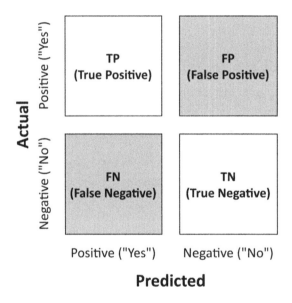

Figure 3.10 – Confusion matrix

The four values reported in the previous confusion matrix are as follows:

- **True positive** (**TP**): The number of predicted positive results that are actually positive

- **True negative** (**TN**): The number of predicted negative results that are actually negative

- **False positive** (**FP**): The number of predicted positive results that are actually negative

- **False negative** (**FN**): The number of predicted negative results that are actually positive

Ideally, we would like to have 100% accuracy, therefore, zero in the gray cells (*FN* and *FP*) of the confusion matrix reported in *Figure 3.10*. In fact, from the confusion matrix, we can calculate the accuracy using the following formula:

$$accuracy = \frac{TP + TN}{TP + FP + TN + FN} \in [0, 1]$$

However, as previously mentioned, we are more interested in alternative performance metrics. These performance indicators are described in the following subsection.

Evaluating recall, precision, and F-score

The first performance metric evaluated is **recall**, defined as follows:

$$Recall = \frac{TP}{TP + FN} \in [0, 1]$$

This metric tells us *how many of all positive ("Yes") samples we predicted correctly*. Recall should be as high as possible.

However, this metric does not consider the misclassification of negative samples. In short, the model could be excellent at classifying positive samples but incapable of classifying negative ones.

For this reason, there is another metric that takes into consideration FPs. It is **precision**, defined as follows:

$$Precision = \frac{TP}{TP + FP} \in [0, 1]$$

This metric tells us *how many predicted positive classes ("yes") were actually positive*. Precision should be as high as possible.

Another key performance metric combines recall and precision with a single formula. It is **F-score**, defined as follows:

$$F - score = \frac{2 \cdot recall \cdot precision}{recall + precision}$$

This formula helps us to evaluate the recall and precision metrics at the same time. Also, a high F-score implies a good model performance.

How to do it...

The following steps will teach us how to visualize the confusion matrix and calculate the recall, precision, and F-score metrics:

1. Visualize the confusion matrix:

```python
y_test_pred = model.predict(x_test)

y_test_pred = (y_test_pred > 0.5).astype("int32")

cm = sklearn.metrics.confusion_matrix(y_test, y_test_pred)

index_names  = ["Actual No Snow", "Actual Snow"]
column_names = ["Predicted No Snow", "Predicted Snow"]

df_cm = pd.DataFrame(cm, index = index_names, columns = column_names)

plt.figure(figsize = (10,7))
sns.heatmap(df_cm, annot=True, fmt='d', cmap="Blues")
plt.figure(figsize = (10,7))
```

The previous code produces the following output:

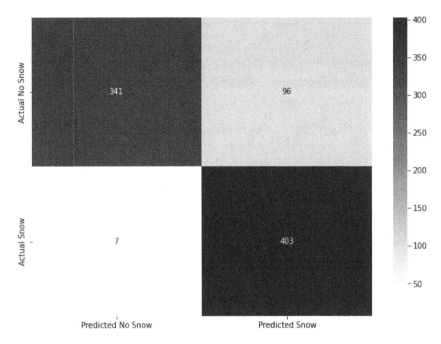

Figure 3.11 – Confusion matrix for the snow forecast model

The confusion matrix is obtained with the following two steps:

A.   Predict the labels on the test dataset using `model.predict()` and threshold the output result at 0.5. The thresholding is required because `model. predict()` returns the output of the sigmoid function, which is a value between zero and one.

B.   Use the `confusion_matrix()` function from the scikit-learn library to calculate the confusion matrix (`cm`).

From *Figure 3.11*, we can see that the samples are mainly distributed in the leading diagonal, and there are more FPs than FNs. Therefore, although the network is suitable for detecting snow, we should expect some false detections.

2.   Calculate the recall, precision, and F-score performance metrics:

```
TN = cm[0][0]
TP = cm[1][1]
FN = cm[1][0]
FP = cm[0][1]

precision = TP / (TP + FP)
recall = TP / (TP + FN)
```

```
f_score = (2 * recall * precision) / (recall + precision)

print("Recall:    ", round(recall, 3))
print("Precision: ", round(precision, 3))
print("F-score:   ", round(f_score, 3))
```

The preceding code prints the following information on the output console:

```
Recall:     0.983
Precision:  0.808
F-score:    0.887
```

Figure 3.12 – Expected results for precision, recall, and F-score

As we can see from the expected results, **Recall** equals **0.983**, so our model can forecast the snow with high confidence. However, the **Precision** is lower, **0.808**. This metric shows that we should expect some false alarms from our model. Finally, the value of **0.887** obtained for the **F-score** tells us that **Recall** and **Precision** are balanced. Therefore, we have a good ML model in our hands capable of forecasting the snow with the input features provided.

The model is now trained and validated. Hence, it is time to make it suitable for microcontroller deployment.

Quantizing the model with the TFLite converter

Exporting the trained network as SavedModel saves the training graphs such as the network architecture, weights, training variables, and checkpoints. Therefore, the generated TF model is perfect for sharing or resuming a training session but not suitable for microcontroller deployment for the following reasons:

- The weights are stored in floating-point format.
- The model keeps information that's not required for the inference.

Since our target device has computational and memory constraints, it is crucial to transform the trained model into something compact.

This recipe will teach how to quantize and convert the trained model into a lightweight, memory-efficient, and easy-to-parse exporting format with **TensorFlow Lite** (**TFLite**). The generated model will then be converted to a C-byte array, suitable for microcontroller deployments.

The following Colab file (see the *Quantizing the model with TFLite converter* section in the following recipe) contains the code referred to in this recipe:

- `preparing_model.ipynb`:

  `https://github.com/PacktPublishing/TinyML-Cookbook/blob/main/Chapter03/ColabNotebooks/preparing_model.ipynb`

Getting ready

The main ingredients used in this recipe are the TFLite converter and quantization.

TFLite (`https://www.tensorflow.org/lite`) is a deep learning framework specifically for inference on edge devices such as smartphones or embedded platforms.

As reported in the following diagram, TFLite provides a set of tools for the following:

- Converting the TF model into a lightweight representation

- Running the model efficiently on the target device

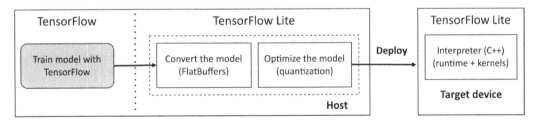

Figure 3.13 – TFLite components

The lightweight model representation used by TFLite is identified with the `.tflite` extension, and it is internally represented as **FlatBuffers** (`https://google.github.io/flatbuffers/`). The FlatBuffers format offers a flexible, easy-to-parse, and memory-efficient structure. The **TFLite converter** is responsible for converting the TF model to FlatBuffers and applying optimizations based on 8-bit integer quantization to reduce the model size and improve latency.

Quantizing the input model

An indispensable technique to make the model suitable for microcontrollers is quantization.

Model quantization, or simply quantization, has three significant advantages:

- It reduces the model size by converting all the weights to lower bit precision.

- It reduces the power consumption by reducing the memory bandwidth.

- It improves inference performance by employing integer arithmetic for all the operations.

This widely adopted technique applies the quantization after training and converts the 32-bit floating-point weights to 8-bit integer values. To understand how quantization works, consider the following C-like function that approximates a 32-bit floating-point value using an 8-bit value:

```
float dequantize(int8 x, float zero_point, float scale) {
    return ((float)x - zero_point) * scale;
}
```

In the proceeding code, x is the quantized value represented as an 8-bit signed integer value, while scale and zero_point are the quantization parameters. The scale parameter is used to map our quantized value to the floating-point domain and vice versa. zero_point is the offset to consider for the quantized range.

To understand why the zero_point could not be zero, consider the following floating-point input distribution that we want to scale to the 8-bit range:

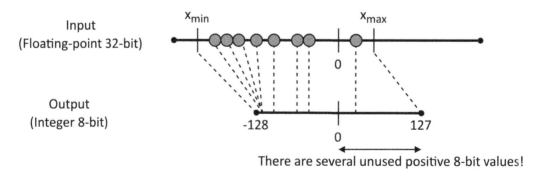

Figure 3.14 – Example where the distribution of the values is shifted toward the negative range

The proceeding figure shows that the input floating-point distribution is not zero-centered but shifted toward the negative range. Therefore, if we simply scaled the floating-point values to 8-bit, we could have the following:

- Multiple negative input values with the same 8-bit counterpart
- Many positive 8-bit values unused

Therefore, it would be inefficient to assign zero to `zero_point` since we could dedicate a larger range to the negative values to reduce their quantization error, defined as follows:

$$\varepsilon = X_{real} - Z_{quantized}$$

When `zero_point` is not zero, we commonly call the quantization **asymmetric** because we assign a different range of values for the positive and negative sides, as shown in the following diagram:

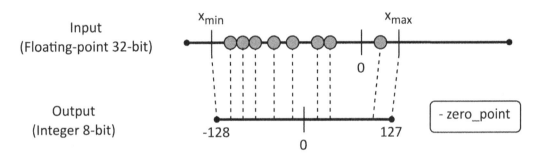

Figure 3.15 – Asymmetric quantization

When `zero_point` is zero, we commonly call the quantization **symmetric** because it is symmetric about zero, as we can see in the following diagram:

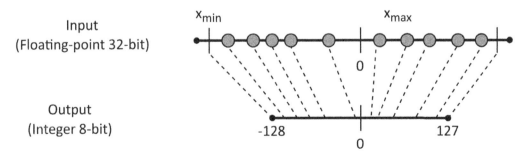

Figure 3.16 – Symmetric quantization

Commonly, we apply symmetric quantization to the model's weights and asymmetric quantization to the input and output of the layers.

The `scale` and `zero_point` values are the only parameters required for quantization and are commonly provided in the following ways:

- **Per-tensor**: The quantization parameters are the same for all tensor elements.

- **Per-channel**: The quantization parameters are different for each feature map of the tensor.

The following diagram visually describes per-tensor and per-channel quantization:

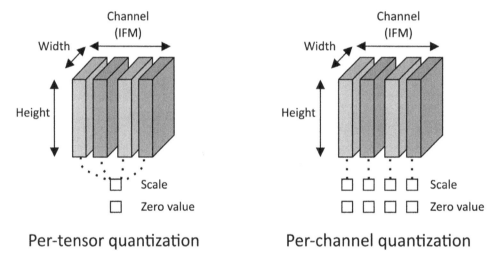

Figure 3.17 – Per-tensor versus per-channel quantization

Commonly, we adopt the per-tensor approach except for the weights and biases of the convolution and depth-wise convolution layers.

How to do it...

The following steps show how to use the TFLite converter to quantize and produce a suitable model for microcontrollers:

1. Select a few hundred samples randomly from the test dataset to calibrate the quantization:

```
def representative_data_gen():
    for i_value in tf.data.Dataset.from_tensor_slices(x_
test).batch(1).take(100):
```

```
i_value_f32 = tf.dtypes.cast(i_value, tf.float32)
yield [i_value_f32]
```

This step is commonly called *generating a representative dataset*, and it is essential to reduce the risk of an accuracy drop in the quantization. In fact, the converter uses this set of samples to find out the range of the input values and then estimate the quantization parameters. Typically, a hundred samples is enough and can be taken from the test or training dataset. In our case, we used the test dataset.

2. Import the TF SavedModel directory into TFLite converter:

```
converter = tf.lite.TFLiteConverter.from_saved_
model("snow_forecast")
```

3. Initialize the TFLite converter for the 8-bit quantization:

```
# Representative dataset
converter.representative_dataset = tf.lite.
RepresentativeDataset(representative_data_gen)
# Optimizations
converter.optimizations = [tf.lite.Optimize.DEFAULT]
# Supported ops
converter.target_spec.supported_ops = [tf.lite.OpsSet.
TFLITE_BUILTINS_INT8]
# Inference input/output type
converter.inference_input_type = tf.int8
converter.inference_output_type = tf.int8
```

In this step, we configure the TFLite converter to apply the 8-bit quantization. The input arguments passed to the tool are as follows:

*   **Representative dataset**: This is the representative dataset generated in the first step.

*   **Optimizations**: This defines the optimization strategy to adopt. At the moment, only DEFAULT optimization is supported, which tries to optimize for both size and latency, minimizing the accuracy drop.

*   **Supported ops**: This forces the adoption of only integer 8-bit operators during the conversion. If our model has unsupported kernels, the conversion will not succeed.

- **Inference input/output type**: This adopts the 8-bit quantization format for the network's input and output. Therefore, we will need to feed the ML model with the quantized input features to run the inference correctly.

Once we have initialized the TFLite converter, we can execute the conversion:

```
tflite_model_quant = converter.convert()
```

4. Save the converted model as .tflite:

```
open("snow_forecast_model.tflite", "wb").write(tflite_
model_quant)
```

5. Convert the TFLite model to a C-byte array with xxd:

```
!apt-get update && apt-get -qq install xxd
!xxd -i snow_forecast_model.tflite > model.h
```

The previous command outputs a C header file (the -i option) containing the TFLite model as an unsigned char array with many hexadecimal numbers. However, in the *Getting ready* section, we mentioned that the model is a file with a .tflite extension. Therefore, why do we need this extra conversion? The conversion to a C-byte array is crucial for deploying the model on microcontrollers because the .tflite format requires an additional software library into our application to load the file from memory. We need to remember that most microcontrollers do not have OS and native filesystem support. Therefore, the C-byte array format allows us to integrate the model directly into the application. The other important reason for this conversion is that the .tflite file does not allow keeping the weights in program memory. Since every byte matters and the SRAM has a limited capacity, keeping the model in program memory is generally more memory efficient when the weights are constant.

Now, you can download the generated model.h file from Colab's left pane. The TFLite model is stored in the snow_forecast_model_tflite array.

Using the built-in temperature and humidity sensor on Arduino Nano

As we know, the Arduino Nano and Raspberry Pi Pico have unique hardware features that make them ideal for tackling different development scenarios. For example, the Arduino Nano have a built-in temperature and humidity sensor so that we do not need external components for our project with this board.

In this recipe, we will show how to read the temperature and humidity sensor data on an Arduino Nano.

The following Arduino sketch contains the code referred to in this recipe:

- `06_sensor_arduino_nano.ino`:

  `https://github.com/PacktPublishing/TinyML-Cookbook/blob/main/Chapter03/ArduinoSketches/06_sensor_arduino_nano.ino`

Getting ready

There are no particular new things to know to accomplish this task. Therefore, this *Getting ready* section will give just an overview of the main characteristics of the built-in temperature and humidity sensor on the Arduino Nano.

The Arduino Nano board integrates the **HTS221** (`https://www.st.com/resource/en/datasheet/HTS221.pdf`) sensor from ST (`https://www.st.com/content/st_com/en.html`) for relative humidity and temperature measurements.

The sensor is ultra-compact (2x2mm) and provides the measurements through two digital serial interfaces. The following table reports the main characteristics of this sensing element:

Relative humidity range	0 – 100 %
Temperature range	-40°C - 120°C
Humidity accuracy	± 3.5 %
Temperature accuracy	± 0.5°C
Current consumption	2uA at 1Hz Output Data Rate (ODR)

Figure 3.18 – Key characteristics of the HTS221 temperature and humidity sensor

As we can see from the table, the sensor is extremely low-power since it has a current power consumption in the range of μA.

How to do it...

Create a new sketch on the Arduino IDE and follow the following steps to initialize and test the temperature and humidity sensor on an Arduino Nano:

1. Include the `Arduino_HTS221.h` C header file in the sketch:

    ```
    #include <Arduino_HTS221.h>
    ```

2. Create function-like macros for reading the temperature and humidity:

    ```
    #define READ_TEMPERATURE() HTS.readTemperature()
    #define READ_HUMIDITY() HTS.readHumidity()
    ```

    The reason for defining the preceding two C macros is because the Raspberry Pi Pico will use different functions to read the temperature and humidity from the sensor. Therefore, it is more practical to have a common interface so that our Arduino Nano and Raspberry Pi Pico applications can share most of their code.

3. Initialize both the serial peripheral and the HTS221 sensor in the `setup()` function:

    ```
    void setup() {
      Serial.begin(9600);
      while (!Serial);
      if (!HTS.begin()) {
        Serial.println("Failed initialization of HTS221!");
        while (1);
      }
    }
    ```

    The serial peripheral will be used to return the classification result.

    > **Important Note**
    >
    > As reported in the FAQ of the Arduino Nano 33 BLE Sense Board, *due to self-heating, when the board is powered by USB, the HTS221 becomes unreliable and shows an offset in each reading that changes with the external temperature.*
    >
    > We recommend disconnecting the USB cable and powering the board with batteries through the VIN pin to obtain reliable measurements. Refer to *Chapter 2, Prototyping with Microcontrollers*, to discover how to power an Arduino Nano with batteries.

Using the DHT22 sensor with the Raspberry Pi Pico

In contrast to the Arduino Nano, the Raspberry Pi Pico requires an external sensor module and an additional software library to measure the temperature and humidity.

In this recipe, we will show how to use the DHT22 sensor with a Raspberry Pico to get temperature and humidity measurements.

The following Arduino sketch contains the code referred to in this recipe:

- `07_sensor_rasp_pico.ino`:

  `https://github.com/PacktPublishing/TinyML-Cookbook/blob/main/Chapter03/ArduinoSketches/07_sensor_rasp_pico.ino`

Getting ready

The temperature and humidity sensor module considered for the Raspberry Pi Pic is the low-cost **AM2302** that you can get either from Adafruit (`https://www.adafruit.com/product/393`) or Amazon.

As shown in the following diagram, the AM2302 module is a through-hole component with three pins that integrates the DHT22 temperature and humidity sensor:

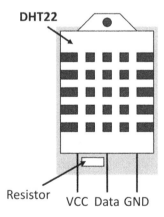

Figure 3.19 – The AM2302 module with the DHT22 sensor

The following table summarizes the key characteristics of the DHT22 sensor:

Relative humidity range	0 – 100 %
Temperature range	-40°C - 80°C
Humidity accuracy	2-5%
Temperature accuracy	± 0.5°C
Current consumption	2.5mA max when requesting data

Figure 3.20 – Key characteristics of the DHT22 temperature and humidity sensor

> Note
>
> DHT11 is another popular temperature and humidity sensor from the
> DHT family. However, we cannot use it in our recipe because it has a good
> temperature accuracy only between 0 °C and 50 °C.

In contrast to the HTS221 sensor on the Arduino Nano, the DHT22 has a digital protocol to read the temperature and humidity values. The protocol must be implemented through the GPIO peripheral and requires precise timing to read the data. Luckily, Adafruit developed a software library (`https://github.com/adafruit/DHT-sensor-library`) for the DHT sensors, so we do not have to worry about it. The library will deal with the low-level software details and provide an API to read the temperature and humidity.

How to do it...

Create a new sketch on the Arduino IDE and follow these steps to use the DHT22 sensor with a Raspberry Pi Pico:

1. Connect the DHT22 sensor to the Raspberry Pi Pico. Use the G10 (row 14) GPIO on the Raspberry Pi Pico for the DHT22 data terminal:

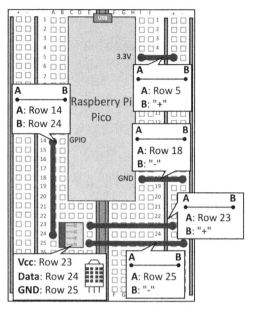

Figure 3.21 – Complete circuit with the Raspberry Pi Pico and the AM2302 sensor module

2. Download the latest release of the DHT sensor software library from `https://www.arduino.cc/reference/en/libraries/dht-sensor-library/`. In the Arduino IDE, import the ZIP file by clicking on the **Libraries** tab on the left pane and **Import**, as shown in the following screenshot:

Figure 3.22 – Import the DHT sensor library in Arduino Web Editor

A pop-up window will tell us that the library has been successfully imported.

3. Include the DHT.h C header file in the sketch:

```
#include <DHT.h>
```

4. Define a global DHT object to interface with the DHT22 sensor:

```
const int gpio_pin_dht_pin = 10;
DHT dht(gpio_pin_dht_pin, DHT22);
```

The DHT object is initialized with the GPIO pin used by the DHT22 data terminal (G10) and the type of DHT sensor (DHT22).

5. Create function-like macros for reading the temperature and humidity:

```
#define READ_TEMPERATURE() dht.readTemperature()
#define READ_HUMIDITY() dht.readHumidity()
```

The function's name must be the same as the ones of the previous recipe. This step ensures a common function interface to measure the temperature and humidity on an Arduino Nano and a Raspberry Pi Pico.

6. Initialize the serial peripheral and the DHT22 sensor in the setup() function:

```
void setup() {
   Serial.begin(9600);
   while(!Serial);
   dht.begin();
   delay(2000);
}
```

The DHT22 can only return new data after two seconds. For this reason, we use delay(2000) to wait for the peripheral to be ready.

Now, the Raspberry Pi Pico can read temperature and humidity sensor data.

Preparing the input features for the model inference

As we know, the model's input features are the scaled and quantized temperature and humidity of the last three hours. Using this data, the ML model can forecast whether it will snow.

In this recipe, we will see how to prepare the input data to feed into our ML model. In particular, this recipe will teach us how to acquire, scale, and quantize the sensor measurements and keep them in temporal order using a **circular buffer**.

The following Arduino sketch contains the code referred to in this recipe:

- `08_input_features.ino`:

  `https://github.com/PacktPublishing/TinyML-Cookbook/blob/main/Chapter03/ArduinoSketches/08_input_features.ino`

Getting ready

Our application will acquire the temperature and humidity every hour to get the necessary input features for the model. However, how can we keep the last three measurements in temporal order to feed the network the correct input?

In this recipe, we will use a circular buffer, a fixed-sized data structure that implements a **First-In-First-Out** (**FIFO**) buffer.

This data structure is well-suited to buffering data streams and can be implemented with an array and a pointer that tells where to store the element in memory. The following diagram shows how a circular buffer with three elements works:

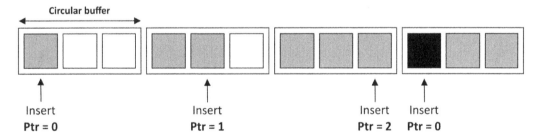

Figure 3.23 – Circular buffer with three elements

As you can see from the preceding diagram, this data structure simulates a ring since the pointer (**Ptr**) is incremented after each data insertion and wraps around when it reaches the end.

How to do it...

The instructions provided in this section apply to both the Arduino Nano and the Raspberry Pi Pico. Follow these steps to see how to create a circular buffer and prepare the input for the model inference:

1. Define two global `int8_t` arrays of size three and an integer variable to implement the circular buffer data structure:

```
#define NUM_HOURS 3
int8_t t_vals [NUM_HOURS] = {0};
int8_t h_vals [NUM_HOURS] = {0};
int cur_idx = 0;
```

These two arrays will be used to keep the scaled and quantized temperature and humidity measurements in temporal order.

2. Define two variables for the `scale` (`float`) and `zero point` (`int32_t`) quantization parameters of the input features:

```
float    tflu_i_scale      = 0.0f;
int32_t tflu_i_zero_point = 0;
```

The following recipe will extract these quantization parameters from the TF model. Please note that `scale` (`tflu_i_scale`) is a floating-point number, while `zero point` (`tflu_i_zero_point`) is a 32-bit integer.

3. Take the average of three temperature and humidity samples, captured every three seconds in the `loop()` function:

```
constexpr int num_reads = 3;
void loop() {
   float t = 0.0f;
   float h = 0.0f;
   for(int i = 0; i < num_reads; ++i) {
      t += READ_TEMPERATURE();
      h += READ_HUMIDITY();
      delay(3000);
   }
   t /= (float)num_reads;
   h /= (float)num_reads;
```

Capturing more than one sample is, in general, a good way to have a robust measurement.

4. Scale the temperature and humidity data with Z-score in the `loop()` function:

```
constexpr float t_mean  = 2.05179f;
constexpr float h_mean  = 82.30551f;
constexpr float t_std   = 7.33084f;
constexpr float h_std   = 14.55707f;
t = (t - t_mean) / t_std;
h = (h - h_mean) / h_std;
```

Z-score requires the mean and standard deviation, which we calculated in the second recipe of this chapter.

5. Quantize the input features in the `loop()` function:

```
t_vals[cur_idx] = (t / tflu_i_scale) + tflu_i_zero_point;
h_vals[cur_idx] = (h / tflu_i_scale) + tflu_i_zero_point;
```

The samples are quantized using the `tflu_i_scale` and `tflu_i_zero_point` input quantization parameters. Remember that the model's input uses the per-tensor quantization schema, so all input features need to be quantized with the same scale and zero-point.

6. Store the temperature and humidity sensor in the circular array:

```
t_vals[cur_idx] = t;
h_vals[cur_idx] = h;
cur_idx = (cur_idx + 1) % NUM_HOURS;
delay(2000);
```

The pointer of the circular buffer (`cur_index`) is updated after each data insertion with the following formula:

$$index_{new} = (index_{current} + 1) \% length_{array}$$

In the preceding formula, $length_{array}$ is the size of the circular buffer, while $index_{current}$ and $index_{new}$ are the pointer's values before and after the data insertion.

Important Note

At the end of the code, we have a delay of two seconds, but it should be one hour in the actual application. The pause of two seconds is used to avoid waiting too long in our experiments.

On-device inference with TFLu

Here we are, with our first ML application on microcontrollers.

In this recipe, we will finally discover how to use **TensorFlow Lite for Microcontrollers** (**TFLu**) to run the TFLite model on an Arduino Nano and a Raspberry Pi Pico.

The following Arduino sketch contains the code referred to in this recipe:

- `09_classification.ino`:

  `https://github.com/PacktPublishing/TinyML-Cookbook/blob/main/Chapter03/ArduinoSketches/09_classification.ino`

Getting ready

To get ready with this last recipe, we need to know how inference with TFLu works.

TFLu was introduced in *Chapter 1, Getting Started with TinyML*, and is the software component that runs TFLite models on microcontrollers.

Inference with TFLu typically consists of the following:

1. **Loading and parsing the model**: TFLu parses the weights and network architecture stored in the C-byte array.

2. **Transforming the input data**: The input data acquired from the sensor is converted to the expected format required by the model.

3. **Executing the model**: TFLu executes the model using optimized DNN functions.

When dealing with microcontrollers, it is necessary to optimize every line of our code to keep the memory footprint at the minimum and maximize performance.

For this reason, TFLu also integrates software libraries to get the best performance from various target processors. For example, TFLu supports **CMSIS-NN** (`https://www.keil.com/pack/doc/CMSIS/NN/html/index.html`), a free and open source software library developed by Arm for optimized DNN operators on Arm Cortex-M architectures. These optimizations are relevant to the critical DNN primitives such as convolution, depth-wise convolution, and the fully connected layer, and are compatible with the Arm processors in the Arduino Nano and Raspberry Pi Pico.

At this point, you might have one question in mind: How can we use TFLu with CMSIS-NN?

We do not need to install additional libraries because TFLu for Arduino comes with CMSIS-NN. Therefore, Arduino will automatically include CMSIS-NN to run the inference faster when using TFLu.

How to do it...

The instructions in this section are applicable to both the Arduino Nano and the Raspberry Pi Pico. The following steps will show how to use TFLu to run the snow forecast TFLite model on our boards:

1. Import the `model.h` file into the Arduino project. As shown in the following screenshot, click on the tab button with the upside-down triangle and click on **Import File into Sketch**.

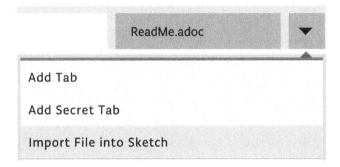

Figure 3.24 – Importing the model.h file into the Arduino project

A folder window will appear from which you can drag and drop the TFLu model's file.

Once the file has been imported, include the C header in the sketch:

```
#include "model.h"
```

2. Include the header files required by TFLu:

```
#include <TensorFlowLite.h>
#include <tensorflow/lite/micro/all_ops_resolver.h>
#include <tensorflow/lite/micro/micro_error_reporter.h>
#include <tensorflow/lite/micro/micro_interpreter.h>
#include <tensorflow/lite/schema/schema_generated.h>
#include <tensorflow/lite/version.h>
```

The main header files are as follows:

*   `all_ops_resolver.h`: To load the DNN operators required for running the ML model

*   `micro_error_reporter.h`: To output the debug information returned by the TFLu runtime

*   `micro_interpreter.h`: To load and execute the ML model

- schema_generated.h: For the schema of the TFLite FlatBuffer format
- version.h: For the versioning of the TFLite schema

For more information about the header files, we recommend reading the *Get started with microcontroller guide* in the TF documentation (https://www.tensorflow.org/lite/microcontrollers/get_started_low_level).

3. Declare the variables required by TFLu:

```
const tflite::Model* tflu_model                = nullptr;
tflite::MicroInterpreter* tflu_interpreter = nullptr;
TfLiteTensor* tflu_i_tensor                    = nullptr;
TfLiteTensor* tflu_o_tensor                    = nullptr;
tflite::MicroErrorReporter tflu_error;
constexpr int tensor_arena_size = 4 * 1024;
byte tensor_arena[tensor_arena_size] __attribute__
((aligned(16)));
```

The global variables declared in this step are as follows:

- tflu_model: The model parsed by the TFLu parser.
- tflu_interpreter: The pointer to TFLu interpreter.
- tflu_i_tensor: The pointer to the model's input tensor.
- tflu_o_tensor: The pointer to the model's output tensor.
- tensor_arena: The memory required by the TFLu interpreter. TFLu does not use dynamic allocation. Therefore, we should provide a fixed amount of memory for the input, output, and intermediate tensors. The arena's size depends on the model and is only determined by experiments. In our case, 4,096 is more than enough.

The preceding variables are generally required in all TFLu-based applications.

4. Load the TFLite model from the C-byte snow_forecast_model_tflite array in the setup() function:

```
tflu_model = tflite::GetModel(snow_forecast_model_
tflite);
```

5. Define a tflite::AllOpsResolver object in the setup() function:

```
tflite::AllOpsResolver tflu_ops_resolver;
```

The TFLu interpreter will use this interface to find the function pointers for each DNN operator.

6. Create the TFLu interpreter in the setup() function:

```
tflu_interpreter = new tflite::MicroInterpreter(tflu_
model, tflu_ops_resolver, tensor_arena, tensor_arena_
size, &tflu_error);
```

7. Allocate the memory required for the model and get the memory pointer of the input and output tensors in the setup() function:

```
tflu_interpreter->AllocateTensors();
tflu_i_tensor = tflu_interpreter->input(0);
tflu_o_tensor = tflu_interpreter->output(0);
```

8. Get the quantization parameters for the input and output tensors in the setup() function:

```
const auto* i_quantization = reinterpret_
cast<TfLiteAffineQuantization*>(tflu_i_tensor-
>quantization.params);
onst auto* o_quantization = reinterpret_
cast<TfLiteAffineQuantization*>(tflu_o_tensor-
>quantization.params);
tflu_i_scale      = i_quantization->scale->data[0];
tflu_i_zero_point = i_quantization->zero_point->data[0];
tflu_o_scale      = o_quantization->scale->data[0];
tflu_o_zero_point = o_quantization->zero_point->data[0];
```

The quantization parameters are returned in the TfLiteAffineQuantization object, containing two arrays for the scale and zero point parameters. Since both input and output tensors adopt a per-tensor quantization, each array stores a single value.

9. Initialize the input tensor with the quantized input features in the loop() function:

```
const int idx0 = cur_idx;
const int idx1 = (cur_idx - 1 + NUM_HOURS) % NUM_HOURS;
const int idx2 = (cur_idx - 2 + NUM_HOURS) % NUM_HOURS;
tflu_i_tensor->data.int8[0] = t_vals[idx2];
tflu_i_tensor->data.int8[1] = t_vals[idx1];
tflu_i_tensor->data.int8[2] = t_vals[idx0];
```

```
tflu_i_tensor->data.int8[3] = h_vals[idx2];
tflu_i_tensor->data.int8[4] = h_vals[idx1];
tflu_i_tensor->data.int8[5] = h_vals[idx0];
```

Since we need the last three samples, we use the following formula to read the elements from the circular buffer:

$$index_{past} = (index_{current} - N + length_{array}) \% length_{array}$$

In the preceding formula, N is the sampling instant and $index_{past}$ is the corresponding circular buffer's pointer. For example, if $t0$ is the current instant, $N = 0$ means the sample at time $t = t0$, $N = 1$ the sample at time $t = t0 - 1$, and $N = 2$ the sample at time $t = t0 - 2$.

10. Run the inference in the loop() function:

```
tflu_interpreter->Invoke();
```

11. Dequantize the output tensor and forecast the weather condition in the loop() function:

```
int8_t out_int8 = tflu_o_tensor->data.int8[0];
float out_f = (out_int8 - tflu_o_zero_point) * tflu_o_
scale;

if (out_f > 0.5) {
    Serial.println("Yes, it snows");
}
else {
    Serial.println("No, it does not snow");
}
```

The dequantization of the output is done with the tflu_o_scale and tflu_o_zero_point quantization parameters retrieved in the setup() function. Once we have the floating-point representation, the output is considered *No* when it is below 0.5; otherwise, it's *Yes*.

Now, compile and upload the program on the microcontroller board. The serial terminal in the Arduino IDE will report **Yes, it snows** or **No, it does not snow**, depending on whether snow is forecast.

To check if the application can forecast snow, you can simply force the temperature to *-10* and the humidity to *100*. The model should return **Yes, it snows** on the serial terminal.

4

Voice Controlling LEDs with Edge Impulse

Keyword spotting (**KWS**) is a technology applied in a wide range of daily-life applications to enable an entirely hands-free experience with the device. The detection of the famous *wake-up* words *OK Google*, *Alexa*, *Hey Siri*, or *Cortana* represents a particular usage of this technology, where the smart assistant continuously listens for the magic phrase before starting to interact with the device.

Since KWS aims to identify utterances from real-time speech, it needs to be on-device, always-on, and running on a low-power system to be effective.

This chapter demonstrates the usage of KWS through **Edge Impulse** by building an application to voice control the **light-emitting diode** (**LED**)-emitting color (**red, green, and blue** (or **RGB**)) and the number of times to make it blink (one, two, and three times).

This TinyML application could find space in smart educational toys to learn both color and number vocabulary with peace of mind regarding privacy and security since it does not require internet connectivity.

This chapter will start focusing on the dataset preparation, showing how to acquire audio data with a mobile phone. Next, we will design a model based on **Mel-frequency cepstral coefficients** (**MFCC**), one of the most popular features for speech recognition. In these recipes, we will show how to extract MFCCs from audio samples, train the **machine learning** (**ML**) model, and optimize the performance with the **EON Tuner**. At the end of the chapter, we will concentrate on finalizing the KWS application on the **Arduino Nano** and the **Raspberry Pi Pico**.

This chapter is intended to show how to develop an **end-to-end** (**E2E**) KWS application with Edge Impulse and get familiar with audio data acquisition and **analog-to-digital converter** (**ADC**) peripherals.

In this chapter, we're going to implement the following recipes:

- Acquiring audio data with a smartphone
- Extracting MFCC features from audio samples
- Designing and training a **neural network** (**NN**) model
- Tuning model performance with EON Tuner
- Live classifications with a smartphone
- Live classifications with the Arduino Nano
- Continuous inferencing on the Arduino Nano
- Building the circuit with the Raspberry Pi Pico to voice control LEDs
- Audio sampling with ADC and timer interrupts on the Raspberry Pi Pico

Technical requirements

To complete all the practical recipes of this chapter, we will need the following:

- An Arduino Nano 33 BLE Sense board
- A Raspberry Pi Pico board
- Smartphone (Android phone or Apple iPhone)
- Micro **Universal Serial Bus** (**USB**) cable
- 1 x half-size solderless breadboard
- 1 x electret microphone amplifier - MAX9814 (Raspberry Pi Pico only)

- 11 x jumper wires (Raspberry Pi Pico only)

- 2 x 220 Ohm resistor (Raspberry Pi Pico only)

- 1 x 100 Ohm resistor (Raspberry Pi Pico only)

- 1 x red LED (Raspberry Pi Pico only)

- 1 x green LED (Raspberry Pi Pico only)

- 1 x blue LED (Raspberry Pi Pico only)

- 1 x push-button (Raspberry Pi Pico only)

- Laptop/PC with either Ubuntu 18.04+ or Windows 10 on x86-64

The source code and additional material are available in the `Chapter04` folder of the GitHub repository (`https://github.com/PacktPublishing/TinyML-Cookbook/tree/main/Chapter04`).

Acquiring audio data with a smartphone

As for all ML problems, data acquisition is the first step to take, and Edge Impulse offers several ways to do this directly from the web browser.

In this recipe, we will learn how to acquire audio samples using a mobile phone.

Getting ready

Acquiring audio samples with a smartphone is the most straightforward data acquisition approach offered by Edge Impulse because it only requires a phone (Android phone or Apple iPhone) with internet connectivity.

However, how many samples do we need to train the model?

Collecting audio samples for KWS

The number of samples depends entirely on the nature of the problem—therefore, no approach fits all. For a situation such as this, 50 samples for each class could be sufficient to get a basic model. However, 100 or more are generally recommended to get better results. We want to give you complete freedom on this choice. However, *remember to get an equal number of samples for each class to obtain a balanced dataset.*

Whichever dataset size you choose, try including different variations in the instances of speech, such as accents, inflations, pitch, pronunciations, and tone. These variations will make the model capable of identifying words from different speakers. Typically, recording audio from persons of different ages and genders should cover all these cases.

Although there are six output classes to identify (red, green, blue, one, two, and three), we should consider an additional class for cases when anyone is speaking or there are unknown words in the speech.

How to do it...

Open the Edge Impulse **Dashboard** and give a name to your project (for example, voice_controlling_leds).

Note

In this recipe, *N* will be used to refer to the number of samples for each output class.

Follow the next steps to acquire audio data with the mobile phone's microphon:

1. Click on **Let's collect some data** from the **Acquire data** section.

    Then, click on **Show QR code** on the **Use your mobile phone** option from the menu:

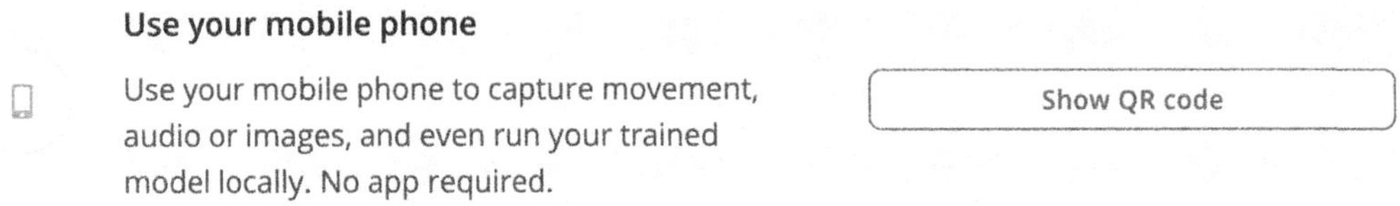

    Use your mobile phone

    Use your mobile phone to capture movement, audio or images, and even run your trained model locally. No app required.

    Show QR code

    Figure 4.1 – Clicking on the Show QR code to pair the mobile phone with Edge Impulse

    Scan the **Quick Response (QR)** code with your smartphone to pair the device with Edge Impulse. A pop-up window on your phone will confirm that the device is connected, as shown in the following screenshot:

Connected as
phone_kseq4mtp

You can collect data from this device
from the **Data acquisition** page in
the Edge Impulse studio.

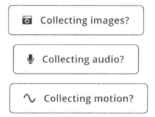

Figure 4.2 – Edge Impulse message on your phone

On your mobile phone, click on **Collecting audio?** and give permission to use the microphone.

Since it is not required to have a laptop and smartphone in the same network, we could collect audio samples anywhere. As we can guess, this approach is well suited to recording sounds from different environments since it only requires a phone with internet connectivity.

2. Record N (for example, 50) utterances for each class (*red*, *green*, *blue*, *one*, *two*, and *three*). Before clicking on **Start recording**, set **Category** to **Training** and enter one of the following labels in the **Label** field, depending on the spoken word:

Class	Red	Green	Blue	One	Two	Three
Label	00_red	01_green	02_blue	03_one	04_two	05_three

Figure 4.3 – Labels for the output categories

Since the label encoding assigns an integer value based on alphabetical ordering to each output category, our proposed names (`00_red`, `01_green`, `02_blue`, `03_one`, `04_two`, and `05_three`) will be helpful to know whether we have a color or a number from the label index easily. For example, if the label index is less than 3, we have a color.

We recommend repeating the same utterance several times in a single recording to avoid uploading too many files into Edge Impulse. For example, you could record audio of 20 **seconds** (**s**) where you repeat the same word 10 times with a 1-s pause in between.

The recordings will be available in the **Data acquisition** section. By clicking on the file, you can visualize the corresponding audio waveform:

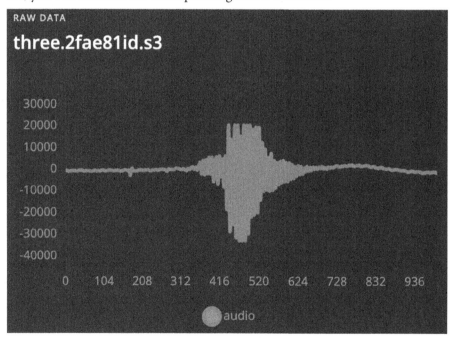

Figure 4.4 – Audio waveform

The raw **audio waveform** is the signal recorded by the microphone and graphically describes the sound-pressure variation over time. The vertical axis reports the amplitude of this vibration, while the horizontal axis reports the time. The higher waveform amplitude implies louder audio as perceived by the human ear.

3. Split the recordings containing repetitions of the utterance in individual samples by clicking on : near the filename and then clicking on **Split sample**, as shown in the following screenshot:

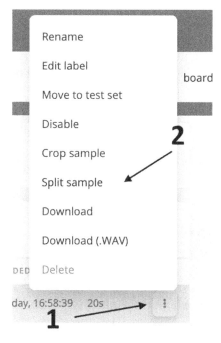

Figure 4.5 – Split sample option

Edge Impulse will automatically detect spoken words, as you can observe from the following screenshot:

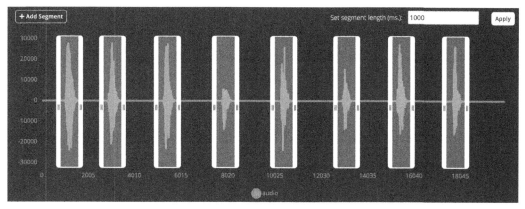

Figure 4.6 – Audio waveform with repetitions of the same utterance

Set the segment length to 1000 **milliseconds (ms)** (1 s), and ensure all the samples are centered within the cutting window. Then, click on **Split** to get the individual samples.

4. Download the keyword dataset from Edge Impulse (`https://cdn.edgeimpulse.com/datasets/keywords2.zip`) and unzip the file. Import *N* random samples from the unknown dataset into the Edge Impulse project. Go to **Data acquisition** and click on the **Upload existing data** button from the **Collect data menu**:

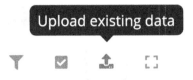

Figure 4.7 – Button to upload existing training data

On the **UPLOAD DATA** page, do the following:

- Set **Upload category** to **Training**.
- Write unknown in the **Enter label** field.

Click on **Begin upload** to import the files into the dataset.

5. Split the samples between training and test datasets by clicking on the **Perform train / test split** button in the **Danger zone** area of the **Dashboard**:

Danger zone

Perform train / test split

Figure 4.8 – Danger zone in Edge Impulse

Edge Impulse will ask you twice if you are sure about this action because the data shuffling is irreversible.

You should now have 80% of the samples assigned to the training/validation set and 20% to the test one.

Extracting MFCC features from audio samples

When building an ML application with Edge Impulse, the **impulse** is responsible for all of the data processing, such as feature extraction and model inference.

In this recipe, we will see how to design an impulse to extract MFCC features from the audio samples.

Getting ready

Let's start this recipe by discussing what an impulse is and examining the MFCC features used for our KWS application.

In Edge Impulse, an impulse is responsible for data processing and consists of two computational blocks, mainly the following:

- **Processing block**: This is the preliminary step in any ML application, and it aims to prepare the data for the ML algorithm.

- **Learning block**: This is the block that implements the ML solution, which aims to learn patterns from the data provided by the processing block.

The processing block determines the ML effectiveness since the raw input data is often not suitable for feeding the model directly. For example, the input signal could be noisy or have irrelevant and redundant information for training the model, just to name a few scenarios.

Therefore, Edge Impulse offers several pre-built processing functions, including the possibility to have custom ones.

In our case, we will use the MFCC feature extraction processing block, and the following subsections will help us learn more about this.

Analyzing audio in the frequency domain

In contrast to vision applications where **convolutional NNs (CNNs)** can make feature extraction part of the learning process, typical speech recognition models do not perform well with raw audio data. Therefore, feature extraction is required and needs to be part of the processing block.

We know from physics that *sound is the vibration of air molecules that propagates as a wave*. For example, if we played a pure single tone, the microphone would record a sine signal:

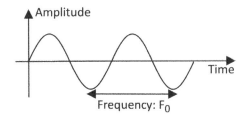

Figure 4.9 – Sine waveform

Although the sounds in nature are far from pure, *every sound can be expressed as the sum of sine waves at different frequencies and amplitudes.*

Since a frequency and amplitude characterize sine waves, we commonly represent the components in the frequency domain through the **power spectrum**:

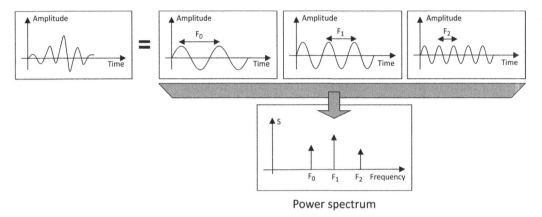

Power spectrum

Figure 4.10 – Representation of a signal in the frequency domain

The power spectrum reports the frequency on the horizontal axis and the power (S) associated with each component on the vertical axis.

The **Discrete Fourier Transform** (**DFT**) is the required mathematical tool to decompose a digital audio waveform in all its constituent sine waves, commonly called **components**.

Now that we are familiar with the frequency representation of an audio signal, let's see what we can generate as an input feature for a CNN.

Generating a mel spectrogram

A **spectrogram** can be considered an audio signal's image representation because it visually shows the power spectrum over time.

A spectrogram is obtained by splitting the audio waveform into smaller segments and applying the DFT on each one, as shown in the following screenshot:

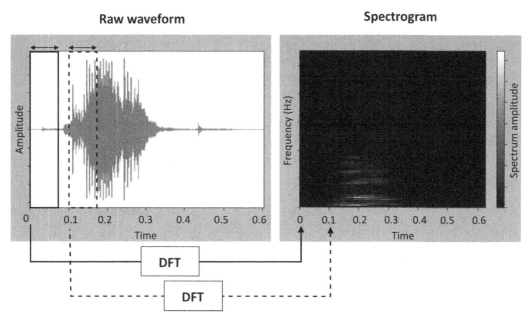

Figure 4.11 – Audio waveform and spectrogram of the red utterance

In the spectrogram, each vertical slice represents the power spectrum associated with each segment—in particular:

- The width reports the time.
- The height reports the frequency.
- The color reports the power spectrum amplitude, so a brighter color implies a higher amplitude.

However, a spectrogram obtained in this way would be ineffective for voice speech recognition because the relevant features are not emphasized. In fact, as we can observe from the preceding screenshot, the spectrogram is dark in almost all regions.

Therefore, the spectrogram is adjusted considering that *humans perceive frequencies and loudness on a logarithmic scale* rather than linearly. These adjustments are as follows:

- **Scaling the frequency (hertz, or Hz) to Mel with the Mel scale filter bank**: The **Mel scale** remaps the frequencies to make them distinguishable and perceived equidistantly. For example, if we played pure tones from 100 Hz to 200 Hz with a 1 Hz step, we could distinctly perceive all 100 frequencies. However, if we conducted the same experiment at higher frequencies (for example, between 7500 Hz and 7600 Hz), we could barely hear all tones. Therefore, not all frequencies are equally important for our ears.

The Mel scale is commonly computed using triangular filters overlapped (**filter bank**) in the frequency domain.

- **Scaling the amplitudes using the decibel (dB) scale**: The human brain does not perceive amplitude linearly but logarithmically, as with frequencies. Therefore, we scale the amplitudes logarithmically to make them visible in the spectrogram.

The spectrogram obtained by applying the preceding transformations is a **mel spectrogram** or **Mel-frequency energy** (**MFE**). The MFE of the *red* word using 40 triangular filters is reported in the following screenshot, where we can now clearly notice the intensity of the frequency components:

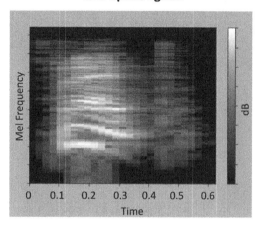

Figure 4.12 – Spectrogram and Mel spectrogram of the red utterance

Although the mel spectrogram works well with audio recognition models, there is also something more efficient for human speech recognition regarding the number of input features—the MFCC.

Extracting the MFCC

MFCC *aims to extract fewer and highly unrelated coefficients from the mel spectrogram.*

The Mel filter bank uses overlapped filters, which makes the components highly correlated. If we deal with human speech, we can decorrelate them by applying the **Discrete Cosine Transform** (**DCT**).

The DCT provides a compressed version of the filter bank. From the DCT output, we can keep the first 2-13 coefficients (cepstral coefficients) and discard the rest because they do not bring additional information for human speech recognition. Hence, the resulting spectrogram has fewer frequencies than the mel spectrogram (13 versus 40).

How to do it...

We start designing our first impulse by clicking on the **Create impulse** option from the left-hand side menu, as shown in the following screenshot:

Figure 4.13 – Create impulse option

In the **Create impulse** section, ensure the time-series data has the **Window size** field set to 1000 ms and the **Window increase** field to 500 ms.

Window increase is a parameter specifically for continuous KWS applications, where there is a continuous audio stream and we do not know when the utterance starts. In this scenario, we should split the audio stream into *windows* (or *segments*) of equal length and execute the ML inference on each one. **Window size** is the temporal length of the window, while **Window increase** is the temporal distance between two consecutive segments, as shown in the following diagram:

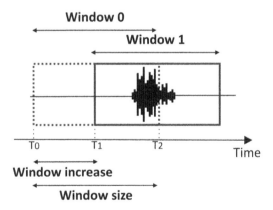

Figure 4.14 – Window size versus Window increase

The **Window size** value depends on the training sample length (1 s) and may affect the accuracy results. On the contrary, the **Window increase** value does not impact the training results but affects the chances of getting a correct start of the utterance. In fact, a smaller **Window increase** value implies a higher probability. However, the suitable **Window increase** value will depend on the model latency.

The following steps show how to design a processing block for extracting MFCC features from recorded audio samples:

1. Click on the **Add a processing block** button and add **Audio (MFCC)**.

2. Click on the **Add a learning block** button and add **Classification (Keras)**.

    The **Output features** block should report the seven output classes to recognize (`00_red`, `01_green`, `02_blue`, `03_one`, `04_two`, `05_three`, and `unknown`), as shown in the following screenshot:

Figure 4.15 – Output features

Save the impulse by clicking on the **Save Impulse** button.

3. Click on **MFCC** from the **Impulse design** category. In the new window, we can play on the parameters affecting the extraction of MFCC features, such as the number of cepstral coefficients, the number of triangular filters applied for the Mel scale, and so on. All the MFCC parameters are kept at their default values.

    At the bottom of the page, there are also two parameters for the **pre-emphasis** stage. The pre-emphasis stage is performed before generating a spectrogram to reduce the effect of noise by increasing energy at the highest frequencies. If the **Coefficient** value is 0, there is no pre-emphasis on the input signal. The pre-emphasis parameters are kept at their default values.

4. Extract the MFCC features from each training sample by clicking on the **Generate features** button:

Parameters | **Generate features**

Figure 4.16 – Generate features button

Edge Impulse will return **Job completed** in the console output at the end of this process.

MFCC features are now extracted from all the recorded audio samples.

There's more...

Once MFCCs have been generated, we can use the **Feature explorer** tool to examine the generated training dataset in a **three-dimensional (3D)** scatter plot, as shown in the following screenshot:

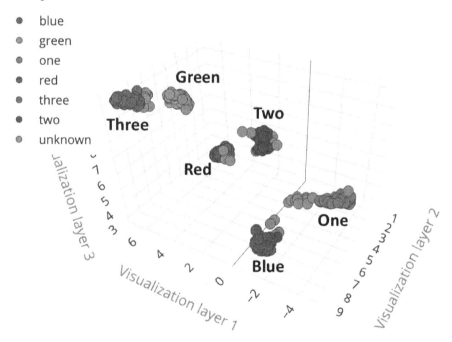

Figure 4.17 – Feature explorer showing the seven output classes

From the **Feature explorer** chart, we should infer whether the input features are suitable for our problem. If so, the output classes (except the unknown output category) should be well separated.

Under the **Feature explorer** area, we find the **On-device performance** section related to MFCC:

Figure 4.18 – MFCC performance on the Arduino Nano 33 BLE Sense board

PROCESSING TIME (latency) and **PEAK RAM USAGE** (data memory) are estimated considering the target device selected in **Dashboard | Project info**:

Figure 4.19 – Target device reported in Project info

From **Project info**, you can change the target device for performance estimation.

Unfortunately, Edge Impulse does not support the Raspberry Pi Pico, so the estimated performance will only be based on the Arduino Nano.

Designing and training a NN model

In this recipe, we will be leveraging the following NN architecture to recognize our words:

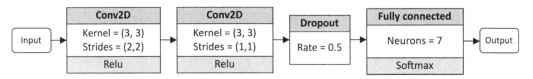

Figure 4.20 – NN architecture

The model has two **two-dimensional** (**2D**) convolution layers, one dropout layer, and one fully connected layer, followed by a softmax activation.

The network's input is the MFCC feature extracted from the 1-s audio sample.

Getting ready

To get ready for this recipe, we just need to know how to design and train a NN in Edge Impulse.

Depending on the learning block chosen, Edge Impulse exploits different underlying ML frameworks for training. For a classification learning block, the framework uses TensorFlow with Keras. The model design can be performed in two ways:

- **Visual mode (simple mode)**: This is the quickest way and through the **user interface** (**UI**). Edge Impulse provides some basic NN building blocks and architecture presets, which are beneficial if you have just started experimenting with **deep learning** (**DL**).

- **Keras code mode (expert mode)**: If we want more control over the network architecture, we can edit the Keras code directly from the web browser.

Once we have designed the model, we can launch the training from the same window.

How to do it...

Click on **Neural Network (Keras)** under **Impulse design** and follow the next steps to design and train the NN presented in *Figure 4.20*:

1. Select the **2D Convolutional** architecture preset and remove the **Dropout** layer between the two convolution layers:

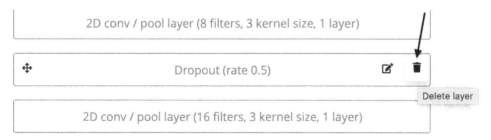

Figure 4.21 – Deleting the dropout layer between the two 2D convolution layers

2. Switch to **Keras (expert)** mode by clicking on ⋮. In the coding area, delete the `MaxPooling2D` layers:

```
        =(input_length, )))
14  model.add(Conv2D(8, kernel_size=3, activation='relu',        Delete
        kernel_constraint=tf.keras.constraints.MaxNorm(1),
        padding='same'))
15  model.add(MaxPooling2D(pool_size=2, strides=2, padding
        ='same'))
16  model.add(Dropout(0.5))
17  model.add(Conv2D(16, kernel_size=3, activation='relu',       Delete
        kernel_constraint=tf.keras.constraints.MaxNorm(1),
        padding='same'))
18  model.add(MaxPooling2D(pool_size=2, strides=2, padding
        ='same'))
19  model.add(Dropout(0.5))
20  model.add(Flatten())
```

Figure 4.22 – Deleting the two pooling layers from the Keras code

Set the strides of the first convolution layer to (2,2):

```
model.add(Conv2D(8, strides=(2,2), kernel_size=3,
activation='relu', kernel_constraint=tf.keras.
constraints.MaxNorm(1), padding='same'))
```

The pooling layer is a subsampling technique that reduces information propagated through the network and lowers the overfitting risk. However, this operator may increase latency and **random-access memory** (**RAM**) usage. In memory-constraint devices such as microcontrollers, memory is a precious resource, and we need to use it as efficiently as possible. Therefore, the idea is to adopt non-unit strides in convolution layers to reduce spatial dimensionality. This approach is typically more performant because we skip the pooling layer computation entirely, and we can have faster convolution layers, given fewer output elements to process.

3. Launch the training by clicking on the **Start training** button:

Figure 4.23 – Start training button

The output console will report the accuracy and loss on the training and validation datasets during training after each epoch.

At the end of the training, we can evaluate the model's performance (accuracy and loss), the confusion matrix, and the estimated on-device performance on the same page.

> **Important Note**
>
> If you achieve 100% accuracy, this is a sign that the model is likely overfitting the data. To avoid this issue, you can either add more data to your training set or reduce the learning rate.

If you are not happy with the model's accuracy, we recommend collecting more data and training the model again.

Tuning model performance with EON Tuner

Developing the most efficient ML pipeline for a given application is always challenging. One way to do this is through iterative experiments. For example, we can evaluate how some target metrics (latency, memory, and accuracy) change depending on the input feature generation and the model architecture. However, this process is time-consuming because there are several combinations, and each one needs to be tested and evaluated. Furthermore, this approach requires familiarity with digital signal processing and NN architectures to know what to tune.

In this recipe, we will use the EON Tuner to find the best ML pipeline for the Arduino Nano.

Getting ready

EON Tuner (`https://docs.edgeimpulse.com/docs/eon-tuner`) is a tool for *automating the discovery of the best ML-based solution* for a given target platform. However, it is not just an **automated ML** (**AutoML**) tool because the processing block is also part of the optimization problem. Therefore, the EON Tuner is an E2E optimizer for discovering the best combination of processing block and ML model for a given set of constraints, such as latency, RAM usage, and accuracy.

How to do it...

Click on the **EON Tuner** from the left-hand side menu and follow the next steps to learn how to find the most efficient ML-based pipeline for our applicatio:

1. Set up the EON Tuner by clicking on the settings wheel icon in the **Target** area:

Figure 4.24 – EON Tuner settings

Edge Impulse will open a new window for setting up the EON Tuner. In this window, set the **Dataset category**, **Target device**, and **Time per inference** values, as follows:

- **Dataset category**: **Keyword spotting**

- **Target device**: **Arduino Nano 33 BLE Sense (Cortex-M4F 64MHz)**

- **Time per inference (ms)**: **100**

Since Edge Impulse does not support the Raspberry Pi Pico yet, we can only tune the performance for the Arduino Nano 33 BLE Sense board.

We set the **Time for inference** value to 100 ms to discover faster solutions than previously obtained in the *Designing and training a NN model* recipe.

2. Save the EON Tuner settings by clicking on the **Save** button.

3. Launch the EON Tuner by clicking on **Start EON Tuner**. The process can take from several minutes up to 6 hours, depending on the dataset size. The tool will show the progress in the progress bar and report the discovered architectures in the same window, as shown in the following screenshot:

Figure 4.25 – EON Tuner reports a confusion matrix for each proposed ML solution

Once the EON Tuner has completed the discovery phase, you will have a collection of ML-based solutions (processing + ML model) to choose from.

4. Select an architecture with higher accuracy and lower window increase by clicking on the **Select** button. Our selected architecture has a 250-ms window increase and uses MFE as an input feature and 1D convolution layers.

    As you can observe, the input feature is not MFCC. The EON Tuner proposes this alternative processing block because it considers the latency of the entire ML pipeline rather than just the model inference. Therefore, it is true that MFE could slow down the model inference because it returns a spectrogram with more features than MFCC. However, MFE is considerably faster than MFCC because it does not require extracting the DCT components.

    Once you have selected an architecture, Edge Impulse will ask you to update the primary model. Click on **Yes** to override the architecture trained in the previous *Designing and training a NN model* recipe. A pop-up window will appear, confirming that the primary model has been updated.

In the end, click on **Retrain model** from the left-hand side panel and click on **Train model** to train the network again.

Live classifications with a smartphone

When we talk of model testing, we usually refer to the evaluation of the trained model on the testing dataset. However, model testing in Edge Impulse is more than that.

In this recipe, we will learn how to test model performance on the test set and show a way to perform live classifications with a smartphone.

Getting ready

Before implementing this recipe, the only thing we need to know is how we can evaluate model performance in Edge Impulse.

In Edge Impulse, we can evaluate the trained model in two ways:

*   **Model testing**: We assess the accuracy using the test dataset. The test dataset provides an unbiased evaluation of model effectiveness because the samples are not used directly or indirectly during training.

*   **Live classification**: This is a unique feature of Edge Impulse whereby we can record new samples either from a smartphone or a supported device (for example, the Arduino Nano).

The live classification approach benefits from testing the trained model in the real world before necessarily deploying the application on the target platform.

How to do it...

Follow the next steps to evaluate model performance with the test dataset and the live classification tool:

1. Click on **Model testing** from the left panel and click on **Classify all**.

   Edge Impulse will take care of extracting the MFE from the test set, running the trained model, and reporting the performance in the confusion matrix.

2. Click on **Live classification** from the left panel and ensure the smartphone is reported in the **Device** list:

Figure 4.26 – Device list showing that the mobile phone is paired with Edge Impulse

   Select **Microphone** from the **Sensor** drop-down list in the **Live classification** section and set the **Sample length (ms)** value to 10000. Keep **Frequency** at the default value (16000 Hz).

3. Click on **Start sampling** and then click on **Give access to the Microphone** on your phone. Record any of our six utterances (*red*, *green*, *blue*, *one*, *two*, and *three*). The audio sample will be uploaded on Edge Impulse once you have completed the recording.

At this point, Edge Impulse will split the recording into 1-second-length samples and test the trained model on each one. The classification results will be reported on the same page and in the following forms:

- **Generic summary**: This reports the number of detections for each output category:

CATEGORY	COUNT
blue	1
green	1
one	1
red	2
three	1
two	1
unknown	29
uncertain	1

Figure 4.27 – Generic summary reporting the number of detections for each keyword

- **Detailed analysis**: This reports the probability of the classes at each timestamp, as shown in the following screenshot:

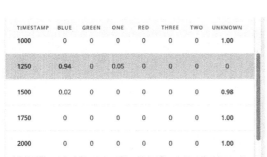 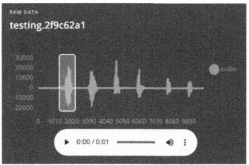

TIMESTAMP	BLUE	GREEN	ONE	RED	THREE	TWO	UNKNOWN
1000	0	0	0	0	0	0	1.00
1250	0.94	0	0.05	0	0	0	0
1500	0.02	0	0	0	0	0	0.98
1750	0	0	0	0	0	0	1.00
2000	0	0	0	0	0	0	1.00

Figure 4.28 – Detailed analysis reporting the probability of the classes at each timestamp

If you click on a table entry, Edge Impulse will show the corresponding audio waveform in the window, as shown in *Figure 4.28*.

Live classifications with the Arduino Nano

If you found live classification with the smartphone helpful, live classification with the Arduino Nano will be even more helpful.

This recipe will show how to pair the Arduino Nano with Edge Impulse to perform live classifications directly from our target platform.

Getting ready

Testing model performance with the sensor used in the final application is a good practice to have more confidence in the accuracy results. Thanks to Edge Impulse, it is possible to perform live classification on the Arduino Nano with a few simple steps that you can also find at the following link: `https://docs.edgeimpulse.com/docs/arduino-nano-33-ble-sense`.

How to do it...

Live classifications with the built-in microphone on the Arduino Nano require installing additional software on your machine. The different tools work on Linux, macOS, and Windows, and are listed here:

- Edge Impulse **command-line interface** (**CLI**): `https://docs.edgeimpulse.com/docs/cli-installation`

- Arduino CLI: `https://arduino.github.io/arduino-cli/0.19/`

Once you have installed the dependencies, follow the next steps to pair the Arduino Nano platform with Edge Impulse:

1. Run `arduino-cli core install arduino:mbed_nano` from Command Prompt or the terminal.

2. Connect the Arduino Nano board to your computer and press the **RESET** button on the platform twice to enter the device in bootloader mode.

   The built-in LED should start blinking to confirm that the platform is in bootloader mode.

3. Download the Edge Impulse firmware for the Arduino Nano from `https://cdn.edgeimpulse.com/firmware/arduino-nano-33-ble-sense.zip` and decompress the file. The firmware will be required to send audio samples from the Arduino Nano to Edge Impulse.

4. In the unzipped folder, execute the *flash script* to upload the firmware on the Arduino Nano. You should use the script accordingly with your **operating system (OS)**—for example, `flash_linux.sh` for Linux.

    Once the firmware has been uploaded on the Arduino Nano, you can press the **RESET** button to launch the program.

5. Execute `edge-impulse-daemon` from Command Prompt or the terminal. The wizard will ask you to log in and select the Edge Impulse project you're working on.

The Arduino Nano should now be paired with Edge Impulse. You can check if the Arduino Nano is paired by clicking on **Devices** from the left-hand side panel, as shown in the following screenshot:

Your devices

These are devices that are connected to the Edge Impulse remote management API, or have posted data to the inge

NAME	ID	TYPE	SENSORS
phone_kseq4mtp		MOBILE_CLIENT	Accelerometer, Microp...
personal		ARDUINO_NANO33...	Built-in accelerometer, ...

Figure 4.29 – List of devices paired with Edge Impulse

As you can see from the preceding screenshot, the Arduino Nano (`personal`) is listed in the **Your devices** section.

Now, go to **Live classification** and select **Arduino Nano 33 BLE Sense board** from the **Device** drop-down list. You can now record audio samples from the Arduino Nano and check if the model works.

> **Important Note**
> If you discover that the model does not work as expected, we recommend adding audio samples recorded with the microphone of the Arduino Nano in the training dataset. To do so, click on **Data acquisition** and record new data using the Arduino Nano device from the right-hand side panel.

Continuous inferencing on the Arduino Nano

As you can guess, the application deployment differs on the Arduino Nano and the Raspberry Pi Pico because the devices have different hardware capabilities.

In this recipe, we will show how to implement a continuous keyword application on the Arduino Nano.

The following Arduino sketch contains the code referred to in this recipe:

- `07_kws_arduino_nano_ble33_sense.ino`:

  `https://github.com/PacktPublishing/TinyML-Cookbook/blob/main/Chapter04/ArduinoSketches/07_kws_arduino_nano_ble33_sense.ino`

Getting ready

The application on the Arduino Nano will be based on the `nano_ble33_sense_microphone_continuous.cpp` example provided by Edge Impulse, which implements a real-time KWS application. Before changing the code, we want to examine how this example works to get ready for the recipe.

Learning how a real-time KWS application works

A real-time KWS application—for example, the one used in the smart assistant—should capture and process all pieces of the audio stream to never miss any events. Therefore, the application needs to *record the audio and run the inference simultaneously* so that we do not skip any information.

On a microcontroller, parallel tasks can be performed in two ways:

- With a **real-time OS** (**RTOS**). In this case, we can use two threads for capturing and processing the audio data.

- With a dedicated peripheral such as **direct memory access** (**DMA**) attached to the ADC. DMA allows data transfer without interfering with the main program running on the processor.

In this recipe, we won't deal with this aspect directly. In fact, the `nano_ble33_sense_microphone_continuous.cpp` example already provides an application where the audio recording and inference run simultaneously through a **double-buffering** mechanism. Double buffering uses two buffers of fixed size, where the following applies:

- One buffer is dedicated to the audio *sampling* task.

- One buffer is dedicated to the *processing* task (feature extraction and ML inference).

Each buffer keeps the number of audio samples required for a window increase recording. Therefore, the buffer size can be calculated through the following formula:

$$Buffer_{size} = SF(Hz) \cdot WI(s)$$

The preceding formula can be defined as the product of the following:

- *SF (Hz)*: Sampling frequency in Hz (for example, 16 **kilohertz** (**kHz**) = 16000 Hz)

- *WI (s)*: Window increase in s (for example, 250 ms = 0.250 s)

For example, if we sample the audio signal at 16 kHz and the window increase is 250 ms, each buffer will have a capacity of 4,000 samples.

These two buffers are continuously switched between *recording* and *processing* tasks, and the following diagram visually shows how:

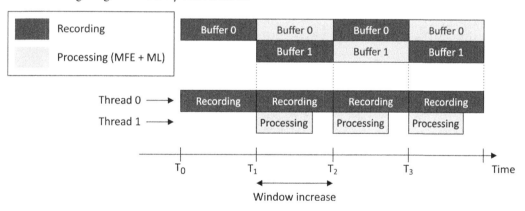

Figure 4.30 – Recording and processing tasks running simultaneously

From the preceding diagram, we can observe the following:

1. The *recording* task starts filling **Buffer 0** at $t=T_0$.

2. At $t=T_1$, **Buffer 0** is full. Therefore, the *processing* task can start the inference using the data in **Buffer 0**. Meanwhile, the *recording* task continues capturing audio data in the background using **Buffer 1**.

3. At $t=T_2$, **Buffer 1** is full. Therefore, the *processing* task must have finished the previous computation before starting a new one.

Keeping the window increase as short as possible has the following benefits:

- Increases the probability of getting the correct beginning of an utterance
- Reduces the computation time of feature extraction because this is only computed on the window increase

However, *the window increase should be long enough to guarantee that the processing task can complete within this time frame.*

At this point, you might have one question in mind: *If we have a window increase of 250 ms, how can the double buffers feed the NN since the model expects a 1-s audio sample?*

The double buffers are not the NN input but the input for an additional buffer containing the samples of the 1-s audio. This buffer stores the data on a **first-in, first-out (FIFO)** basis and provides the actual input to the ML model, as shown in the following diagram:

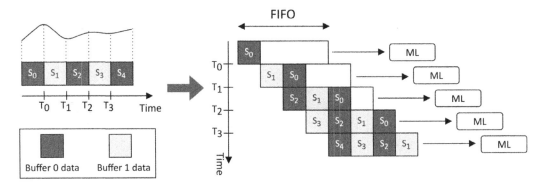

Figure 4.31 – The FIFO buffer is used to feed the NN model

Therefore, every time we start a new processing task, the sampled data is copied into the FIFO queue before running the inference.

How to do it...

With the following steps, we will make some changes to the `nano_ble33_sense_microphone_continuous.cpp` file to control the built-in RGB LEDs on the Arduino Nano with our voice:

1. In Edge Impulse, click on **Deployment** from the left-hand side menu and select **Arduino Library** from the **Create library** options, as shown in the following screenshot:

Deploy your impulse

You can deploy your impulse to any device. This makes the model run without an internet connection, minimizes latency, and runs with minimal power consumption. Read more.

Create library

Turn your impulse into optimized source code that you can run on any device.

| C++ library | Arduino library | Cube.MX CMSIS-PACK |

Figure 4.32 – Create library options in Edge Impulse

Next, click on the **Build** button at the bottom of the page and save the ZIP file on your machine. The ZIP file is an Arduino library containing the KWS application, the routines for feature extraction (MFCC and MFE), and a few ready-to-use examples for the Arduino Nano 33 BLE Sense board.

2. Open the Arduino **integrated development environment** (**IDE**) and import the library created by Edge Impulse. To do so, click on the **Libraries** tab from the left pane and then click on the **Import** button, as shown in the following screenshot:

Figure 4.33 – Import library in Arduino Web Editor

Once imported, open the `nano_ble33_sense_microphone_continuous` example from **Examples | FROM LIBRARIES | <name_of_your_project>_ INFERENCING**.

In our case, **<name_of_your_project>** is `VOICE_CONTROLLING_LEDS`, which matches the name given to our Edge Impulse project.

In the file, the `EI_CLASSIFIER_SLICES_PER_MODEL_WINDOW` C macro defines the window increase in terms of the number of frames processed per model window. We can keep it at the default value.

3. Declare and initialize a global array of `mbed::DigitalOut` objects to drive the built-in RGB LEDs:

```
mbed::DigitalOut rgb[] = {p24, p16, p6};
#define ON 0
#define OFF 1
```

The initialization of `mbed::DigitalOut` requires the `PinName` value of the RGB LEDs. The pin names can be found in the Arduino Nano 33 BLE Sense board schematic (`https://content.arduino.cc/assets/NANO33BLE_V2.0_sch.pdf`):

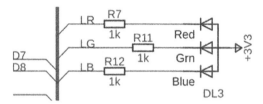

Figure 4.34 – The built-in RGB LEDs are powered by a current-sinking circuit (`https://content.arduino.cc/assets/NANO33BLE_V2.0_sch.pdf`)

The RGB LEDs—identified with the labels **LR**, **LG**, and **LB**—are controlled by a **current-sinking** circuit and are connected to **P0.24**, **P0.16**, and **P0.06**:

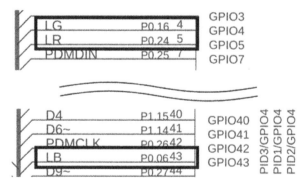

Figure 4.35 – The RGB LEDs are connected to P0.24, P0.16, and P0.06 (`https://content.arduino.cc/assets/NANO33BLE_V2.0_sch.pdf`)

Therefore, the **general-purpose input/output (GPIO)** *pin must supply 0 volts (V) (LOW) to turn on the LEDs*. To avoid using numerical values, we can use the `#define ON 0` and `#define OFF 1` C defines to turn the LEDs on and off.

4. Define an integer global variable (`current_color`) to keep track of the last detected color. Initialize it to `0` (*red*):

```
size_t current_color = 0;
```

5. Initialize the built-in RGB LEDs in the `setup()` function by turning on just `current_color`:

```
rgb[0] = OFF; rgb[1] = OFF; rgb[2] = OFF; rgb[current_
color] = ON;
```

6. In the `loop()` function, set to `false` the **moving average (MA)** flag in the `run_classifier_continuous()` function:

```
run_classifier_continuous(&signal, &result, debug_nn,
false);
```

The `run_classifier_continuous()` function is responsible for the model inference. The MA is disabled by passing `false` after the `debug_nn` parameter. However, *why do we disable this functionality*?

MA is an effective method to filter out false detections when the window increase is small. For example, consider the word *bluebird*. This word contains *blue*, but it is not the utterance we want to recognize. However, when running continuous inference with a slight window increase, there is the benefit of processing small pieces of the word at a time. Therefore, the *blue* word may be detected with high confidence in one piece but not in the others. So, *the goal of the MA is to average the results of classifications over time to avoid false detections*.

As we can guess, the output class must have multiple high-rated classifications when using the MA. Therefore, *what happens if the window increase is significant*?

When the window increase is significant (for example, greater than 100 ms), we process fewer segments per second, and then the moving average could filter out all the classifications. Since our window increase will be between 250 ms and 500 ms (depending on the ML architecture chosen), we recommend you disable it to avoid filtering out the classifications.

7. Remove the code after `run_classifier_continuous()` till the end of the `loop()` function.

8. In the `loop()` function and after `run_classifier_continuous()`, write the code to return a class with higher probability:

```
size_t ix_max = 0;
float   pb_max = 0.0f;
for (size_t ix = 0; ix < EI_CLASSIFIER_LABEL_COUNT; ix++)
{
  if(result.classification[ix].value > pb_max) {
    ix_max = ix;
    pb_max = result.classification[ix].value;
  }
}
```

In the preceding code snippet, we iterate through all the output classes (`EI_CLASSIFIER_LABEL_COUNT`) and keep the index (`ix`) with the maximum classification value (`result.classification[ix].value`). `EI_CLASSIFIER_LABEL_COUNT` is a C define provided by Edge Impulse and is equal to the number of output categories.

9. If the probability of the output category (`pb_max`) is higher than a fixed threshold (for example, *0.5*) and the label is not unknown, check whether it is a color. If the label is a color and different from the last one detected, turn off `current_color` and turn on `new_color`:

```
size_t new_color = ix_max;
if (new_color != current_color) {
  rgb[current_color] = OFF;
  rgb[new_color] = ON;
  current_color = new_color;
}
```

If the label is a number, blink the `current_color` LED for the recognized number of times:

```
const size_t num_blinks = ix_max0 - 2;
for(size_t i = 0; i < num_blinks; ++i) {
  rgb[current_color] = OFF;
  delay(1000);
  rgb[current_color] = ON;
  delay(1000);
}
```

Compile and upload the sketch on the Arduino Nano. You should now be able to change the color of the LED or make it blink with your voice.

Building the circuit with the Raspberry Pi Pico to voice control LEDs

The Raspberry Pi Pico has neither a microphone nor RGB LEDs onboard for building a KWS application. Therefore, voice controlling the RGB LEDs on this platform requires building an electronic circuit.

This recipe aims to prepare a circuit with the Raspberry Pi Pico, RGB LEDs, a push-button, and an electret microphone with a MAX9814 amplifier.

Getting ready

The application we have considered for the Raspberry Pi Pico is not based on continuous inferencing. Here, we would like to use a button to start the audio recording of 1 s and then run the model inference to recognize the utterance. The spoken word, in turn, will be used to control the status of the RGB LEDs.

In the following subsection, we will learn more about using the electret microphone with the MAX9814 amplifier.

Introducing the electret microphone amplifier with the MAX9814 amplifier

The microphone put into action in this recipe is the low-cost **electret microphone amplifier – MAX9814**. You can buy the microphone from the following distributors:

- *Pimoroni*: https://shop.pimoroni.com/products/adafruit-electret-microphone-amplifier-max9814-w-auto-gain-control

- *Adafruit*: https://www.adafruit.com/product/1713

The signal coming from the microphone is often tiny and requires amplification to be adequately captured and analyzed.

For this reason, our microphone is coupled with the **MAX9814** chip (https://datasheets.maximintegrated.com/en/ds/MAX9814.pdf), an amplifier with built-in **automatic gain control** (**AGC**). AGC allows the capturing of speech in environments where the background audio level changes unpredictably. Therefore, the MAX9814 automatically adapts the amplification gain to make the voice always distinguishable.

The amplifier requires a *supply voltage between 2.7V and 5.5V* and produces an output with a maximum **peak-to-peak voltage (Vpp)** of *2Vpp on a 1.25V direct current (DC) bias.*

> **Note**
>
> Vpp is the full height of the waveform.

Therefore, the device can be connected to ADC, expecting input signals between 0V and 3.3V.

As shown in the following diagram, the microphone module has five holes at the bottom for inserting the header strip:

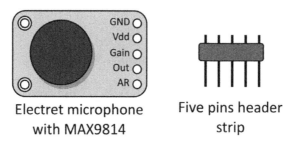

Figure 4.36 – Electret microphone with MAX9814

The header strip is required for mounting the device on the breadboard, and it typically needs to be soldered.

> **Tip**
>
> If you are not familiar with soldering, we recommend reading the following tutorial:
>
> ```
> https://learn.adafruit.com/adafruit-agc-electret-
> microphone-amplifier-max9814/assembly
> ```

In the following subsection, you will discover how to connect this device with the Raspberry Pi Pico.

Connecting the microphone to the Raspberry Pi Pico ADC

The voltage variations produced by the microphone require conversion to a digital format.

The RP2040 microcontroller on the Raspberry Pi Pico has four ADCs to carry out this conversion, but only three of them can be used for external inputs because one is directly connected to the internal temperature sensor.

The pin reserved for the ADCs are shown here:

ADC name	ADC0	ADC1	ADC2
Pin	GP26	GP27	GP28

Figure 4.37 – ADC pins

The expected voltage range for the ADC on the Raspberry Pi Pico is between 0V and 3.3V, perfect for the signal coming from our electret microphone.

How to do it...

Let's start by placing the Raspberry Pi Pico on the breadboard. We should mount the platform vertically, as we did in *Chapter 2*, *Prototyping with Microcontrollers*.

Once you have placed the device on the breadboard, ensure the USB cable is not connected to power and follow the next steps to build the electronic circuit:

1. Place the RGB LEDs on the breadboard:

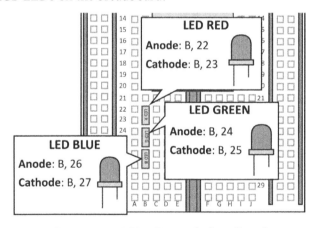

Figure 4.38 – RGB LEDs on the breadboard

Put the resistor in series to the LEDs by connecting one of the two terminals to the LED cathode and the other one to GND. The following table reports which resistor to use with each LED:

LED	Red	Green	Blue
Resistance (Ohm)	220	220	100

Figure 4.39 – Resistors used with the RGB LEDs

The resistances have been chosen to guarantee at least a ~3 milliampere (mA) forward current through each LED.

The following diagram shows how you can connect the resistors in series to the LEDs:

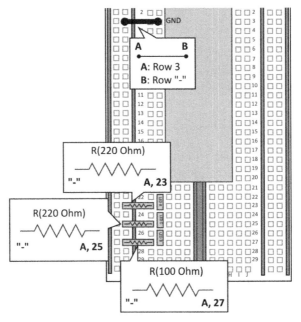

Figure 4.40 – Resistors in series to LEDs

As you can observe, you can plug the microcontroller's GND into the - rail to insert the resistor's terminal into the negative bus rail.

2.   Connect the RGB LEDs' anode to the GPIO pins:

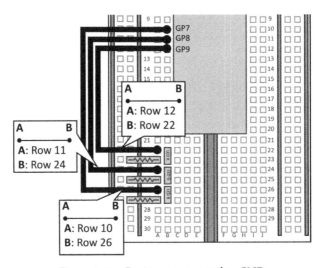

Figure 4.41 – Resistors connected to GND

As shown in the previous diagram, the GPIOs used to drive the LEDs are **GP9** (red), **GP8** (green), and **GP7** (blue).

Since the resistor is connected between the LED cathode and GND, the *LEDs are powered by a current sourcing circuit.* Therefore, we should supply *3.3V (HIGH)* to turn them on.

3. Place the push-button on the breadboard:

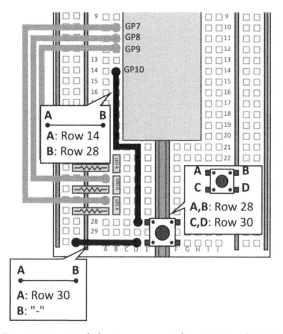

Figure 4.42 – Push-button connected to GP10 and GND

The GPIO used for the push-button is **GP10**.

Since our circuits will require several jumper wires, we place the device at the bottom of the breadboard to have enough space to press it.

4.   Place the electret microphone on the breadboard:

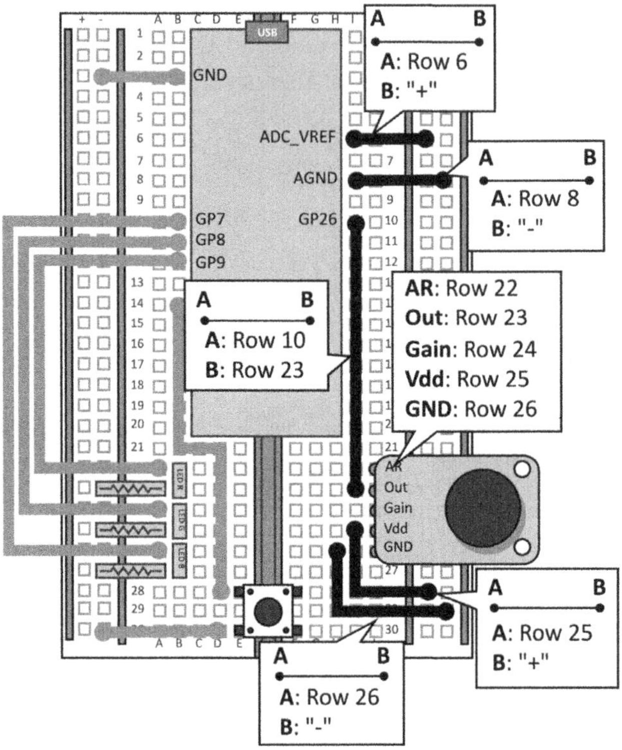

Figure 4.43 – Electret microphone mounted on the breadboard

The ADC pin is **GP26**. Out of the five pins on the microphone module, we only need to connect three of them, which are outlined as follows:

- **Vdd** (3.3V): This is the supply voltage of the amplifier. **Vdd** must be stable and equal to the ADC supply voltage. These conditions are required to reduce the noise on the analog signal coming from the microphone.

- **Vdd** should be connected to ADC_VREF, the ADC reference voltage produced on the Raspberry Pi Pico.

- **GND**: This is the ground of the circuit amplifier and should be the same as the ADC peripheral. Since analog signals are more susceptible to noise than digital ones, the Raspberry Pi Pico offers a dedicated ground for ADCs: the **analog ground (AGND)**. **GND** should be connected to **AGND** to decouple the analog circuit from the digital one.

- **Out**: This is the amplified analog signal coming from the microphone module and should be connected to **GP26** to sample it with the **ADC0** peripheral.

The following table reports the connections to make between the Raspberry Pi Pico and the electret microphone with the MAX9814 amplifier:

Mic with MAX9814 - Pin	Vdd	GND	Out
Raspberry Pi Pico - Pin	ADC_VREF	AGND	GP26

Figure 4.44 – Electret microphone connections

The remaining two terminals of the microphone are used to set the `gain` and the `attach&release` ratio. These settings are not required for this recipe, but you can discover more in the MAX9814 datasheet (`https://datasheets.maximintegrated.com/en/ds/MAX9814.pdf`).

At this point, you can plug the Raspberry Pi Pico into your computer through the Micro USB cable because the circuit is ready to implement our KWS application.

Audio sampling with ADC and timer interrupts on the Raspberry Pi Pico

All the components are now mounted on the breadboard. Therefore, there is nothing left for us to write our KWS application.

The application consists of recording 1-s audio and running the ML inference when pressing the push-button. The classification result will be shown through the RGB LEDs, similar to what we have done in the *Continuous inferencing on the Arduino Nano* recipe.

The following Arduino sketch and Python script contains the code referred to in this recipe:

- `09_kws_raspberrypi_pico.ino`:

  `https://github.com/PacktPublishing/TinyML-Cookbook/blob/main/Chapter04/ArduinoSketches/09_kws_raspberrypi_pico.ino`

- `09_debugging.py`:

  `https://github.com/PacktPublishing/TinyML-Cookbook/blob/main/Chapter04/PythonScripts/09_debugging.py`

Getting ready

The application on the Raspberry Pi Pico will be based on the Edge Impulse `nano_ble33_sense_microphone.cpp` example, where the user speaks at well-defined times and the application executes the ML model to guess the spoken word.

In contrast to what we implemented in the *Continuous inferencing on the Arduino Nano* recipe, the audio recording and processing task can be performed sequentially because the push-button will tell us the beginning of the utterance.

The following subsection will introduce the approach considered in this recipe to sample the audio signal with ADC and timer interrupts.

Audio sampling with ADC and timer interrupts on the Raspberry Pi Pico

The RP2040 microcontroller on the Raspberry Pi Pico has *four* ADCs with *12-bit* resolution and a maximum sampling frequency of 500 kHz (or 500 **kilosamples per second (kS/s)**).

The ADC will be configured in *one-shot* mode, which means that the ADC will provide the sample as soon as we make the request.

The timer peripheral will be initialized to trigger interrupts at the same frequency as the sampling rate. Therefore, the **interrupt service routine (ISR)** will be responsible for sampling the signal coming from the microphone and storing the data in an audio buffer.

Since the ADC maximum frequency is 500 kHz, the minimum time between two consecutive conversions is 2 **microseconds (us)**. This constraint is largely met because the audio signal is sampled at 16 kHz, which means every 62.5 us.

How to do it...

Open the `nano_ble33_sense_microphone` example from **Examples | FROM LIBRARIES | <name_of_your_project>_INFERENCING**, and make the following changes to implement the KWS application on the Raspberry Pi Pico:

1. Delete all the references to the PDM library, such as the header file (`#include <PDM.h>`) and calls to PDM class methods since these are only required for the built-in microphone of the Arduino Nano.

    Remove the code within the `microphone_inference_record()` function.

2. Declare and initialize a global array of mbed::DigitalOut objects to drive the RGB LEDs:

```
mbed::DigitalOut rgb[] = {p9, p8, p7};
```

Declare and initialize a global mbed::DigitalOut object to drive the built-in LED:

```
mbed::DigitalOut led_builtin(p25);
#define ON 1
#define OFF 0
```

Since a current sourcing circuit powers all LEDs, we need to supply 3.3V (*HIGH*) to turn them on.

3. Define an integer global variable (current_color) to keep track of the last detected color. Initialize it to 0 (*red*):

```
size_t current_color = 0;
```

Initialize the RGB LEDs in the setup() function by turning on current_color only:

```
rgb[0] = OFF; rgb[1] = OFF; rgb[2] = OFF; rgb[current_
color] = ON; led_builtin = OFF;
```

4. Declare and initialize the global mbed::DigitalIn object to read the push-button state:

```
mbed::DigitalIn button(p10);
#define PRESSED 0
```

Set the button mode to PullUp in the setup() function:

```
button.mode(PullUp);
```

Since the button is directly connected to GND and the GPIO pin, we must enable the internal pull-up resistor by enabling the PullUp button mode. Therefore, the numerical value returned by mbed::DigitalIn is 0 when the button is pressed.

5. Add the "hardware/adc.h" header file to use the ADC peripheral:

```
#include "hardware/adc.h"
```

Initialize the ADC (**GP26**) peripheral in the setup() function using the Raspberry Pi Pico **application programming interface** (**API**):

```
adc_init(); adc_gpio_init(26); adc_select_input(0);
```

Raspberry Pi offers a dedicated API for the RP2040 microcontroller in the *Raspberry Pi Pico SDK* (`https://raspberrypi.github.io/pico-sdk-doxygen/index.html`).

Since the Raspberry Pi Pico SDK is integrated into the Arduino IDE, we don't need to import any library. We just need to include the header file (`"hardware/adc.h"`) in the sketch to use the ADC's API.

The ADC is initialized by calling the following functions in `setup()`:

A. `adc_init()`, to initialize the ADC peripheral.

B. `adc_gpio_init(26)`, to initialize the GPIO used by the ADC. This function needs the GPIO pin number attached to the ADC peripheral. Therefore, we pass 26 because ADC0 is attached to **GP26**.

C. `adc_select_input(0)`, to initialize the ADC input. The ADC input is the reference number of the ADC attached to the selected GPIO. Therefore, we pass 0 because we use **ADC0**.

By calling the preceding functions, we initialize the ADC in *one-shot* mode.

6. Declare a global `mbed::Ticker` object to use the timer peripheral:

```
mbed::Ticker timer;
```

The `timer` object will be used *to fire the timer interrupts at the frequency of the audio sampling rate* (16 kHz).

7. Write the timer ISR to sample the audio coming from the microphone:

```
#define BIAS_MIC ((int16_t)(1.25f * 4095) / 3.3f)
volatile int  ix_buffer       = 0;
volatile bool is_buffer_ready = false;
void timer_ISR() {
   if(ix_buffer < EI_CLASSIFIER_RAW_SAMPLE_COUNT) {
      int16_t v = (int16_t)((adc_read() - BIAS_MIC));
      inference.buffer[ix_buffer] = v;
      ++ix_buffer;
   }
   else {
      is_buffer_ready = true;
   }
}
```

The ISR samples the microphone's signal with the `adc_read()` function, which returns a value from `0` to `4096` because of the ADC resolution. Since the signal generated by the MAX9814 amplifier has a bias of 1.25V, we should subtract the corresponding digital sample from the measurement. The relationship between the voltage sample and the converted digital sample is provided with the following formula:

$$DS = \frac{(2^{resolution} - 1) \cdot VS}{VREF}$$

Here, the following applies:

- *DS* is the digital sample.

- *resolution* is the ADC resolution.

- *VS* is the voltage sample.

- *VREF* is the ADC supply voltage reference (for example, `ADC_VREF`).

Therefore, a 12-bit ADC with a VREF of 3.3V converts the 1.25V bias to `1552`.

Once we have subtracted the bias from the measurement, we can store it in the audio buffer (`inference.buffer[ix_buffer] = v`) and then increment the buffer index (`++ix_buffer`).

The audio buffer needs to be dynamically allocated in `setup()` with `microphone_inference_start()`, and it can keep the number of samples required for a 1-s recording. The `EI_CLASSIFIER_RAW_SAMPLE_COUNT` C define is provided by Edge Impulse to know the number of samples in 1-s audio. Since we sample the audio stream with a sampling rate of 16 kHz, the audio buffer will contain 16,000 `int16_t` samples.

The ISR sets `is_buffer_ready` to `true` when the audio buffer is full (`ix_buffer` is greater than or equal to `EI_CLASSIFIER_RAW_SAMPLE_COUNT`).

`ix_buffer` and `is_buffer_ready` are global because they are used by the main program to know when the recording is ready. Since ISR changes these variables, we must declare them `volatile` to prevent compiler optimizations.

8. Write the code in `microphone_inference_record()` to record 1 s of audio:

```
bool microphone_inference_record(void) {
    ix_buffer = 0;
    is_buffer_ready = false;
    led_builtin = ON;
```

```
    unsigned int sampling_period_us = 1000000 / 16000;
    timer.attach_us(&timer_ISR, sampling_period_us);
    while(!is_buffer_ready);
    timer.detach();
    led_builtin = OFF;
    return true;
}
```

In `microphone_inference_record()`, we set `ix_buffer` to 0 and `is_buffer_ready` to `false` every time we start a new recording.

The user will know when the recording starts through the built-in LED light (`led_builtin = ON`).

At this point, we initialize the `mbed::Ticker` object to fire the interrupts with a frequency of 16 kHz. To do so, we call the `attach_us()` method, which requires the following:

- The ISR to call when the interrupt is triggered (`&timer_ISR`).

- The interval time for us to fire the interrupt. Since we sample the audio signal at 16 kHz, we pass 62us (`unsigned int sampling_period_us = 1000000 / 16000`).

The `while(!is_buffer_ready)` statement is used to check whether the audio recording is finished.

When the recording ends, we can stop generating the timer interrupts (`timer.detach()`) and turn off the built-in LED (`led_builtin = OFF`).

9. Check whether we are pressing the button in the `loop()` function:

```
if(button == PRESSED) {
```

If so, wait for almost a second (for example, 700 ms) to avoid recording the mechanical sound of the pressed button:

```
delay(700);
```

We recommend not releasing the push-button until the end of the recording to also prevent a mechanical sound when releasing it.

Next, record 1 s of audio with the `microphone_inference_record()` function and execute the model inference by calling `run_classifier()`:

```
microphone_inference_record();


signal_t signal;
signal.total_length = EI_CLASSIFIER_RAW_SAMPLE_COUNT;
signal.get_data = &microphone_audio_signal_get_data;
ei_impulse_result_t result = { 0 };


run_classifier(&signal, &result, debug_nn);
```

After the `run_classifier()` function, you can use the same code written in the *Continuous inferencing on the Arduino Nano* recipe to control the RGB LEDs.

However, before ending the `loop()` function, wait for the button to be released:

```
while(button == PRESSED);
}
```

Now, compile and upload the sketch on the Raspberry Pi Pico. When the device is ready, press the push-button, wait for the built-in LED light, and try to speak loud and close to the microphone to control the RGB LEDs with your voice.

You should now be able to control the RGB LEDs with your voice!

There's more...

What can we do if the application does not work? We may have different reasons, but one could be related to the recorded audio. For example, *how can we know if the audio is recorded correctly*?

To debug the application, we have implemented the `09_debugging.py` Python script (`https://github.com/PacktPublishing/TinyML-Cookbook/blob/main/Chapter04/PythonScripts/09_debugging.py`) to generate an audio file (`.wav`) from the audio captured by the Raspberry Pi Pico.

The Python script works locally on your machine and only needs the `PySerial`, `uuid`, `Struct`, and `Wave` modules in your environment.

The following steps show how to use the Python script for debugging the application on the Raspberry Pi Pico:

1. Import the `09_kws_raspberrypi_pico.ino` sketch (`https://github.com/PacktPublishing/TinyML-Cookbook/blob/main/Chapter04/ArduinoSketches/09_kws_raspberrypi_pico.ino`) in the Arduino IDE and set the `debug_audio_raw` variable to `true`. This flag will allow the Raspberry Pi Pico to transmit audio samples over the serial whenever we have a new recording.

2. Compile and upload the `09_kws_raspberrypi_pico.ino` sketch on the Raspberry Pi Pico.

3. Run the `09_debugging.py` Python script, providing the following input arguments:

   * `--label`: The label assigned to the recorded utterance. The label will be the prefix for the filename of the generated `.wav` audio files.

   * `--port`: Device name of the serial peripheral used by the Raspberry Pi Pico. The port's name depends on the OS—for example, `/dev/ttyACM0` on **GNU**/Linux or `COM1` on Windows. The easiest way to find out the serial port's name is from the device drop-down menu in the Arduino IDE:

Figure 4.45 – Device drop-down menu in Arduino Web Editor

Once the Python script has been executed, it will parse the audio samples transmitted over the serial to produce a `.wav` file whenever you press the push-button.

You can listen to the audio file with any software capable of opening `.wav` files.

If the audio level of the `.wav` file is too low, try speaking loud and close to the microphone when recording.

However, suppose the audio level is acceptable, and the application still does not work. In that case, the ML model is probably not generic enough to deal with the signal of the electret microphone. To fix this problem, you can expand the training dataset in Edge Impulse with the audio samples obtained from this microphone. For this scope, upload the generated `.wav` audio files in the **Data acquisition** section of Edge Impulse and train the model again. Once you have prepared the model, you just need to build a new Arduino library and import it into the Arduino IDE.

If you are wondering how this script works, don't worry. In the following chapter, you will learn more about it.

5

Indoor Scene Classification with TensorFlow Lite for Microcontrollers and the Arduino Nano

Computer vision is what made convolutional neural networks hugely popular. Without this deep learning algorithm, tasks such as object recognition, scene understanding, and pose estimation would be really challenging. Nowadays, many modern camera applications are powered by **machine learning** (**ML**), and we just need to take the smartphone to see them in action. Computer vision also finds space in microcontrollers, although with limitations given the reduced onboard memory.

In this chapter, we will see the benefit of adding sight to our tiny devices by recognizing indoor environments with the **OV7670** camera module in conjunction with the Arduino Nano 33 BLE Sense board.

In the first part, we will learn how to acquire images from the OV7670 camera module. We will then focus on the model design, applying **transfer learning** with the **Keras** API to recognize kitchens and bathrooms. Finally, we will deploy the quantized **TensorFlow Lite (TFLite)** model on an Arduino Nano with the help of **TensorFlow Lite for Microcontrollers (TFLu)**.

The goal of this chapter is to show how to apply transfer learning with TensorFlow and learn the best practices of using a camera module with a microcontroller.

In this chapter, we're going to implement the following recipes:

- Taking pictures with the OV7670 camera module
- Grabbing camera frames from the serial port with Python
- Converting QQVGA images from YCbCr422 to RGB888
- Building the dataset for indoor scene classification
- Applying transfer learning with Keras
- Preparing and testing the quantized TFLite model
- Reducing RAM usage by fusing crop, resize, rescale, and quantize

Technical requirements

To complete all the practical recipes of this chapter, we will need the following:

- An Arduino Nano 33 BLE Sense board
- A micro-USB cable
- 1 x half-size solderless breadboard
- 1 x OV7670 camera module
- 1 x push-button
- 18 x jumper wires (male to female)
- A laptop/PC with either Ubuntu 18.04+ or Windows 10 on x86-64

The source code and additional materials are available in Chapter05 (https://github.com/PacktPublishing/TinyML-Cookbook/tree/main/Chapter05).

Taking pictures with the OV7670 camera module

Adding sight to the Arduino Nano is our first step to unlocking computer vision applications.

In this first recipe, we will build an electronic circuit to take pictures from the OV7670 camera module using the Arduino Nano. Once we have assembled the circuit, we will use the Arduino pre-built `CameraCaptureRawBytes` sketch to transmit the pixel values over the serial.

The following Arduino sketch contains the code referred to in this recipe:

* `01_camera_capture.ino`:

    `https://github.com/PacktPublishing/TinyML-Cookbook/blob/main/Chapter05/ArduinoSketches/01_camera_capture.ino`

Getting ready

The **OV7670** camera module is the main ingredient required in this recipe to take pictures with the Arduino Nano. It is one of the most affordable cameras for TinyML applications – you can buy it from various distributors for less than $10. Cost is not the only reason we went for this sensor, though. Other factors make this device our preferred option, such as the following:

* **Frame resolution and color format support**: Since microcontrollers have limited memory, we should consider cameras capable of transferring low-resolution images. The OV7670 camera unit is a good choice because it can output **QVGA** (320x240) and **QQVGA** (160x120) pictures. Furthermore, the device can encode the images in different color formats, such as **RGB565**, **RGB444**, and **YUCbCr422**.

* **Software library support**: Camera units can be complicated to control without a software driver. Therefore, vision sensors with software library support are generally recommended to make the programming straightforward. The OV7670 has a support library for the Arduino Nano 33 BLE Sense board (`https://github.com/arduino-libraries/Arduino_OV767X`), which is already integrated into the Arduino Web Editor.

These factors, along with voltage supply, power consumption, frame rate, and interface, are generally pondered when choosing a vision module for TinyML applications.

How to do it...

Let's start this recipe by taking a half breadboard with 30 rows and 10 columns and mounting the Arduino Nano vertically among the left and right terminal strips, as shown in the following figure:

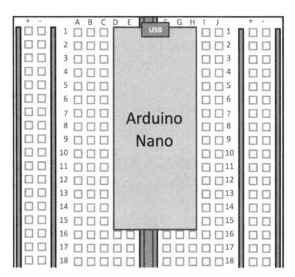

Figure 5.1 – The Arduino Nano mounted vertically between the left and right terminal strips

The following steps will show how to assemble the circuit with the Arduino Nano, OV7670 module, and a push-button:

1. Connect the OV7670 camera module to the Arduino Nano by using 16 male-to-female jumper wires, as illustrated in the following diagram:

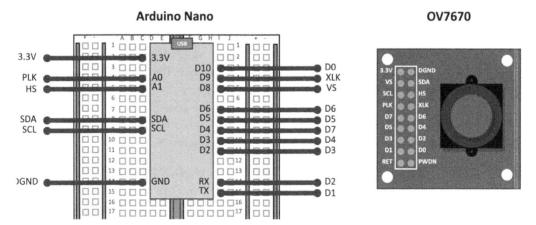

Figure 5.2 – Wiring between the Arduino Nano and OV7670

Although the OV7670 has 18 pins, we only need to connect 16 of them.

The OV7670 camera module is connected to the Arduino Nano following the arrangement needed for the `Arduino_OV767X` support library.

> **Tip**
>
> You can find the pin arrangement required by the `Arduino_OV767x` support library at the following link:
>
> `https://github.com/arduino-libraries/Arduino_OV767X/blob/master/src/OV767X.h`

2. Add a push-button on the breadboard and connect it to **P0.30** and **GND**:

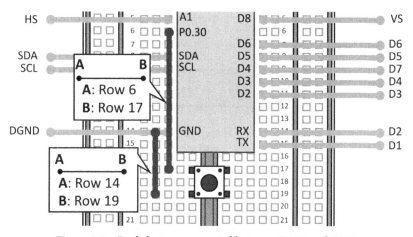

Figure 5.3 – Push-button connected between P0.30 and GND

The push-button does not need an additional resistor because we will employ the microcontroller pull-up one.

Now, open the Arduino IDE and follow these steps to implement a sketch to take pictures whenever we press the push-button:

1. Open the `CameraCaptureRawBytes` sketch from **Examples->FROM LIBRARIES->ARDUINO_OV767X**:

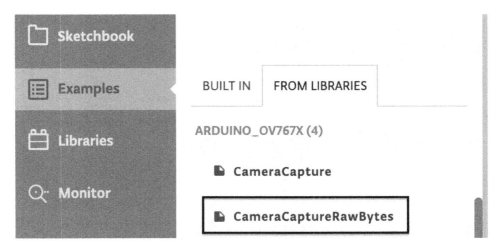

Figure 5.4 – CameraCaptureRawBytes sketch

Copy the content of `CameraCaptureRawBytes` in a new sketch.

2. Declare and initialize a global `mbed::DigitalIn` object to read the push-button state:

```
mbed::DigitalIn  button(p30);
#define PRESSED 0
```

Next, set the button mode to `PullUp` in the `setup()` function:

```
button.mode(PullUp);
```

3. Set the baud rate of the serial peripheral to `115600` in the `setup()` function:

```
Serial.begin(115600);
```

4. Add an `if` statement in the `loop()` function to check whether the push-button is pressed. If the button is pressed, take a picture from the OV7670 camera and send the pixel values over the serial:

```
if(button == PRESSED) {
    Camera.readFrame(data);
    Serial.write(data, bytes_per_frame);
}
```

> **Note**
>
> The variables' names in the pre-built `CameraCaptureRawBytes` are in **PascalCase**, so the first letter of each word is capitalized. To keep consistency with the lowercase naming convention used in the book, we have renamed `BytesPerFrame` to `bytes_per_frame`.

Compile and upload the sketch on the Arduino Nano. Now, you can open the serial monitor by clicking on **Monitor** from the **Editor** menu. From there, you will see all the pixels values transmitted whenever you press the push-button.

Grabbing camera frames from the serial port with Python

In the previous recipe, we showed how to take images from the OV7670, but we didn't present a method for displaying them.

This recipe will use Python to parse the pixel values transmitted serially to display the captured pictures on the screen.

The following Arduino sketch and Python script contain the code referred to in this recipe:

- `02_camera_capture_qvga_rgb565.ino`:

  `https://github.com/PacktPublishing/TinyML-Cookbook/blob/main/Chapter05/ArduinoSketches/02_camera_capture_qvga_rgb565.ino`

- `02_parse_camera_frame.py`:

  `https://github.com/PacktPublishing/TinyML-Cookbook/blob/main/Chapter05/PythonScripts/02_parse_camera_frame.py`

Getting ready

In contrast to all Python programs developed so far, we will write the Python script on our local machine to access the serial port used by the Arduino Nano.

Parsing serial data with Python requires little effort with the `pySerial` library, which can be installed through the `pip` Python package manager:

```
$ pip install pyserial
```

However, `pySerial` will not be the only module required for this recipe. Since we need to create images from the data transmitted over the serial, we will use the Python `Pillow` library (**PIL**) to facilitate this task.

The PIL module can be installed with the following `pip` command:

```
$ pip install Pillow
```

However, what data format should we expect from the microcontroller?

Transmitting RGB888 images over the serial

To simplify the parsing of the pixels transmitted over the serial, we will make some changes in the Arduino sketch of the previous recipe to send images in **RGB888** format. This format packs the pixel in 3 bytes, using 8 bits for each color component.

Using RGB888 means that our Python script can directly create the image with PIL without extra conversions.

However, it is a good practice to transmit the image with **metadata** to simplify the parsing and check communication errors.

In our case, the metadata will provide the following information:

1. *The beginning of the image transmission*: We send the `<image>` string to signify the beginning of the communication.

2. *The image resolution*: We send the image resolution as a string of digits to say how many RGB pixels will be transmitted. The width and height will be sent on two different lines.

3. *The completion of the image transmission*: Once we have sent all pixel values, we transmit the `</image>` string to notify the end of the communication.

The pixel values will be sent right after the image resolution metadata and following the top to bottom, left to right order (**raster scan order**):

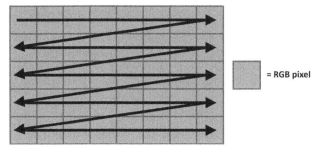

Figure 5.5 – Raster scan order

The color components will be sent as strings of digits terminated with a newline character (\n) and following the RGB ordering. Therefore, the red channel comes first and the blue one last, as shown in the following diagram:

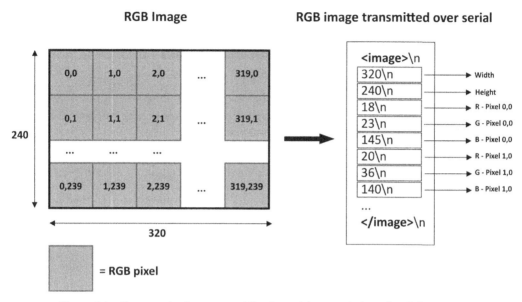

Figure 5.6 – Communication protocol for the serial transmission of an RGB image

As you can observe from the preceding illustration, the pixel values are transmitted following the raster scanning order. Each color component is sent as a string of digits terminated with a newline character (\n).

However, the OV7670 camera is initialized to output images in the RGB565 color format. Therefore, we need to convert the camera pixels to RGB888 before sending them over the serial.

Learning how to convert RGB565 to RGB888

As you may have noticed, **RGB565** is the format used in the camera initialization of the CameraCaptureRawBytes sketch:

```
Camera.begin(QVGA, RGB565, 1)
```

RGB565 packs the pixel in 2 bytes, reserving 5 bits for the red and blue components and 6 bits for the green one:

Figure 5.7 – RGB565 color format

This color format finds applicability mainly in embedded systems with limited memory capacity since it reduces the image size. However, memory reduction is achieved *by reducing the dynamic range of the color components.*

How to do it...

In the following steps, we will see what to change in the Arduino sketch of the previous recipe to send the RGB888 pixels over the serial. Once the sketch is implemented, we will write a Python script to display the image transmitted over the serial on the screen:

1. Write a function to convert the RGB565 pixel to RGB888:

```
void rgb565_rgb888(uint8_t* in, uint8_t* out) {
    uint16_t p = (in[0] << 8) | in[1];
    out[0] = ((p >> 11) & 0x1f) << 3;
    out[1] = ((p >> 5) & 0x3f) << 2;
    out[2] = (p & 0x1f) << 3;
}
```

The function takes 2 bytes from the input buffer to form the 16-bit RGB565 pixel. The first byte (in[0]) is left-shifted by eight positions to place it in the higher half of the uint16_t p variable. The second byte (in[1]) is set in the lower part:

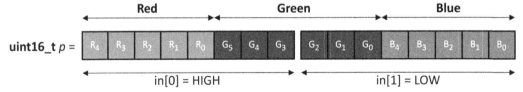

Figure 5.8 – The RGB565 pixel is formed with in[0] and in[1] bytes

Once we have the 16-bit pixel, we get the 8-bit color components from p by right-shifting each channel towards the beginning of the least significant byte:

- The 8-bit red channel (out[0]) is obtained by shifting p by 11 positions so that **R0** is the first bit of the uint16_t variable. After, we clear all the non-red bits by applying a bitmask with 0x1F (all bits cleared except the first five).

- The 8-bit green channel (out[1]) is obtained by shifting p by five positions so that **G0** is the first bit of the uint16_t variable. After, we clear all the non-green bits by applying a bitmask with 0x3F (all bits cleared except the first six).

- The 8-bit blue channel (out[2]) is obtained without shifting because **B0** is already the first bit of the uint16_t variable. Therefore, we just need to clear the non-blue bits by applying a bitmask with 0x1F (all bits cleared except the first five).

In the end, we perform an extra left-shifting to move the most significant bit of each channel to the eighth position of the byte.

2. Enable testPattern in the setup() function:

```
Camera.testPattern();
```

The Camera module will always return a fixed image with color bands when the test pattern mode is enabled.

3. In the loop() function, replace Serial.write(data, bytes_per_frame) with the routine to send the RGB888 pixels over the serial:

```
Camera.readFrame(data);
uint8_t rgb888[3];
Serial.println("<image>");
Serial.println(Camera.width());
Serial.println(Camera.height());
const int bytes_per_pixel = Camera.bytesPerPixel();
for(int i = 0; i < bytes_per_frame; i+=bytes_per_pixel) {
    rgb565_rgb888(&data[i], &rgb888[0]);
    Serial.println(rgb888[0]);
    Serial.println(rgb888[1]);
    Serial.println(rgb888[2]);
}
Serial.println("</image>");
```

The communication starts by sending the <image> string and the resolution of the image (Camera.width(), Camera.height()) over the serial.

Next, we iterate all bytes stored in the camera buffer and apply the RGB565 to RGB888 conversion with the rgb565_rgb888() function. Every color component is then sent as a string of digits with the newline character (\n).

When we complete the conversion, we send the </image> string to signify the end of the data transmission.

Now, you can compile and upload the sketch on the Arduino Nano.

4. On your computer, create a new Python script and import the following modules:

```
import numpy as np
import serial
from PIL import Image
```

5. Initialize pySerial with the port and baud rate used by the Arduino Nano's microcontroller:

```
port = '/dev/ttyACM0'
baudrate = 115600
ser = serial.Serial()
ser.port     = port
ser.baudrate = baudrate
```

The easiest way to check the serial port name is from the device drop-down menu in the Arduino IDE:

Figure 5.9 – Device drop-down menu in the Arduino Web Editor

In the preceding screenshot, the serial port name is **/dev/ttyACM0**.

Then, open the serial port and discard the content in the input buffer:

```
ser.open()
ser.reset_input_buffer()
```

6. Create a utility function to return a line from the serial port as a string:

```
def serial_readline():
    data = ser.readline
    return data.decode("utf-8").strip()
```

The string transmitted by the Arduino Nano over the serial is encoded in **UTF-8** and terminates with the newline character. Therefore, we decode the UTF-8 encoded bytes and remove the newline character with `.decode("utf-8")` and `.strip()`.

7. Create a 3D NumPy array to store the pixel values transmitted over the serial. Since the Arduino Nano will send the frame resolution, you can initialize the width and height with `1` and resize the NumPy array later when parsing the serial stream:

```
width  = 1
height = 1
num_ch = 3
image = np.empty((height, width, num_ch), dtype=np.uint8)
```

8. Use a `while` loop to read the serial data line by line:

```
while True:
    data_str = serial_readline()
```

Check whether we have the `<image>` metadata:

```
    if str(data_str) == "<image>":
```

If so, parse the frame resolution (width and height) and resize the NumPy array accordingly:

```
        w_str = serial_readline()
        h_str = serial_readline()
        w = int(w_str)
        h = int(h_str)
        if w != width or h != height:
            if w * h != width * height:
                image.resize((h, w, num_ch))
            else:
                image.reshape((h, w, num_ch))
            width  = w
            height = h
```

9. Once you know the frame resolution, parse the pixel values transmitted over the serial, and store them in the NumPy array:

```
for y in range(0, height):
    for x in range(0, width):
        for c in range(0, num_ch):
            data_str = serial_readline()
            image[y][x][c] = int(data_str)
```

To have a more efficient solution, you may consider the following alternative code without nested `for` loops:

```
for i in range(0, width * height * num_ch):
    c = int(i % num_ch)
    x = int((i / num_ch) % width)
    y = int((i / num_ch) / width)
    data_str = serial_readline()
    image[y][x][c] = int(data_str)
```

10. Check if the last line contains the `</image>` metadata. If so, display the image on the screen:

```
data_str = serial_readline()
if str(data_str) == "</image>":
    image_pil = Image.fromarray(image)
    image_pil.show()
```

Keep the Arduino Nano connected to your machine and run the Python script. Now, whenever you press the push-button, the Python program will parse the data transmitted over the serial and, after a few seconds, show an image with eight color bands, as reported at the following link:

`https://github.com/PacktPublishing/TinyML-Cookbook/blob/main/Chapter05/test_qvga_rgb565.png`

If you do not get the image with the test pattern just described, we recommend checking the wiring between the camera and the Arduino Nano.

Converting QQVGA images from YCbCr422 to RGB888

When compiling the previous sketch on Arduino, you may have noticed the **Low memory available, stability may occur** warning in the Arduino IDE output log.

The Arduino IDE returns this warning because the QVGA image with the RGB565 color format needs a buffer of 153.6 KB, which is roughly 60% of the SRAM available in the microcontroller.

In this recipe, we will show how to acquire an image at a lower resolution and use the **YCbCr422** color format to prevent image quality degradation.

The following Arduino sketch contains the code referred to in this recipe:

- `03_camera_capture_qqvga_ycbcr422.ino`:

  `https://github.com/PacktPublishing/TinyML-Cookbook/blob/main/Chapter05/ArduinoSketches/03_camera_capture_qqvga_ycbcr422.ino`

Getting ready

The main ingredients to reduce the image size are behind the resolution and color format.

Images are well known for requiring big chunks of memory, which might be a problem when dealing with microcontrollers.

Lowering the image resolution is a common practice to reduce the image memory size. Standard resolution images adopted on microcontrollers are generally smaller than QVGA (320x240), such as **QQVGA** (160x120) or **QQQVGA** (80x60). Even lower-resolution images exist, but they are not always suitable for computer vision applications.

Color encoding is the other lever to reduce the image memory size. As we saw in the previous recipe, the RGB565 format saves memory by lowering the color components' dynamic range. However, the OV7670 camera module offers an alternative and more efficient color encoding: **YCbCr422**.

Converting YCbCr422 to RGB888

YCbCr422 is digital color encoding that does not express the pixel color in terms of red, green, and blue intensities but rather in terms of *brightness* (*Y*), *blue-difference* (*Cb*), and *red-difference* (*Cr*) chroma components.

The OV7670 camera module can output images in YCbCr422 format, which means that Cb and Cr are shared between two consecutive pixels on the same scanline. Therefore, 4 bytes are used to encode 2 pixels:

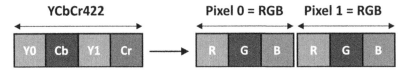

Figure 5.10 – 4 bytes in YCbCr422 format packs 2 RGB888 pixels

Although YCbCr422 still needs 2 bytes per pixel as RGB565, it offers better image quality.

The following table reports the formulas to accomplish the color conversion from YCbCr422 to RGB888 using just integer arithmetic operations:

Color	Formula
Red	$R_i = Y_i + Cr + (Cr \gg 2) + (Cr \gg 3) + (cr \gg 5) \in [0, 255]$
Green	$G_i = Y_i - (Cb \gg 2) - (Cb \gg 4) - (Cb \gg 5) - (Cr \gg 1) - (Cr \gg 3) - (Cr \gg 5) \in [0, 255]$
Blue	$B_i = Y_i + Cb + (Cb \gg 1) + (Cb \gg 2) + (Cb \gg 6) \in [0, 255]$

Figure 5.11 – Table reporting the formulas to convert YCbCr422 to RGB888

The i subscript in $\mathbf{R}_i$, $\mathbf{G}_i$, $\mathbf{B}_i$, and $\mathbf{Y}_i$ represents the pixel index, either 0 (the first pixel) or 1 (the second pixel).

How to do it...

Open the Arduino sketch written in the previous recipe and make the following changes to acquire QQVGA YCbCr422 images from the OV7670 camera module:

1. Resize the camera buffer (`data`) to accommodate a QQVGA image in YCbCr422 color format:

```
byte data[160 * 120 * 2];
```

The QQVGA resolution makes the buffer four times smaller than the one used in the previous recipe.

2. Write a function to get an RGB888 pixel from the Y, Cb, and Cr components:

```
template <typename T>
inline T clamp_0_255(T x) {
  return std::max(std::min(x, (T)255)), (T)(0));
}


void ycbcr422_rgb888(int32_t Y, int32_t Cb,
                     int32_t Cr, uint8_t* out) {
  Cr = Cr - 128;
  Cb = Cb - 128;
  out[0] = clamp_0_255((int)(Y + Cr + (Cr >> 2) +
                        (Cr >> 3) + (Cr >> 5)));
  out[1] = clamp_0_255((int)(Y - ((Cb >> 2) + (Cb >> 4) +
                        (Cb >> 5)) - ((Cr >> 1) +
                        (Cr >> 3) + (Cr >> 4)) +
                        (Cr >> 5)));
  out[2] = clamp_0_255((int)(Y + Cb + (Cb >> 1) +
                        (Cb >> 2) + (Cb >> 6)));
}
```

The function returns two pixels because the Cb and Cr components are shared between two pixels.

The conversion is performed using the formulas provided in the *Getting ready* section.

Attention

Please note that the OV7670 driver returns the Cr component before the Cb one.

---

3. Initialize the OV7670 camera to capture QQVGA frames with YCbCr422 (YUV422) color format in the setup() function:

```
if (!Camera.begin(QQVGA, YUV422, 1)) {
  Serial.println("Failed to initialize camera!");
  while (1);
}
```

Unfortunately, the OV7670 driver interchanges YCbCr422 with YUV422, leading to some confusion. The main difference between YUV and YCbCr is that YUV is for analog TV. Therefore, although we pass `YUV422` to `Camera.begin()`, we actually initialize the device for YCbCr422.

4. In the `loop()` function, remove the statement that iterates over the RGB565 pixels stored in the previous camera buffer. Next, write a routine to read 4 bytes from the `YCbCr422` camera buffer and return two RGB888 pixels:

```
const int step_bytes = Camera.bytesPerPixel() * 2;
for(int i = 0; i < bytes_per_frame; i+=step_bytes) {
  const int32_t Y0 = data[i + 0];
  const int32_t Cr = data[i + 1];
  const int32_t Y1 = data[i + 2];
  const int32_t Cb = data[i + 3];
  ycbcr422_to_rgb888_i(Y0, Cb, Cr, &rgb888[0]);
  Serial.println(rgb888[0]);
  Serial.println(rgb888[1]);
  Serial.println(rgb888[2]);
  ycbcr422_to_rgb888_i(Y1, Cb, Cr, &rgb888[0]);
  Serial.println(rgb888[0]);
  Serial.println(rgb888[1]);
  Serial.println(rgb888[2]);
}
```

Compile and upload the sketch on the Arduino Nano. Execute the Python script and press the push-button on the breadboard. After a few seconds, you should see on the screen, again, an image with eight color bands, as reported at the following link: `https://github.com/PacktPublishing/TinyML-Cookbook/blob/main/Chapter05/test_qqvga_ycbcr422.png`.

The image should be smaller but with more vivid colors than the one captured with the RGB565 format.

Building the dataset for indoor scene classification

Now that we can capture frames from the camera, it is time to create the dataset for classifying indoor environments.

In this recipe, we will construct the dataset by collecting the kitchen and bathroom images with the OV7670 camera.

The following Python script contains the code referred to in this recipe:

- `04_build_dataset.py`:

  `https://github.com/PacktPublishing/TinyML-Cookbook/blob/main/Chapter05/PythonScripts/04_build_dataset.py`

Getting ready

Training a deep neural network from scratch for image classification commonly requires a dataset with 1,000 images per class. As you might guess, this solution is impractical for us since collecting thousands of pictures takes a lot of time.

Therefore, we will consider an alternative ML technique: **transfer learning**.

Transfer learning is a popular method that uses a **pre-trained** model to train a deep neural network with a small dataset. This ML technique will be used in the following recipe and only requires a dataset with just 20 samples per class to get a basic working model.

How to do it...

Before implementing the Python script, remove the test pattern mode (`Camera.testPattern()`) in the Arduino sketch so that you can get live images. After that, compile and upload the sketch on the platform.

The Python script implemented in this recipe will reuse part of the code developed in the earlier *Grabbing camera frames from the serial port with Python* recipe. The following steps will show what changes to make in the Python script to save the captured images as `.png` files and build a dataset for recognizing kitchens and bathrooms:

1. Import the **UUID** Python module:

   ```
   import uuid
   ```

   UUID will be used to produce unique filenames for `.png` files.

2. Add a variable at the beginning of the program for the label's name:

   ```
   label = "test"
   ```

   The label will be the prefix for the filename of the `.png` files.

3. After receiving the image over the serial, crop it into a square shape and display it on the screen:

```
crop_area = (0, 0, height, height)
image_pil = Image.fromarray(image)
image_cropped = image_pil.crop(crop_area)
image_cropped.show()
```

We crop the acquired image from the serial port into a square shape because the pre-trained model will consume an input with a square aspect ratio. We crop the left side of the image by taking an area with dimensions matching the height of the original picture, as shown in the following figure:

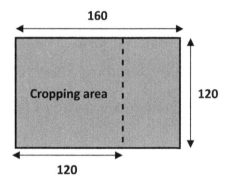

Figure 5.12 – Cropping area

The picture is then displayed on the screen.

4. Ask the user if the image can be saved and read the response with the Python input() function. If the user types y from the keyboard, ask for the label's name and save the image as a .png file:

```
key = input("Save image? [y] for YES: ")
  if key == 'y':
    str_label = "Write label or leave it blank to use
[{}]: ".format(label)
    label_new = input(str_label)
    if label_new != '':
      label = label_new
    unique_id = str(uuid.uuid4())
    filename = label + "_"+ unique_id + ".png"
    image_cropped.save(filename)
```

If the user leaves the label empty, the program will use the last label provided.

The filename for the `.png` file is `<label>_<unique_id>`, where `<label>` is the label chosen by the user and `<unique_id>` is the unique identifier generated by the UUID library.

5. Acquire 20 images of kitchens and the bathrooms with the OV7670 camera. Since we only take a few pictures per class, we recommend you point the camera to specific elements of the rooms.

    Remember to take 20 pictures for the `unknown` class as well, representing cases where we have neither a kitchen nor a bathroom.

Once you have acquired all the images, put them in separate subdirectories, matching the name of the corresponding class, as shown in the following directory structure:

Figure 5.13 – Example of a directory structure

In the end, generate a `.zip` file with the three folders.

Transfer learning with Keras

Transfer learning is an effective technique for getting immediate results with deep learning when dealing with small datasets.

In this recipe, we will apply transfer learning alongside the MobileNet v2 pre-trained model to recognize indoor environments.

The following Colab notebook (the *Transfer learning with Keras* section) contains the code referred to in this recipe:

*   `prepare_model.ipynb`:

    `https://github.com/PacktPublishing/TinyML-Cookbook/blob/main/Chapter05/ColabNotebooks/prepare_model.ipynb`

Getting ready

Transfer learning exploits a pre-trained model to obtain a working ML model in a short time.

When doing image classification with transfer learning, the pre-trained model (**convolution based network**) is coupled with a trainable classifier (**head**), as shown in the following figure:

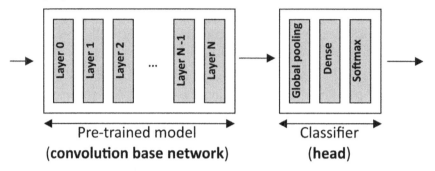

Figure 5.14 – Model architecture with transfer learning

As you can observe from the previous illustration, the pre-trained model is the backbone of feature extraction and feeds the classifier, commonly made of global pooling, dense, and softmax layers.

In our scenario, we will only train the classifier. Hence, the *pre-trained model will be frozen and act as a fixed feature extractor.*

Keras provides different pre-trained models, such as VGG16, ResNet50, InceptionV3, MobileNet, and so on. Therefore, which one should we use?

When considering a pre-trained model for TinyML, model size is the metric to keep in mind to fit the deep learning architecture into memory-constrained devices.

From the list of pre-trained models offered by Keras (`https://keras.io/api/applications/`), **MobileNet v2** is the network with fewer parameters and tailored for being deployed on target devices with reduced computational power.

Exploring the MobileNet network design choices

MobileNet v2 is the second generation of MobileNet networks and, compared to the previous one (**MobileNet v1**), it has half as many operations and higher accuracy.

This model is the perfect place to take a cue from the architectural choices that made MobileNet networks small, fast, and accurate for edge inferencing.

One of the successful design choices that made the first generation of MobileNet networks suitable for edge inferencing was the adoption of **depthwise convolution**.

As we know, traditional convolution layers are well known for being computationally expensive. Furthermore, when dealing with 3x3 or greater kernel sizes, this operator typically needs extra temporary memory to lower the computation to a matrix multiplication routine.

The idea behind MobileNet v1 was to replace standard convolution 2D with **depthwise separable convolution**, as shown in the following diagram:

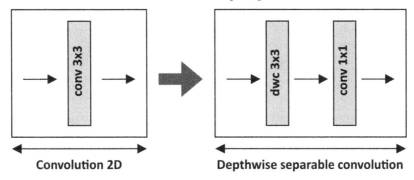

Figure 5.15 – Depthwise separable convolution

As you can observe from the preceding illustration, depthwise separable convolution consists of a depthwise convolution with a 3x3 filter size followed by a convolution layer with a 1x1 kernel size (also known as **pointwise convolution**). This solution brings less trainable parameters, less memory usage, and a lower computational cost.

> **Tip**
> *Chapter 7, Running a Tiny CIFAR-10 Model on a Virtual Platform with the Zephyr OS* will provide more information on the benefits given by depthwise separable convolution.

The computational cost on MobileNet v2 was reduced further by *performing the convolutions on tensors with fewer channels.*

From an ideal computational perspective, all the layers should work on tensors with few channels (**feature maps**) to improve the model latency. Practically, and from an accuracy perspective, it means that our compact tensors can keep the relevant features for the problem we want to solve.

Depthwise separable convolution alone cannot help because a reduction in the number of **feature maps** causes a drop in the model accuracy. Therefore, MobileNet v2 introduced the **bottleneck residual block** to keep the number of channels used in the network smaller:

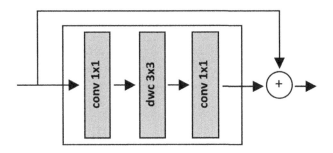

Figure 5.16 – Bottleneck residual block

The bottleneck residual block acts as a *feature compressor*. As illustrated in the preceding diagram, the input is processed by the pointwise convolution, which *expands* (or increases) the number of features maps. Then, the convolution's output feeds the depthwise separable convolution layer to compress the features in fewer output channels.

How to do it...

Create a new Colab notebook. Next, upload the `.zip` file containing the dataset (`dataset.zip`) by using the upload button at the top of the file explorer:

Figure 5.17 – Upload button at the top of the file explorer

Now, follow these steps to apply transfer learning with the MobileNet v2 pre-trained model:

1. Unzip the dataset:

```python
import zipfile
with zipfile.ZipFile("dataset.zip", 'r') as zip_ref:
    zip_ref.extractall(".")
data_dir = "dataset"
```

2. Prepare the training and validation datasets:

```python
train_ds = tf.keras.utils.image_dataset_from_directory(
    data_dir,
    validation_split=0.2,
    subset="training",
    seed=123,
    interpolation="bilinear",
    image_size=(48, 48))

val_ds = tf.keras.utils.image_dataset_from_directory(
    data_dir,
    validation_split=0.2,
    subset="validation",
    seed=123,
    interpolation="bilinear",
    image_size=(48, 48))
```

3. The preceding code resizes the input images to 48x48 with the bilinear interpolation and produces the training and validation datasets with an 80/20 split.

4. Rescale the pixel values from [0, 255] to [-1, 1]:

```python
rescale = tf.keras.layers.Rescaling(1./255, offset= -1)
train_ds = train_ds.map(lambda x, y: (rescale(x), y))
val_ds    = val_ds.map(lambda x, y: (rescale(x), y))
```

The reason for rescaling the pixels values from [0, 255] to [-1, 1] is because the pre-trained model expects this interval data range for the input tensor.

5. Import the MobileNet v2 pre-trained model with the weights trained on the *ImageNet* dataset and `alpha=0.35`. Furthermore, set the input image at the lowest resolution allowed by the pre-trained model (*48, 48, 3*) and exclude the top (fully-connected) layers:

```
base_model = MobileNetV2(input_shape=(48, 48, 3),
                         include_top=False,
                         weights='imagenet',
                         alpha=0.35)
```

Keras offers more than one variant of MobileNet v2. From the list of MobileNet v2 Keras models (`https://github.com/keras-team/keras-applications/blob/master/keras_applications/mobilenet_v2.py`), we choose *mobilenet_v2_0.35_96*, which has the smallest input size (`48,48,3`) and the smallest alpha value (`0.35`).

6. Freeze the weights so that you do not update these values during training:

```
base_model.trainable = False
feat_extr = base_model
```

7. Augment the input data:

```
augmen = tf.keras.Sequential([
tf.keras.layers.experimental.preprocessing.
RandomFlip('horizontal'),  tf.keras.layers.experimental.
preprocessing.RandomRotation(0.2),])
```

```
train_ds = train_ds.map(lambda x, y: (augmen(x), y))
val_ds = val_ds.map(lambda x, y: (augmen(x), y))
```

Since we don't have a large dataset, we recommend artificially applying some random transformations on the images to prevent overfitting.

8. Prepare the classification head with a global pooling followed by a dense layer with a softmax activation:

```
global_avg_layer = tf.keras.layers.
GlobalAveragePooling2D()
```

```
dense_layer = tf.keras.layers.Dense(3,
                              activation='softmax')
```

9. Build the model architecture:

```
inputs = tf.keras.Input(shape=MODEL_INPUT_SIZE)
x = global_avg_layer(feat_extr.layers[-1].output)
x = tf.keras.layers.Dropout(0.2)(x)
outputs = dense_layer(x)
model = tf.keras.Model(inputs=feat_extr.inputs,
                        outputs=outputs)
```

We recommend passing `training=False` to the feature extractor module to not update the batch normalization layers' internal variables (mean and variance) in MobileNet v2.

10. Compile the model with a `0.0005` learning rate:

```
lr = 0.0005
model.compile(
optimizer=tf.keras.optimizers.Adam(learning_rate=lr),
loss=tf.losses.SparseCategoricalCrossentropy(from_
logits=False),
metrics=['accuracy'])
```

The default learning rate used by TensorFlow is 0.001. The reason for reducing the learning rate to 0.0005 is to prevent overfitting.

11. Train the model with 10 epochs:

```
model.fit(
    train_ds,
    validation_data=val_ds,
    epochs=10)
```

The expected accuracy on the validation dataset should be around 90% or more.

12. Save the TensorFlow model as `SavedModel`:

```
model.save("indoor_scene_recognition")
```

The model is now ready to be quantized with the TFLite converter.

Preparing and testing the quantized TFLite model

As we know from *Chapter 3*, *Building a Weather Station with TensorFlow Lite for Microcontrollers*, the model requires quantization to 8 bits to run more efficiently on a microcontroller. However, how do we know if the model can fit into the Arduino Nano? Furthermore, how do we know if the quantized model preserves the accuracy of the floating-point variant?

These questions will be answered in this recipe, where we will show how to evaluate the program memory utilization and the accuracy of the quantized model generated by the TFLite converter. After analyzing the memory usage and accuracy validation, we will convert the TFLite model to a C-byte array.

The following Colab notebook (the *Preparing and testing the quantized TFLite model* section) contains the code referred to in this recipe:

- `prepare_model.ipynb`:

  `https://github.com/PacktPublishing/TinyML-Cookbook/blob/main/Chapter05/ColabNotebooks/prepare_model.ipynb`

Getting ready

The model's memory requirement and accuracy evaluation should always be done to avoid unpleasant surprises when deploying the model on the target device. For example, the C-byte array generated from the TFLite model is typically a constant object stored in the microcontroller program memory. However, the program memory has a limited capacity, and usually, it does not exceed 1 MB.

The memory requirement is not the only problem we may encounter, though. Quantization is an effective technique to reduce the model size and significantly improve latency. However, the adoption of arithmetic with limited precision may change the model's accuracy. For this reason, it is crucial to assess the accuracy of the quantized model to be sure that the application works as expected. Unfortunately, TFLite does not provide a built-in function to evaluate the accuracy of the test dataset. Hence, we will need to run the quantized TFLite model through the Python TFLite interpreter over the test samples to check how many are correctly classified.

How to do it...

Let's start by collecting some test samples with the OV7670 camera module. You can follow the same steps presented in the early *Building the dataset for indoor scene classification* recipe. You just need to take a few pictures (for example, *10*) for each output class and create a `.zip` file (`test_samples.zip`) with the same folder structure we had for the training dataset.

Next, upload the `.zip` file in Colab and follow the following steps to evaluate the accuracy of the quantized model and examine the model size:

1. Unzip the `test_samples.zip` file:

    ```
    with zipfile.ZipFile("test_samples.zip", 'r') as zip_ref:
        zip_ref.extractall(".")
    test_dir = "test_samples"
    ```

2. Resize the test images to 48x48 with bilinear interpolation:

    ```
    test_ds = tf.keras.utils.image_dataset_from_directory(
        test_dir,
        interpolation="bilinear",
        image_size=(48, 48))
    ```

3. Rescale the pixels values from [0, 255] to [-1, 1]:

    ```
    test_ds = test_ds.map(lambda x, y: (rescale(x), y))
    ```

4. Convert the TensorFlow model to TensorFlow Lite format (**FlatBuffers**) with the TensorFlow Lite converter tool. Apply the 8-bit quantization to the entire model except for the output layer:

    ```
    repr_ds = test_ds.unbatch()

    def representative_data_gen():
      for i_value, o_value in repr_ds.batch(1).take(60):
        yield [i_value]


    TF_MODEL = "indoor_scene_recognition"


    converter = tf.lite.TFLiteConverter.from_saved_model(TF_
    MODEL)
    converter.representative_dataset = tf.lite.
    ```

```
RepresentativeDataset(representative_data_gen)
converter.optimizations = [tf.lite.Optimize.DEFAULT]
converter.target_spec.supported_ops = [tf.lite.OpsSet.
TFLITE_BUILTINS_INT8]
converter.inference_input_type = tf.int8


tfl_model = converter.convert()
```

The conversion is done in the same way we did it in *Chapter 3*, *Building a Weather Station with TensorFlow Lite for Microcontrollers*, except for the output data type. In this case, the output is kept in floating-point format to avoid the dequantization of the output result.

5. Get the TFLite model size in bytes:

```
print(len(tfl_model), "bytes")
```

The generated TFLite object (`tfl_model`) is what we deploy on the microcontroller, which contains the model architecture and the weights of the trainable layers. Since the weights are constant, the TFLite model can be stored in the microcontroller program memory, and the length of the `tfl_model` object provides its memory usage. The expected model size is 627880, roughly 63% of the total program memory.

6. Initialize the TFLite interpreter:

```
interpreter = tf.lite.Interpreter(model_content=tfl_
model)
interpreter.allocate_tensors()
```

Unfortunately, TFLite does not offer pre-built functions to evaluate the model accuracy as the TensorFlow counterpart. Therefore, we require running the quantized TensorFlow Lite model in Python to evaluate the accuracy of the test dataset. The Python TFLite interpreter is responsible for loading and executing the TFLite model.

7. Get the input quantization parameters:

```
i_details = interpreter.get_input_details()[0]
o_details = interpreter.get_output_details()[0]
i_quant = i_details["quantization_parameters"]
i_scale      = i_quant['scales'][0]
i_zero_point = i_quant['zero_points'][0]
```

8. Evaluate the accuracy of the quantized TFLite model:

```
test_ds0 = test_ds.unbatch()
num_correct_samples = 0
num_total_samples   = len(list(test_ds0.batch(1)))

for i_value, o_value in test_ds0.batch(1):
    i_value = (i_value / i_scale) + i_zero_point
    i_value = tf.cast(i_value, dtype=tf.int8)
    interpreter.set_tensor(i_details["index"], i_value)
    interpreter.invoke()
    o_pred = interpreter.get_tensor(o_details["index"])[0]
    if np.argmax(o_pred) == o_value:
      num_correct_samples += 1
print("Accuracy:", num_correct_samples/num_total_samples)
```

9. Convert the TFLite model to a C-byte array with xxd:

```
open("model.tflite", "wb").write(tflite_model)
!apt-get update && apt-get -qq install xxd
!xxd -c 60 -i model.tflite > indoor_scene_recognition.h
```

The command generates a C header file containing the TensorFlow Lite model as an unsigned char array. Since the Arduino Web Editor truncates C files exceeding 20,000 lines, we recommend passing the -c 60 option to xxd. This option increases the number of columns per line from 16 (the default) to 60 to have roughly 10,500 lines in the file.

You can now download the indoor_scene_recognition.h file from Colab's left pane.

Reducing RAM usage by fusing crop, resize, rescale, and quantize

In this last recipe, we will deploy the application on the Arduino Nano. However, a few extra operators are needed to recognize indoor environments with our tiny device.

In this recipe, we will learn how to fuse crop, resize, rescale, and quantize operators to reduce RAM usage. These extra operators will be needed to prepare the TFLite model's input.

The following Arduino sketch contains the code referred to in this recipe:

- `07_indoor_scene_recognition.ino`:

  `https://github.com/PacktPublishing/TinyML-Cookbook/blob/main/Chapter05/ArduinoSketches/07_indoor_scene_recognition.ino`

Getting ready

To get ready for this recipe, we need to know what parts of the application affect RAM usage.

RAM usage is impacted by the variables allocated during the program execution, such as the input, output, and intermediate tensors of the ML model. However, the model is not solely responsible for memory utilization. In fact, the image acquired from the OV7670 camera needs to be processed with the following operations to provide the appropriate input to the model:

1. Convert the color format from YCbCr422 to RGB888.

2. Crop the camera frame to match the input shape aspect ratio of the TFLite model.

3. Resize the camera frame to match the expected input shape of the TFLite model.

4. Rescale the pixel values from [0, 255] to [-1, 1].

5. Quantize the floating-point pixel values.

Each of the preceding operations reads values from a buffer and returns the computation result in a new one, as shown in the following figure:

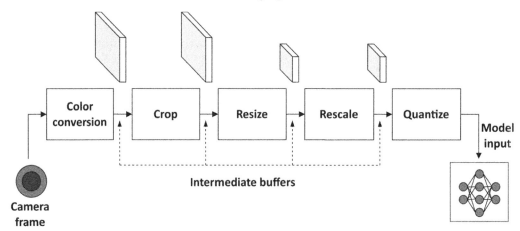

Figure 5.18 – Input preparation pipeline

Therefore, RAM usage is also affected by the camera frame and intermediate buffers passed from one operation to the next.

Our goal is to execute the processing pipeline described previously using as small intermediate buffers as possible.

To achieve this goal, the data propagated throughout the pipeline must represent a portion of the entire input to be processed. By adopting this technique, commonly called **operator fusion**, the camera frame will be the only considerable chunk of memory to reside in RAM in addition to the input, output, and intermediate tensors of the TFLite model.

Before showing how to implement this final recipe, let's see how to implement resizing in more detail.

Resizing with bilinear interpolation

Resizing is an image processing function used to alter the image's resolution (width and height), as shown in the following figure:

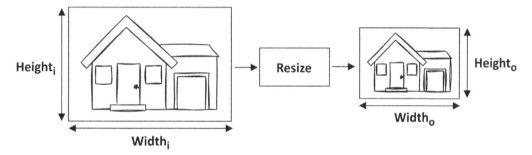

Figure 5.19 – Resize operation

The resulting image is created from the pixels of the input image. Generally, the following formulas are applied to map the spatial coordinates of the output pixels with the corresponding input ones:

$$x_i = x_o \cdot ScaleX \quad ScaleX = \frac{width_i}{width_o}$$

$$y_i = y_o \cdot ScaleY \quad ScaleY = \frac{height_i}{height_o}$$

From the previous two formulas, (x_i, y_i) are the spatial coordinates of the input pixel, (x_o, y_o) are the spatial coordinates of the output pixel, $(width_i, height_i)$ are the dimensions of the input image, and $(width_o, height_o)$ are the dimensions of the output image. As we know, a digital image is a grid of pixels. However, when applying the preceding two formulas, we don't always get an integer spatial coordinate, which means that the actual input sample doesn't always exist. This is one of the reasons why image quality degrades *whenever we change the resolution of an image*. However, some interpolation techniques exist to alleviate the problem, such as **nearest-neighbor**, **bilinear**, or **bicubic** interpolation.

Bilinear interpolation is the technique adopted in this recipe to improve the image quality of the resized image. As shown in the following diagram, this method takes the four closest pixels to the input sampling point in a 2x2 grid:

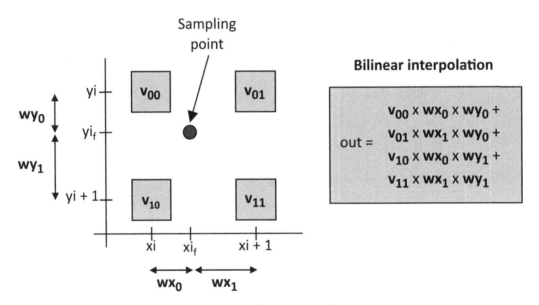

Figure 5.20 – Bilinear interpolation

The interpolation function calculates the output pixel with a weighted average of the four nearest pixels to the input sampling point, as described by the formula in the previous figure.

In our case, we have shown an example of bilinear interpolation applied to a single color component image. However, this method works regardless of the number of color components since we can interpolate the values independently.

How to do it...

Unplug the USB cable from the Arduino Nano and remove the push-button from the breadboard. After that, open the Arduino IDE and copy the sketch developed in the *Converting QQVGA images from YCbCr422 to RGB888* recipe in a new project. Next, import the `indoor_scene_recognition.h` header file into the Arduino IDE.

In the sketch, remove the code in the `loop()` function and all the references to the push-button usages.

The following are the necessary steps to recognize indoor environments with the Arduino Nano:

1. Include the `indoor_scene_recognition.h` header file:

    ```
    #include "indoor_scene_recognition.h"
    ```

2. Include the header files for using the TFLu runtime:

    ```
    #include <TensorFlowLite.h>
    #include <tensorflow/lite/micro/all_ops_resolver.h>
    #include <tensorflow/lite/micro/micro_error_reporter.h>
    #include <tensorflow/lite/micro/micro_interpreter.h>
    #include <tensorflow/lite/schema/schema_generated.h>
    #include <tensorflow/lite/version.h>
    ```

    The header files are the same ones described in *Chapter 3, Building a Weather Station with TensorFlow Lite for Microcontrollers*.

3. Declare the variables related to TFLu initialization/runtime as global:

    ```
    const tflite::Model* tflu_model            = nullptr;
    tflite::MicroInterpreter* tflu_interpreter = nullptr;
    TfLiteTensor* tflu_i_tensor                = nullptr;
    TfLiteTensor* tflu_o_tensor                = nullptr;
    tflite::MicroErrorReporter tflu_error;
    constexpr int tensor_arena_size = 144000;
    uint8_t *tensor_arena = nullptr;
    float    tflu_scale     = 0.0f;
    int32_t tflu_zeropoint = 0;
    ```

4. The variables reported in the preceding code are the same ones used in *Chapter 3, Building a Weather Station with TensorFlow Lite for Microcontrollers*, with the only exception being the output quantization parameters since they are not required in this case. The tensor arena size is set to 144000 to accommodate the input, output, and intermediate tensors of the TFLite model.

5. Declare and initialize the resolutions of the cropped camera frame and input shape as global variables:

```
int height_i = 120; int width_i = hi;
int height_o = 48; int width_o = 48;
```

Since we crop the camera frame before resizing it, we can make cropping simpler by taking a square area matching the height of the camera frame on the left side.

6. Declare and initialize the resolution scaling factors to resize the camera frame as global variables:

```
float scale_x = (float)width_i / (float)width_o;
float scale_y = scale_x;
```

7. Write the function to calculate the bilinear interpolation for a single color component pixel:

```
uint8_t bilinear_inter(uint8_t v00, uint8_t v01,
                       uint8_t v10, uint8_t v11,
                       float xi_f, float yi_f,
                       int xi, int yi) {
    const float wx1  = (xi_f - xi);
    const float wx0  = (1.f - wx1);
    const float wy1  = (yi_f - yi);
    const float wy0  = (1.f - wy1);
    return clamp_0_255((v00 * wx0 * wy0) +
                       (v01 * wx1 * wy0) +
                       (v10 * wx0 * wy1) +
                       (v11 * wx1 * wy1));
}
```

The preceding function calculates the distance-based weights and applies the bilinear interpolation formula described in the *Getting ready* section of this recipe.

8. Write the function to rescale the pixel values from `[0,255]` to `[-1,1]`:

```
float rescaling(float x, float scale, float offset) {
    return (x * scale) - offset;
}
```

Next, write the function to quantize the input image:

```
int8_t quantize(float x, float scale, float zero_point) {
    return (x / scale) + zero_point;
}
```

> **Tip**
>
> Since rescaling and quantizing are executed one after the other, you may think of fusing them in a single function to make the implementation more efficient in terms of arithmetic instructions executed.

9. In the `setup()` function, dynamically allocate the memory for the tensor arena:

```
tensor_arena = (uint8_t *)malloc(tensor_arena_size);
```

We allocate the tensor arena with the `malloc()` function to place the memory in the **heap**. As we know, the heap is the area of RAM related to the dynamic memory and can only be released explicitly by the user with the `free()` function. The heap is opposed to the **stack** memory, where the data **lifetime** is limited to the **scope**. The stack and heap memory sizes are defined in the **startup** code, executed by the microcontroller when the system resets. Since the stack is typically much smaller than the heap, it is preferable to allocate the TFLu working space in the heap because the tensor arena takes a significant portion of RAM (144 KB).

10. Load the `indoor_scene_recognition` model, initialize the TFLu interpreter, and allocate the tensors: shankar

```
tflu_model = tflite::GetModel(
    indoor_scene_recognition);
tflite::AllOpsResolver tflu_ops_resolver;

tflu_interpreter = new tflite::MicroInterpreter(tflu_
model, tflu_ops_resolver, tensor_arena, tensor_arena_
size, &tflu_error);

    tflu_interpreter->AllocateTensors();
```

Next, get the pointers to the input and output tensors:

```
tflu_i_tensor = tflu_interpreter->input(0);
tflu_o_tensor = tflu_interpreter->output(0);
```

Finally, get the input quantization parameters:

```
const auto* i_quantization =
  reinterpret_cast<TfLiteAffineQuantization*>(
  tflu_i_tensor->quantization.params);
tflu_scale     = i_quantization->scale->data[0];
tflu_zeropoint = i_quantization->zero_point->data[0];
}
```

11. Iterate over the spatial coordinates of the MobileNet v2 input shape in the `loop()` function. Then, calculate the corresponding sampling point position for each output coordinate. Next, round down to the nearest integer value the sampling point coordinate:

```
for (int yo = 0; yo < height_o; yo++) {
  float yi_f = (yo * scale_y);
  int yi = (int)std::floor(yi_f);
  for(int xo = 0; xo < width_o; xo++) {
    float xi_f = (xo * scale_x);
    int xi = (int)std::floor(xi_f);
```

As you can observe from the code, we iterate over the spatial coordinates of the MobileNet v2 input shape (48x48). For each `xo` and `yo`, we calculate the sampling position (`xi_f` and `yi_f`) in the camera frame required for the resize operation. Since we apply bilinear interpolation to resize the image, we round down to the nearest integer `xi_f` and `yi_f` to get the spatial coordinates of the top-left pixel in the 2x2 sampling grid.

Once you have the input coordinates, calculate the camera buffer offsets to read the four YCbCr422 pixels needed for the bilinear interpolation:

```
int x0 = xi;
int y0 = yi;
int x1 = std::min(xi + 1, width_i - 1);
int y1 = std::min(yi + 1, height_i - 1);
int stride_in_y = Camera.width() * bytes_per_pixel;
int ix_y00 = x0 * sizeof(int16_t) + y0 * stride_in_y;
```

```
int ix_y01 = x1 * sizeof(int16_t) + y0 * stride_in_y;
int ix_y10 = x0 * sizeof(int16_t) + y1 * stride_in_y;
int ix_y11 = x1 * sizeof(int16_t) + y1 * stride_in_y;
```

12. Read the Y component for each of the four pixels:

```
int Y00 = data[ix_y00];
int Y01 = data[ix_y01];
int Y10 = data[ix_y10];
int Y11 = data[ix_y11];
```

Next, read the red-difference components (Cr):

```
int offset_cr00 = xi % 2 == 0? 1 : -1;
int offset_cr01 = (xi + 1) % 2 == 0? 1 : -1;
int Cr00 = data[ix_y00 + offset_cr00];
int Cr01 = data[ix_y01 + offset_cr01];
int Cr10 = data[ix_y10 + offset_cr00];
int Cr11 = data[ix_y11 + offset_cr01];
```

After, read the blue-difference components (Cb):

```
int offset_cb00 = offset_cr00 + 2;
int offset_cb01 = offset_cr01 + 2;
int Cb00 = data[ix_y00 + offset_cb00];
int Cb01 = data[ix_y01 + offset_cb01];
int Cb10 = data[ix_y10 + offset_cb00];
int Cb11 = data[ix_y11 + offset_cb01];
```

13. Convert the YCbCr422 pixels to RGB888:

```
uint8_t rgb00[3], rgb01[3], rgb10[3], rgb11[3];
ycbcr422_rgb888(Y00, Cb00, Cr00, rgb00);
ycbcr422_rgb888(Y01, Cb01, Cr01, rgb01);
ycbcr422_rgb888(Y10, Cb10, Cr10, rgb10);
ycbcr422_rgb888(Y11, Cb11, Cr11, rgb11);
```

14. Iterate over the channels of the RGB pixels:

```
uint8_t c_i; float c_f; int8_t c_q;
for(int i = 0; i < 3; i++) {
```

For each color component, apply bilinear interpolation:

```
c_i = bilinear(rgb00[i], rgb01[i],
               rgb10[i], rgb11[i],
               xi_f, yi_f, xi, yi);
```

Next, rescale and quantize the color component:

```
c_f = rescale((float)c, 1.f/255.f, -1.f);
c_q = quantize(c_f, tflu_scale, tflu_zeropoint);
```

In the end, store the quantized color component in the input tensor of the TFLite model and close the `for` loop that iterates over the spatial coordinates of the MobileNet v2 input shape:

```
      tflu_i_tensor->data.int8[idx++] = c_q;
    }
  }
}
```

15. Run the model inference and return the classification result over the serial:

```
TfLiteStatus invoke_status = tflu_interpreter->Invoke();
  size_t ix_max = 0;
  float  pb_max = 0;
  for (size_t ix = 0; ix < 3; ix++) {
    if(tflu_o_tensor->data.f[ix] > pb_max) {
      ix_max = ix;
      pb_max = tflu_o_tensor->data.f[ix];
    }
  }
  const char *label[] = {"bathroom", "kitchen",
"unknown"};
  Serial.println(label[ix_max]);
```

Compile and upload the sketch on the Arduino Nano. Your application should now recognize your rooms and report the classification result in the serial monitor!

6
Building a Gesture-Based Interface for YouTube Playback

Gesture recognition is a technology that interprets human gestures to allow people to interact with their devices without touching buttons or displays. This technology is now in various consumer electronics (for example, smartphones and game consoles) and involves two principal ingredients: a sensor and a software algorithm.

In this chapter, we will show you how to use **accelerometer** measurements in conjunction with **machine learning** (**ML**) to recognize three hand gestures with the Raspberry Pi Pico. These recognized gestures will then be used to play/pause, mute/unmute, and change YouTube videos on our PC.

We will start by collecting the accelerometer data to build the gesture recognition dataset. In this part, we will learn how to interface with the **I2C protocol** and use the **Edge Impulse data forwarder** tool. Next, we will focus on the Impulse design, where we will build a spectral-features-based fully connected neural network for gesture recognition. Finally, we will deploy the model on a Raspberry Pi Pico and implement a Python program with **PyAutoGUI** to build a touchless interface for YouTube video playback.

This chapter aims to help you develop an end-to-end gesture recognition application with Edge Impulse and the Raspberry Pi Pico so that you can learn how to use I2C peripheral, get acquainted with inertial sensors, write a multithreading program in **Arm Mbed OS**, and discover how to filter out redundant classification results during model inference.

In this chapter, we're going to cover the following recipes:

- Communicating with the MPU-6050 IMU through I2C
- Acquiring accelerometer data
- Building the dataset with the Edge Impulse data forwarder tool
- Designing and training the ML model
- Live classifications with the Edge Impulse data forwarder tool
- Gesture recognition on the Raspberry Pi Pico with Arm Mbed OS
- Building a touchless interface with PyAutoGUI

Technical requirements

To complete all the practical recipes in this chapter, you will need the following:

- A Raspberry Pi Pico
- A micro-USB cable
- 1 x half-size solderless breadboard
- 1 x MPU-6050 IMU
- 4 x jumper wires
- A laptop/PC with either Ubuntu 18.04+ or Windows 10 on x86-64

The source code for this chapter and additional material are available in Chapter06 (https://github.com/PacktPublishing/TinyML-Cookbook/tree/main/ Chapter06).

Communicating with the MPU-6050 IMU through I2C

The dataset is the core part of any ML project because it has implications regarding the model's performance. However, recording sensor data is often a challenging task in TinyML since it requires low-level interfacing with the hardware.

In this recipe, we will use the **MPU-6050 Inertial Measurement Unit** (**IMU**) to teach the fundamentals behind a common communication protocol for sensors: the **Inter-Integrated Circuit** (**I2C**). By the end of this recipe, we will have an Arduino sketch to read out the MPU-6050 address.

The following Arduino sketch contains the code that will be referred to in this recipe

- `01_i2c_imu_addr.ino`:

  `https://github.com/PacktPublishing/TinyML-Cookbook/blob/main/Chapter06/ArduinoSketches/01_i2c_imu_addr.ino`.

Getting ready

For this recipe, we need to know what an IMU sensor is and how to retrieve its measurements with the I2C communication protocol.

The IMU sensor is an electronic device that's capable of measuring accelerations, angular rates, and, in some cases, body orientations through a combination of integrated sensors. This device is at the heart of many technologies in various industries, including automotive, aerospace, and consumer electronics, to give position and orientation estimates. For example, IMU allows the screen of a smartphone to **auto-rotate** and enables **augmented reality/virtual reality** (**AR/VR**) use cases.

The following subsection provides more details about the MPU-6050 IMU.

Introducing the MPU-6050 IMU

MPU-6050 (`https://invensense.tdk.com/products/motion-tracking/6-axis/mpu-6050/`) is an IMU that combines a three-axis accelerometer and three-axis gyroscope sensors to measure accelerations and the angular rate of the body. This device has been on the market for several years, and due to its low-cost and high performance, it is still a popular choice for DIY electronic projects based on motion sensors.

The MPU-6050 IMU can be found via various distributors, such as *Adafruit, Amazon, Pimoroni,* and *PiHut,* and it is available in different form factors. In this recipe, we have considered the compact breakout board that's offered by *Adafruit* (`https://learn.adafruit.com/mpu6050-6-dof-accelerometer-and-gyro/overview`), which can be powered by 3.3V and does not require additional electronic components.

> **Important Note**
>
> Unfortunately, the IMU module comes with unsoldered header strips. Therefore, if you are not familiar with soldering, we recommend reading the following tutorial:
>
> `https://learn.adafruit.com/adafruit-agc-electret-microphone-amplifier-max9814/assembly`

The MPU-6050 IMU can communicate through the **I2C** serial communication protocol with the microcontroller. The following subsection describes some of the main features worth mentioning of I2C.

Communicating with I2C

I2C is a communication protocol that's based on two wires, commonly called **SCL (clock signal)** and **SDA (data signal)**.

The protocol has been structured to allow communication between a **primary device** (for example, the microcontroller) and numerous **secondary devices** (for example, the sensors). Each secondary device is identified with a permanent 7-bit address.

> **Important Note**
>
> The I2C protocol refers to the terms master and slave rather than primary and secondary devices. In this book, we have decided to rename those terms so that the language is more inclusive and to remove unnecessary references to slavery.

The following diagram shows how the primary and secondary devices are connected:

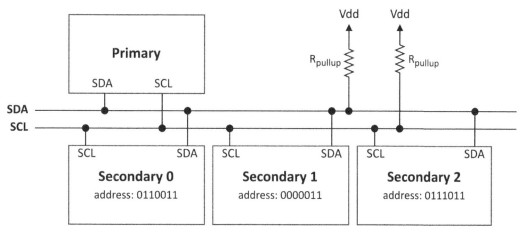

Figure 6.1 – I2C communication

As we can see, there are only two signals (SCL and SDA), regardless of the number of secondary devices. SCL is only produced by the primary device and is used by all I2C devices to sample the bits that are transmitted over the data signal. Both the primary and secondary devices can transmit data over the SDA bus.

The pull-up resistors (**Rpullup**) are required because the I2C device can only drive the signal to *LOW* (logic level *0*). In our case, the pull-up resistors are not needed because they are integrated into the MPU-6050 breakout board.

From a communication protocol perspective, *the primary device always starts the communication* by transmitting as follows:

1. 1 bit at *LOW* (logical level *0*) on SDA (start condition).

2. The 7-bit address of the target secondary device.

3. 1 bit for the read or write intention (**R/W flag**). Logic level *0* indicates that the primary device will send the data over SDA (**write mode**). Otherwise, logical level *1* means that the primary device will read the data that's transmitted by the secondary device over SDA (**read mode**).

The following diagram shows an example of a bit command sequence in the scenario where the primary device in *Figure 6.1* starts communicating with secondary 0:

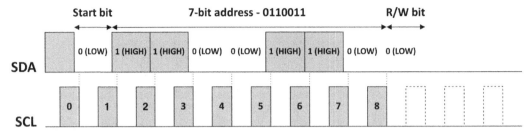

Figure 6.2 – Bit command sequence transmitted by the primary device

The secondary device that matches the 7-bit address will then respond with 1 bit at logical level *0* (**ACK**) over the SDA bus.

If the secondary device responds with the ACK, the primary device can either transmit or read the data in chunks of 8 bits accordingly with the R/W flag set.

In our context, *the microcontroller is the primary device*, and it uses the R/W flag to do the following:

- **Read data from the sensor**: The microcontroller requests what it wants to read (**write mode**) before the MPU-6050 IMU transmits the data (**read mode**).

- **Program an internal feature of the IMU**: The microcontroller only uses **write mode** to set an operating mode of MPU-6050 (for example, the sampling frequency of the sensors).

At this point, you may have a question in mind: *what do we read and write with the primary device?*

The primary device reads and writes specific registers on the secondary device. Therefore, the secondary device works like a form of memory where each register has a unique 8-bit memory address.

> **Tip**
>
> The register map for MPU-6050 is available at the following link:
>
> ```
> https://invensense.tdk.com/wp-content/
> uploads/2015/02/MPU-6000-Register-Map1.pdf
> ```

How to do it...

Let's start this recipe by taking a breadboard with 30 rows and 10 columns and mounting the Raspberry Pi Pico vertically among the left and right terminal strips. We should place the microcontroller platform in the same way as we did in *Chapter 2, Prototyping with Microcontrollers*.

Next, place the accelerometer sensor module at the bottom of the breadboard. Ensure that the breadboard's notch is in the middle of the two headers, as shown in the following diagram:

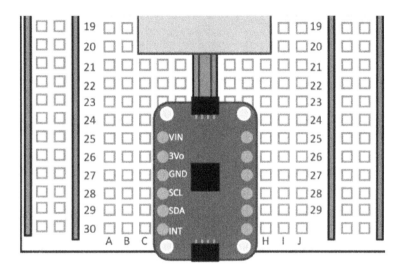

Figure 6.3 – MPU-6050 mounted at the bottom of the breadboard

As you can see, the I2C pins are located on the left terminal strips of the MPU-6050 module.

The following steps will show you how to connect the accelerometer module with the Raspberry Pi Pico and write a basic sketch to read the ID (address) of the MPU-6050 device:

1. Take four jumper wires and connect the MPU-6050 IMU to the Raspberry Pi Pico, as reported in the following table:

MPU-6050	VIN	GND	SCL	SDA
Raspberry Pi Pico	3V3	GND	GP7 (SCL1)	GP6 (SDA1)

Figure 6.4 – Connections between the MPU-6050 IMU and the Raspberry Pi Pico

The following diagram should help you visualize how to do the wiring:

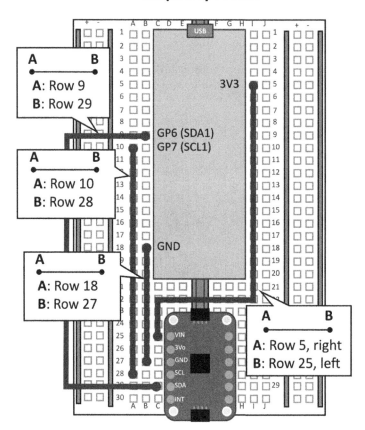

Figure 6.5 – Connections between the MPU-6050 IMU and Raspberry Pi Pico

As we mentioned in the *Getting ready* section of this recipe, we do not need pull-up resistors on **SDA** and **SCL** because they have already been integrated into the IMU's breakout board.

2. Create a new sketch in the Arduino IDE. Declare and initialize the `mbed::I2C` object with the **SDA** and **SCL** pins:

```
#define I2C_SDA p6
#define I2C_SCL p7
I2C i2c(I2C_SDA, I2C_SCL);
```

The initialization of the I2C peripheral only requires the pins that are dedicated to the **SDA** (p6) and **SCL** (p7) buses.

3. Use a C define to keep the 7-bit address of the MPU-6050 IMU (0x68):

```
#define MPU6050_ADDR_7BIT 0x68
```

Next, use a C define to keep the 8-bit address required that's for mbed::I2C. The 8-bit address can easily be obtained by left-shifting the 7-bit address by one bit:

```
#define MPU6050_ADDR_8BIT (0x68 << 1) //0xD1
```

4. Implement a utility function to read the data from an MPU-6050 register:

```
void read_reg(int addr_i2c, int addr_reg, char *buf, int
length) {
    char data = addr_reg;
    i2c.write(addr_i2c, &data, 1);
    i2c.read(addr_i2c, buf, length);
    return;
}
```

As per the I2C protocol, we need to transmit the address of the MPU-6050 IMU and then send the address of the register to read. So, we must use the write() method of the mbed::I2C class, which needs three input arguments, as follows:

- The 8-bit address of the secondary device (addr_i2c)
- A char array containing the registered address (char data = addr_reg)
- The number of bytes to transmit (1 since we're only sending the registered address)

After sending the request to read the data from the register, we can get the data that's been transmitted by MPU-6050 with the read() method of the mbed::I2C class, which needs the following input arguments:

- The 8-bit address of the secondary device (addr_i2c)
- A char array to store the received data (buf)
- The size of the array (length)

The function will return once the read is complete.

5. In the setup() function, initialize the I2C frequency at the maximum speed that's supported by MPU-6050 (400 KHz):

```
void setup() {
    i2c.frequency(400000);
```

6. In the setup() function, use read_reg() to read the WHO_AM_I register (0x75) of the MPU-6050 IMU. Transmit the MPU-6050 found message over the serial if the WHO_AM_I register contains the 7-bit device address (0x68):

```
#define MPU6050_WHO_AM_I 0x75
Serial.begin(115600);
while(!Serial);
char id;
read_reg(MPU6050_ADDR_8BIT, MPU6050_WHO_AM_I, &id, 1);
if(id == MPU6050_ADDR_7BIT) {
    Serial.println("MPU-6050 found");
} else {
    Serial.println("MPU-6050 not found");
    while(1);
}
}
```

Compile and upload the sketch on the Raspberry Pi Pico. Now, you can open the serial **Monitor** from the **Editor** menu. If the Raspberry Pi Pico can communicate with the MPU-6050 device, it will transmit the **MPU-6050 found** string over serial.

Acquiring accelerometer data

The accelerometer is one of the most common sensors that's incorporated into the IMU.

In this recipe, we will develop an application to read the accelerometer measurements from the MPU-6050 IMU with a frequency of 50 Hz. The measurements will then be transmitted over the serial so that they can be acquired with the Edge Impulse data forwarder tool in the following recipe.

The following Arduino sketch contains the code that's referred to in this recipe

- `02_i2c_imu_read_acc.ino0`:

  `https://github.com/PacktPublishing/TinyML-Cookbook/blob/main/Chapter06/ArduinoSketches/02_i2c_imu_read_acc.ino`.

Getting ready

The accelerometer is a sensor that measures accelerations on one, two, or three spatial axes, denoted as X, Y, and Z.

In this and the following recipes, we will use the **three-axis accelerometer** that's integrated into the MPU-6050 IMU to measure the accelerations of three orthogonal directions.

However, how does the accelerometer work, and how can we take the measurements from the sensor?

Let's start by explaining the basic underlying working principle of this sensor. Consider the following system, which has a mass attached to a spring:

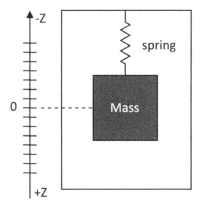

Figure 6.6 – Mass-spring system

The preceding diagram models the physical principle of an accelerometer working on a single spatial dimension (that is, a **one-axis accelerometer**).

What happens if we place the accelerometer on the table?

In this case, we will see the mass go down because of the constant gravitational force. Therefore, the lower spring on the *Z-axis* would have a displacement from the rest position, as shown in the following diagram:

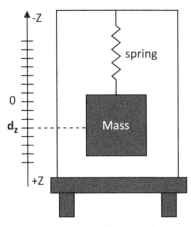

Figure 6.7 – The mass-spring system under the influence of gravitational force

From physics class, we know that **Hooke's law** gives the **spring force (restoring force)**:

$$F = k \cdot d_z$$

Here, F is the force, k is the elastic constant, and d_z is the displacement.

From **Newton's second law**, we also know that the force that's applied on the mass is as follows:

$$F = m \cdot a$$

Here, F is the force, m is the mass, and a is the acceleration.

Under the $F = m \cdot a = k \cdot d_z$ constraint, we can infer that the spring displacement, d_z, is proportional to the acceleration.

Hence, when a one-axis accelerometer is placed on the table, it returns ~9.81 m/s², which is the object's acceleration when it's falling under the influence of gravity. The 9.81 m/s² acceleration is commonly denoted with the g symbol (9.81 m/s² = 1 g).

As we can imagine, the spring goes up and down whenever we move the accelerometer (even slightly). Therefore, the spring displacement is the physical quantity that's acquired by the sensor to measure acceleration.

An accelerometer that's working on two or three spatial dimensions can still be modeled with the mass-spring system. For example, a three-axis accelerometer can be modeled with three mass-spring systems so that each one returns the acceleration for a different axis.

Of course, we made some simplifications while explaining the device's functionality. Still, the core mechanism that's based on the mass-spring system is designed in silicon through the **micro-electromechanical systems (MEMS)** process technology.

Most accelerometers have a programmable measurement range (or scale) that can vary from ±1 g (±9.81 m/s²) to ±250 g (±2,452.5 m/s²). This range is also proportional to the **sensitivity**, which is commonly expressed as the **least-significant bit over g (LSB/g)** and defined as *the minimum acceleration to cause a change in the numerical representation.* Therefore, the higher the sensitivity, the smaller the minimum detectable acceleration.

In the MPU-6050 IMU, we can program the measurement range through the `ACCEL_CONFIG` register (`0x1C`). The following table reports the corresponding sensitivity for each one:

Measurement range (g)	±2g	±4g	±8g	±16g
Sensitivity (LSB/g)	16384	8192	4096	2048
ACCEL_CONFIG register value	0x00	0x01	0x02	0x03

Figure 6.8 – Measurement range versus sensitivity on MPU-6050

As we can see, the smaller the measurement range, the higher the sensitivity. A **±2 g** range is typically enough for acquiring accelerations due to hand movements.

The measurements that are returned by the MPU-6050 IMU are in 16-bit integer format and stored in two 8-bit registers. These two registers' names are marked with the _H and _L suffixes to identify the high and low bytes of the 16-bit variable. The following diagram shows the names and addresses of each register:

Address	Register
3B	ACCEL_XOUT_H
3C	ACCEL_XOUT_L
3D	ACCEL_YOUT_H
3E	ACCEL_YOUT_L
3F	ACCEL_ZOUT_H
40	ACCEL_ZOUT_L

Figure 6.9 – Registers for the accelerometer measurements in the MPU-6050 IMU

As you can see, the registers are placed at consecutive memory addresses, starting with `ACCEL_XOUT_H` at `0x3B`. To read all the accelerometer measurements without sending the address of each register, we can simply access `ACCEL_XOUT_H` and read 6 bytes.

How to do it...

Let's keep working on the sketch from the previous recipe. The following steps will show you how to extend the program to read accelerometer data from the MPU-6050 IMU and transmit the measurements over the serial:

1. Implement a utility function to write one byte into an MPU-6050 register:

    ```
    void write_reg(int addr_i2c, int addr_reg, char v) {
        char data[2] = {addr_reg, v};
        i2c.write(addr_i2c, data, 2);
        return;
    }
    ```

    As shown in the preceding code, we use the `write()` method of the `mbed::I2C` class to transmit the following details:

    I.   The MPU-6050 address

    II.   The register address to access

    III. The byte to store into the register

    The `write_reg()` function will be required to initialize the MPU-6050 device.

2. Implement a utility function to read the accelerometer data from MPU-6050. To do so, create a function called `read_accelerometer()` with three input floating-point arrays:

    ```
    void read_accelerometer(float *x, float *y, float *z) {
    ```

    The x, y, and z arrays will contain the sampled accelerations for the three orthogonal spatial directions.

3. In the `read_accelerometer()` function, read the accelerometer measurements from the MPU-6050 IMU:

    ```
    char data[6];
    #define MPU6050_ACCEL_XOUT_H 0x3B
    read_reg(MPU6050_ADDR_8BIT, MPU6050_ACCEL_XOUT_H, data, 6);
    ```

    Next, combine the low and high byte of each measurement to get the 16-bit data format representation:

    ```
    int16_t ax_i16 = (int16_t)(data[0] << 8 | data[1]);
    int16_t ay_i16 = (int16_t)(data[2] << 8 | data[3]);
    int16_t az_i16 = (int16_t)(data[4] << 8 | data[5]);
    ```

Once you have these 16-bit values, divide the numbers by the sensitivity that's been assigned to the selected measurement range and multiply it by g (9.81 m/s^2). Then, store the accelerations in the x, y, and z arrays:

```
const float sensitivity = 16384.f;
const float k = (1.f / sensitivity) * 9.81f;
*x = (float)ax_i16 * k;
*y = (float)ay_i16 * k;
*z = (float)az_i16 * k;
return;
}
```

The preceding code converts the raw data into an m/s^2 numerical value. The sensitivity is 16384 because the MPU-6050 IMU will operate in the **±2 g** range.

4. In the setup() function, ensure that the MPU-6050 IMU is not in sleep mode:

```
#define MPU6050_PWR_MGMT_1 0x6B
#define MPU6050_ACCEL_CONFIG 0x1C
if (id == MPU6050_ADDR_7BIT) {
  Serial.println("MPU6050 found");
  write_reg(MPU6050_ADDR_8BIT, MPU6050_PWR_MGMT_1, 0);
```

When the IMU is in sleep mode, the sensor does not return any measurements. To ensure the MPU-6050 IMU is not in this operating mode, we need to clear the sixth bit (*bit* 6) of the PWR_MGMT_1 register. This can easily be done by clearing the PWR_MGMT_1 register directly.

5. In the setup() function, set the accelerometer measurement range of the MPU-6050 IMU to **±2 g**:

```
  write_reg(MPU6050_ADDR_8BIT, MPU6050_ACCEL_CONFIG, 0);
}
```

6. In the loop() function, sample the accelerometer measurements with a frequency of 50 Hz (50 three-axis accelerometer samples per second) and transmit them over the serial. Send the data with one line per accelerometer reading and the three-axis measurements (ax, ay, and az) comma-separated:

```
#define FREQUENCY_HZ   50
#define INTERVAL_MS    (1000 / (FREQUENCY_HZ + 1))
#define INTERVAL_US    INTERVAL_MS * 1000
void loop() {
```

```
mbed::Timer timer;
timer.start();
float ax, ay, az;
read_accelerometer(&ax, &ay, &az);
Serial.print(ax);
Serial.print(",");
Serial.print(ay);
Serial.print(",");
Serial.println(az);
timer.stop();
using std::chrono::duration_cast;
using std::chrono::microseconds;
auto t0 = timer.elapsed_time();
auto t_diff = duration_cast<microseconds>(t0);
uint64_t t_wait_us = INTERVAL_US - t_diff.count();
int32_t t_wait_ms = (t_wait_us / 1000);
int32_t t_wait_leftover_us = (t_wait_us % 1000);
delay(t_wait_ms);
delayMicroseconds(t_wait_leftover_us);
}
```

In the preceding code, we did the following:

I.   Started the mbed::Timer before reading the accelerometer measurements to take the time required to acquire the samples.

II.   Read the accelerations with the read_accelerometer() function.

III. Stopped mbed::Timer and retrieved the elapsed time in microseconds (μs).

IV.   Calculated how much time the program needs to wait before the next accelerometer reading. This step will guarantee the 50 Hz sampling rate.

V.   Paused the program.

The program is paused with the delay() function, followed by delayMicroseconds(), due to the following reasons:

* delay() alone would be inaccurate since this timer needs the input argument in ms.

* delayMicroseconds() works up to *16 383 μs*, which is insufficient for a sampling frequency of 50 Hz (*2,000 μs*).

So, we find out how much time to wait in milliseconds by dividing `t_wait_us` by 1,000. Then, we calculate the remaining time to wait in microseconds by calculating the remainder of the `t_wait_us / 1000` division (`t_wait_us % 1000`).

The format that's used to send the accelerometer data over the serial (one line per reading with the three-axis measurements comma-separated) will be necessary to accomplish the task presented in the following recipe.

Compile and upload the sketch to the Raspberry Pi Pico. Next, open the serial monitor and check whether the microcontroller transmits the accelerometer measurements. If so, lay the breadboard flat on the table. The expected acceleration for the Z-axis (third number of each row) should be roughly equal to the acceleration due to gravity (9.81 m/s^2), while the accelerations for the other axes should be approximately close to zero, as shown in the following diagram:

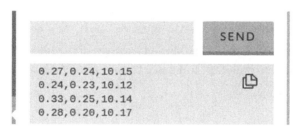

Figure 6.10 – Accelerations displayed in the Arduino serial monitor

As you can see, the accelerations could be affected by offset and noise. However, we don't need to worry about the accuracy of the measurements because the deep learning model will be capable of recognizing our gestures.

Building the dataset with the Edge Impulse data forwarder tool

Any ML algorithm needs a dataset, and for us, this means getting data samples from the accelerometer.

Recording accelerometer data is not as difficult as it may seem at first glance. This task can easily be carried out with Edge Impulse.

In this recipe, we will use the Edge Impulse data forwarder tool to take the accelerometer measurements when we make the following three movements with the breadboard:

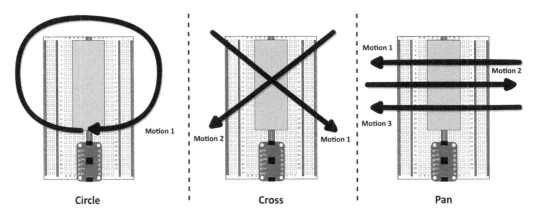

Figure 6.11 – Gestures to recognize – circle, cross, and pan

As shown in the preceding diagram, we should ensure that the breadboard is vertical, have our Raspberry Pi Pico in front of us, and make the movements that are shown by the arrows.

Getting ready

An adequate dataset for gesture recognition requires at least 50 samples for each output class. The three gestures that we've considered for this project are as follows:

- *Circle*: For moving the board clockwise in a circular motion.
- *Cross*: For moving the board from the top left to the bottom right and then from the right top to the bottom left.
- *Pan*: For moving the board horizontally to the left, then right, and then left again.

Each gesture should be performed by placing the breadboard vertically and with the Raspberry Pi Pico in front of us. Since we will consider training samples with a duration of 2.5 seconds, we recommend completing each movement in roughly 2 seconds.

Although we have three output classes to identify, an additional one is required to cope with the *unknown* movements and the case where there are no gestures (for example, the breadboard lying flat on the table).

In this recipe, we will use the Edge Impulse data forwarder to build our dataset. This tool allows us to quickly acquire the accelerations from any device that's capable of transmitting data over the serial and import the sample directly in Edge Impulse.

The data forwarder will run on your computer, so you will need to have the **Edge Impulse CLI** installed. If you haven't installed the Edge Impulse CLI yet, we recommend following the instructions in the official documentation: `https://docs.edgeimpulse.com/docs/cli-installation`.

How to do it...

Compile and upload the sketch that we developed in the previous recipe on your Raspberry Pi Pico. Ensure the Arduino serial monitor is closed; the serial peripheral on your computer can only communicate with one application at a time.

Next, open Edge Impulse and create a new project. Edge Impulse will ask you to write the name of the project. In our case, we have named the project `gesture_recognition`.

Now, follow these steps to build the dataset with the data forwarder tool:

1. Run the `edge-impulse-data-forwarder` program on your computer with a `50` Hz frequency and `115600` baud rate:

    ```
    $ edge-impulse-data-forwarder -- frequency 50 --baud-rate
    115600
    ```

    The data forwarder will ask you to authenticate on Edge Impulse, select the project you are working on, and give your Raspberry Pi Pico a name (for example, you can call it **pico**).

    Once you have configured the tool, the program will start parsing the data that's being transmitted over the serial. The data forwarder protocol expects one line per sensor reading with the three-axis accelerations either comma (,) or tab separated, as shown in the following diagram:

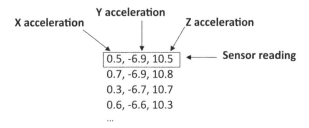

Figure 6.12 – Data forwarder protocol

Since our Arduino sketch complies with the protocol we just described, the data forwarder will detect the three-axis measurements that are being transmitted over the serial and ask you to assign a name. You can call them *ax*, *ay*, and *az*.

2. Open Edge Impulse and click on the **Data acquisition** tab from the left-hand side menu.

As shown in the following screenshot, use the **Record new data** area to record *50* samples for each gesture (*circle*, *cross*, and *pan*):

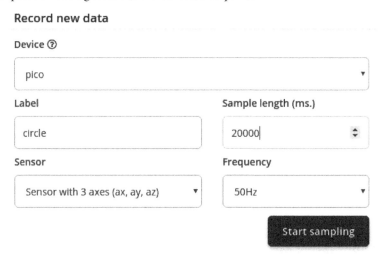

Figure 6.13 – The Record new data window in Edge Impulse

The **Device** and **Frequency** fields should already report the name of the device that's connected to the data forwarder (**pico**), as well as the sampling frequency (**50Hz**).

For each gesture, enter the label's name in the **Label** field (for example, **circle** for the circle gesture) and the duration of the recording in **Sample length (ms.)**.

Although each sample has a duration of 2.5 seconds, you can conveniently acquire 20 seconds of data where you repeat the same gestures multiple times, as shown in the following screenshot:

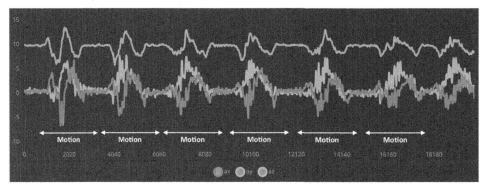

Figure 6.14 – A single recording with multiple motions of the same type

However, we recommend waiting 1 or 2 seconds between movements to help Edge Impulse recognize the motions in the following step.

3. Split the recording into samples of 2.5 seconds by clicking on ⋮ near the filename and then clicking **Split sample**, as shown in the following screenshot:

	SAMPLE NAME	LABEL	ADDED	LENGTH	
☐	**circle.json.2jam5jrk**	circle	Today, 15:2...	20s	⋮
☐	circle.json.2j930h3c	circle	To	Rename	
☐	circle.json.2j910pi...	circle	Ye	Edit label	
				Move to test set	
☐	circle.json.2j910pi...	circle	Ye	Disable	
☐	circle.json.2j910pi...	circle	Ye	Crop sample	
☐	circle.json.2j910pi...	circle	Ye	Split sample	
				Download	

Figure 6.15 – The Split sample option in Edge Impulse

Set **segment length (ms.)** to **2500** (2.5s) in the new window and click **Apply**. Edge Impulse will detect the motions and put a cutting window of 2.5 seconds on each one, as shown in the following screenshot:

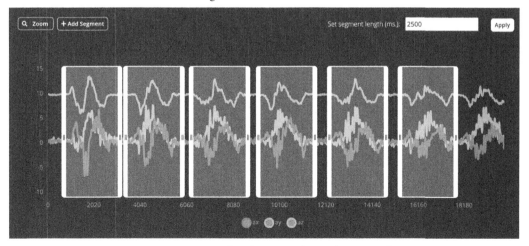

Figure 6.16 – Sample splits in windows of 2.5 seconds

If Edge Impulse does not recognize a motion in the recording, you can always add the window manually by clicking the **Add Segment** button and clicking on the area you want to cut.

Once all the segments have been selected, click **Split** to get the individual samples.

4. Use the **Record new data** area to record 50 random motions for the *unknown* class. To do so, acquire 40 seconds of accelerometer data where you move the breadboard randomly and lay it flat on the table.

5. Split the *unknown* recording into samples of 2.5 seconds by clicking on ⋮ near the filename and then **Split sample**. In the new window, add 50 cutting windows and click on **Split** when you are done.

6. Split the samples between the training and test datasets by clicking on the **Perform train/test split** button in the **Danger zone** area of the dashboard.

    Edge Impulse will ask you twice if you are sure that you want to perform this action. This is because the data shuffling operation is irreversible.

The dataset is now ready, with 80% of the samples assigned to the training/validation set and 20% to the test set.

Designing and training the ML model

With the dataset in our hands, we can start designing the model.

In this recipe, we will develop the following architecture with Edge Impulse:

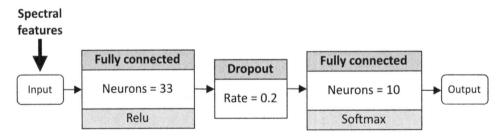

Figure 6.17 – Fully connected neural network to train

As you can see, the spectral features are the input for the model, which consists of just two fully connected layers.

Getting ready

In this recipe, we want to explain why the tiny network shown in the preceding diagram recognizes gestures from accelerometer data.

When developing deep neural network architectures, we commonly feed the model with raw data to leave the network to learn how to extract the features automatically.

This approach proved to be effective and incredibly accurate in various applications, such as image classification. However, there are some applications where hand-crafted engineering features offer similar accuracy results to deep learning and help reduce the architecture's complexity. This is the case for gesture recognition, where we can use features from the frequency domain.

> **Note**
>
> If you are not familiar with frequency domain analysis, we recommend reading *Chapter 4, Voice Controlling LEDs with Edge Impulse*.

The benefits of spectral features will be described in more detail in the following subsection.

Using spectral analysis to recognize gestures

Spectral analysis allows us to discover characteristics of the signal that are not visible in the time domain. For example, consider the following two signals:

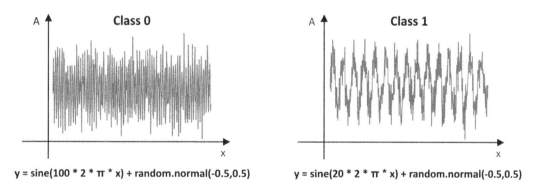

Figure 6.18 – Two signals in the time domain

These two signals are assigned to two different classes: **class 0** and **class 1**.

What features would you use in the time domain to discriminate class 0 from class 1?

Whatever set of features you may consider, they must be shift-invariant and robust to noise to be effective. Although there may be a set of features to distinguish class 0 from class 1, the solution would be straightforward if we considered the problem in the frequency domain, as shown by their power spectrums in the following diagram:

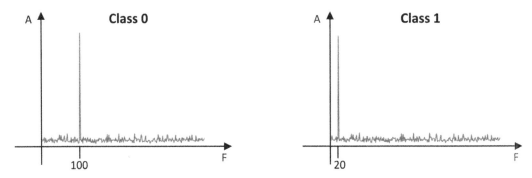

Figure 6.19 – Frequency representations of the class 0 and class 1 signals

As we can see, the two signals have different **dominant frequencies**, defined as the components with the highest magnitude. In other words, *the dominant frequencies are the components that carry more energy.*

Although signals from an accelerometer are not the same as class 0 and class 1, they still have repetitive patterns that make the frequency components suitable for a classification problem.

However, the frequency representation also offers another benefit related to the possibility of getting a compressed representation of the original signal.

For example, let's consider our dataset samples, which are three-axis accelerations that we acquired with a frequency of 50 Hz for 2.5 seconds. Each instance contains 375 data points (125 data points per axis). Now, let's apply the **Fast Fourier Transform** (**FFT**) with 128 output frequencies (**FFT length**) on each sample. This domain transformation produces 384 data points (128 data points per axis). Hence, FFT appears to be reducing the amount of data. However, as we saw in the previous example with class 0 and class 1, not all frequencies bring meaningful information. Therefore, we could just extract the frequencies that get the most energy (dominant frequencies) to reduce the amount of data and then facilitate signal pattern recognition.

For gesture recognition, we commonly produce spectral features by doing the following:

1.   Applying a low-pass filter to the frequency domain to filter out the highest frequencies. This step generally makes feature extraction more robust against noise.

2. Extracting the frequency components with the highest magnitude. Commonly, we take the three frequencies with the highest peak.

3. Extracting the power features in the power spectrum. Generally, these features are the **root mean square** (**RMS**) and the **power spectral density** (**PSD**), which describe the power that's present in an interval of frequencies.

In our case, we will extract the following features for each accelerometer axis:

*   One value for the RMS

*   Six values for extracting the frequencies with the highest peak (three values for the frequency and three values for the magnitude)

*   Four values for the PSD

Therefore, we would only get 33 features, which means a data reduction of over 11 times compared to the original signal, which is enough to feed a tiny fully connected neural network.

How to do it...

Click on the **Create Impulse** tab from the left-hand side menu. In the **Create Impulse** section, set **Window size** to 2500ms and **Window increase** to 200ms.

As we saw in *Chapter 4*, *Voice Controlling LEDs with Edge Impulse*, the **Window increase** parameter is required to run ML inference at regular intervals. This parameter plays a crucial role in a continuous data stream since we do not know when the event may start. Therefore, the idea is to split the input data stream into fixed windows (or segments) and execute the ML inference on each one. **Window size** is the temporal length of the window, while **Window increase** is the temporal distance between two consecutive segments.

The following steps will show how to design the neural network shown in *Figure 6.17*:

1. Click the **Add a processing block** button and look for **Spectral Analysis**:

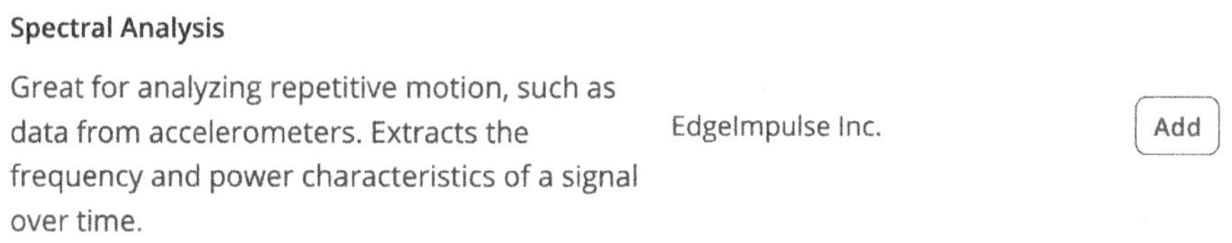

Spectral Analysis

Great for analyzing repetitive motion, such as data from accelerometers. Extracts the frequency and power characteristics of a signal over time.   EdgeImpulse Inc.   [Add]

Figure 6.20 – The Spectral Analysis processing block

Click the **Add** button to integrate the processing block into Impulse.

2.   Click the **Add a learning block** button and add **Classification (Keras)**.

Output features block should report the four output classes we must recognize (**circle**, **cross**, **pan**, and **unknown**), as shown in the following screenshot:

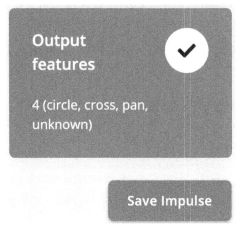

Figure 6.21 – Output classes

Save the Impulse by clicking the **Save Impulse** button.

3.   Click on the **Spectral features** button from the Impulse design category:

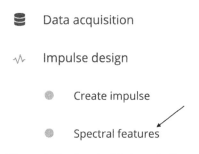

Figure 6.22 – Spectral features button

In the new window, we can play with the parameters that are affecting the feature extraction, such as the following:

  • **The type of filter to apply to the input signal**: We can either select a low-pass or high-pass filter and then set the **cut-off** frequency, the frequency at which attenuation occurs due to the filter increasing rapidly. Since we want to filter out the contribution of the noise, we should use a low-pass filter.

  • **The parameters that are affecting the spectral power features being extracted**: This includes the FFT length, the number of frequency components with the highest peak to extract, and the power edges that are required for the PSD.

We can keep all the parameters at their default values and click on the **Generate features** button to extract the spectral features from each training sample. Edge Impulse will return the **Job completed** message in the output log when the feature extraction process ends.

4. Click on the **Neural Network (Keras)** button under the **Impulse design** section and add a **Dropout layer** with a 0.2 ratio between the fully connected layers. Ensure that the first fully connected layer has **33** neurons while the other has **10** neurons, as shown in the following screenshot:

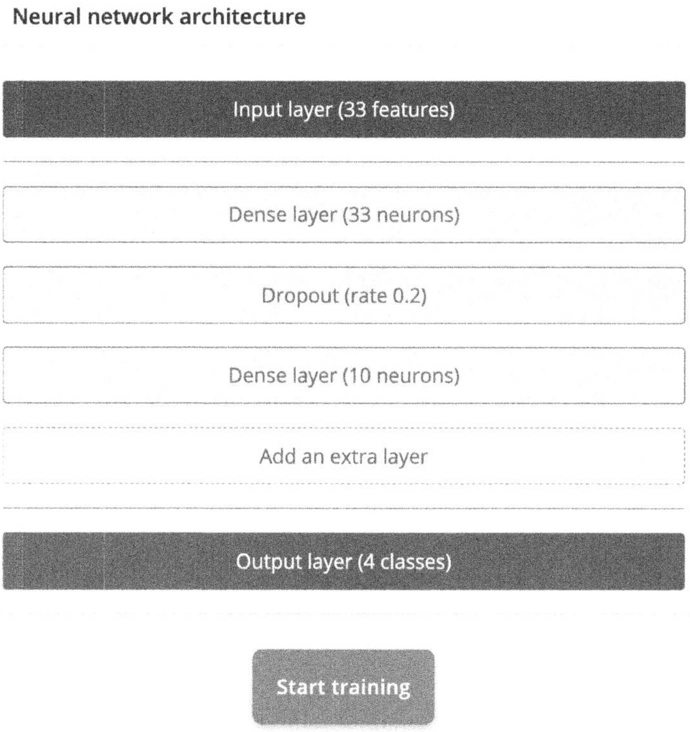

Neural network architecture

Input layer (33 features)

Dense layer (33 neurons)

Dropout (rate 0.2)

Dense layer (10 neurons)

Add an extra layer

Output layer (4 classes)

Start training

Figure 6.23 – Neural network architecture

Set the number of training epochs to 100 and click on **Start training**.

The output console will report the accuracy and loss on the training and validation datasets during training after each epoch.

Now, let's evaluate the model's performance on the test dataset. To do so, click the **Model testing** button from the left panel and then click **Classify all**.

Edge Impulse will provide this progress in **Model testing output** and generate the confusion matrix once the process is completed:

ACCURACY
88.46%

	CIRCLE	CROSS	PAN	UNKNOWN	UNCERTAIN
CIRCLE	81.8%	0%	0%	0%	18.2%
CROSS	0%	100%	0%	0%	0%
PAN	0%	0%	100%	0%	0%
UNKNOWN	0%	0%	0%	73.3%	26.7%
F1 SCORE	0.90	1.00	1.00	0.85	

Figure 6.24 – Model testing results

As you can see, our tiny model, which is made up of just two fully connected layers, achieved 88% accuracy!

Live classifications with the Edge Impulse data forwarder tool

Model testing is the step we should always take before exporting the final application to the target platform. Deploying on microcontrollers is error-prone because the code may contain bugs, the integration could be incorrect, or the model could not work reliably in the field. Therefore, model testing is necessary to exclude at least ML from the source of failures.

In this recipe, we will learn how to perform live classifications via Edge Impulse using the Raspberry Pi Pico.

Getting ready

The most effective way to evaluate the behavior of an ML model is to test the model's performance on the target platform.

In our case, we have already got a head start because the dataset was built with the Raspberry Pi Pico. Therefore, the accuracy of the test dataset should already give us a clear indication of how the model behaves. However, there are cases where the dataset may not be built on top of sensor data coming from the target device. When this happens, the model that's been deployed on the microcontroller could behave differently from what we expect. Usually, the reason for this performance degradation is due to sensor specifications. Fundamentally, sensors can be of the same type but have different specifications, such as offset, accuracy, range, sensitivity, and so on.

Thanks to the Edge Impulse data forwarder tool, it is straightforward to discover how the model performs on our target platform.

How to do it...

Ensure your Raspberry Pi Pico is still running the program we developed in the *Acquiring accelerometer data* recipe and that the `edge-impulse-data-forwarder` program is running on your computer. Next, click the **Live classification** tab and check whether the device (for example, **pico**) is being reported in the **Device** drop-down list, as shown in the following screenshot:

Figure 6.25 – The Device dropdown menu in Edge Impulse

If the device is not listed, follow the steps provided in the *How to do it…* subsection of the *Acquiring accelerometer data* recipe to pair your Raspberry Pi Pico with Edge Impulse again.

Now, follow these steps to evaluate the model's performance with the live classification tool:

1. In the **Live classification** window, select **Sensor with 3 axes** from the **Sensor** drop-down list and set **Sample length (ms)** to 20000. Keep **Frequency** at the default value (50 Hz).

2. With your Raspberry Pi Pico in front of you, click **Start sampling** and wait for the **Sampling…** message to appear on the button.

   When the recording begins, make any of the three movements that the model can recognize (*circle*, *cross*, or *pan*). The sample will be uploaded to Edge Impulse when the recording ends.

Edge Impulse will then split the recording into samples of 2.5 seconds and test the trained model on each. The classification results will be reported on the same page, similar to what we saw in *Chapter 4, Voice Controlling LEDs with Edge Impulse*.

Gesture recognition on Raspberry Pi Pico with Arm Mbed OS

Now that the model is ready, we can deploy it on the Raspberry Pi Pico.

In this recipe, we will build a continuous gesture recognition application with the help of Edge Impulse, Arm Mbed OS, and an algorithm to filter out redundant or spurious classification results.

The following Arduino sketch contains the code that will be referred to in this recipe:

- `06_gesture_recognition.ino`:

  `https://github.com/PacktPublishing/TinyML-Cookbook/blob/main/Chapter06/ArduinoSketches/06_gesture_recognition.ino`.

Getting ready

In this recipe, we will make our Raspberry Pi Pico capable of recognizing gestures with the help of the library that's generated by Edge Impulse for Arduino IDE. In *Chapter 4, Voice Controlling LEDs with Edge Impulse*, we used a pre-built example to accomplish this. However, here, we will implement the entire program from scratch.

Our goal is to develop a continuous gesture recognition application, which means that the accelerometer data sampling and ML inference must be performed concurrently. This approach guarantees that we capture and process all the pieces of the input data stream so that we don't miss any events.

The main ingredients we will need to accomplish our task are as follows:

- Arm Mbed OS for writing a multithreading program
- An algorithm to filter out redundant classification results

Let's start by learning how to perform concurrent tasks easily with the help of **real-time operating system** (**RTOS**) APIs in Arm Mbed OS.

Creating working threads with RTOS APIs in Arm Mbed OS

Any Arduino sketches that have been developed for the Arduino Nano 33 BLE Sense board and Raspberry Pi Pico are built on top of Arm Mbed OS, an open source RTOS for Arm Cortex-M microcontrollers. So far, we have only used Mbed APIs for interfacing with peripherals such as GPIO and I2C. However, Arm Mbed OS also offers functionalities that are typical of a canonical OS, such as **managing threads** to perform different tasks concurrently.

Once the thread has been created, we just need to bind the thread to the function that we want to run and execute it when we are ready.

> **Tip**
>
> If you are interested in learning more about the functionalities of Arm Mbed OS, we recommend reading the official documentation, which can be found at the following link: `https://os.mbed.com/docs/mbed-os/v6.15/bare-metal/index.html`.

A thread in a microcontroller is a piece of a program that runs independently on a single core. Since all the threads run on the same core, the scheduler is responsible for deciding on what to execute and for how long. Mbed OS uses a **pre-emptive scheduler** and uses a **round-robin priority-based scheduling** algorithm (`https://en.wikipedia.org/wiki/Round-robin_scheduling`). Therefore, every thread is assigned to a priority that's provided by us when we create the thread object through the RTOS API of Mbed OS (`https://os.mbed.com/docs/mbed-os/v6.15/apis/thread.html`). The supported priority values can be found at `https://os.mbed.com/docs/mbed-os/v6.15/apis/thread.html`.

For this recipe, we will need two threads:

- **Sampling thread**: The thread that's responsible for acquiring the accelerations from the MPU-6050 IMU with a frequency of 50 Hz
- **Inference thread**: The thread that's responsible for running model inference after every 200 ms

However, as we mentioned at the beginning of this *Getting ready* section, a multithreading program is not the only ingredient that's required to build our gesture recognition application. A filtering algorithm will also be necessary to filter out redundant and spurious predictions.

Filtering out redundant and spurious predictions

Our gesture recognition application employs a sliding window-based approach over a continuous data stream to determine whether we have a motion of interest. The idea behind this approach is to split the data stream into smaller windows of a fixed size and execute the ML inference on each one.. As we already know, ML is a powerful tool for gathering robust classification results, especially if we use temporal shifts on the input data. Therefore, neighboring windows will have similar and high probability scores, leading to multiple and redundant detections.

In this recipe, we will adopt a **test and trace filtering algorithm** to make our application robust against spurious detections. Conceptually, this filtering algorithm only wants to consider the ML output class as valid if the last **N** predictions (for example, the last four) reported the following:

- The same output class but it's different from the *unknown* one.

- The probability score is above a fixed **threshold** (for example, greater than 0.7).

To visually understand how this algorithm works, look at the following diagram:

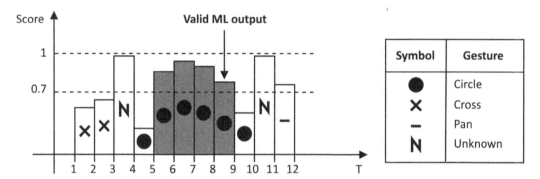

Figure 6.26 – Example of a valid ML prediction

In the preceding diagram, each rectangular bar is the predicted class at a given time, where the following occurs:

- The symbol represents the predicted output class

- The bar's height is the probability score associated with the predicted class

Therefore, considering *N* as four and the *probability threshold* as 0.7, we can consider the ML output class as valid only at **T=8**. The previous four classification results returned *circle* and had probability scores greater than 0.7.

How to do it...

Click on **Deployment** from the left-hand side menu and select **Arduino Library** from the **Create library** options, as shown in the following screenshot:

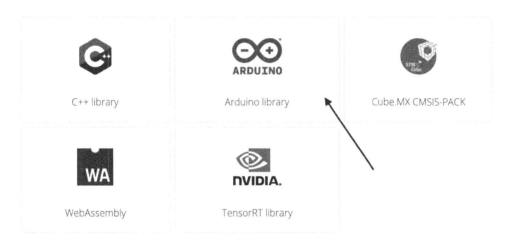

Build firmware

Or get a ready-to-go binary for your development board that includes your impulse.

Figure 6.27 – Edge Impulse deployment section

Then, click on the **Build** button at the bottom of the page. Save the ZIP file on your computer.

Next, import the library into the Arduino IDE. After that, copy the sketch that we developed in the *Acquiring accelerometer data* recipe in a new sketch. Follow these steps to learn how to extend this code to make the Raspberry Pi Pico capable of recognizing our three gestures:

1. Include the `<edge_impulse_project_name>_inferencing.h` header file in the sketch. For example, if the Edge Impulse project's name is `gesture_recognition`, you should include the following information:

```
#include <gesture_recognition_inferencing.h>
```

   This header file is the only requirement for using the constants, functions, and C macros that have been built by Edge Impulse specifically for our project.

2. Declare two floating-point arrays (`buf_sampling` and `buf_inference`) that have 375 elements each:

```
#define INPUT_SIZE EI_CLASSIFIER_DSP_INPUT_FRAME_SIZE
float buf_sampling[INPUT_SIZE] = { 0 };
float buf_inference[INPUT_SIZE];
```

   In the preceding code, we used the Edge Impulse `EI_CLASSIFIER_DSP_INPUT_FRAME_SIZE` C macro definition to get the number of input samples that are required for 2.5 seconds of accelerometer data (375).

   The `buf_sampling` array will be used by the *sampling thread* to store the accelerometer data, while the `buf_inference` array will be used by the *inference thread* to feed the input to the model.

3. Declare an RTOS thread with a low priority schedule for running the ML model:

```
rtos::Thread inference_thread(osPriorityLow);
```

   The *inference thread* should have a lower priority (`osPriorityLow`) than the *sampling thread* because it has a longer execution time due to ML inference. Therefore, a low priority schedule for the inference thread will guarantee that we do not miss any accelerometer data samples.

4. Create a C++ class to implement the test and trace filtering algorithm. Make the filtering parameters (*N* and *probability threshold*) and the variables that are needed to trace the ML predictions (*counter* and the *last output valid class index)* as `private` members:

```
class TestAndTraceFilter {
private:
    int32_t        _n {0};
    float          _thr {0.0f};
    int32_t        _counter {0};
    int32_t        _last_idx_class {-1};
    const int32_t  _num_classes {3};
```

The algorithm mainly needs two variables to trace the classification results. These variables are as follows:

- `_counter`: This variable is used to keep track of how many times we had the same classification with a probability score above the fixed threshold (`_thr`).

- `_last_idx_class`: This variable is used to find the output class index of the last inference.

In this recipe, we will assign `-1` to the `_last_idx_class` variable when the last inference returns either *unknown* or a probability score below the fixed threshold (`_thr`).

5. Declare the invalid output index class (`-1`) as a `public` member:

```
public:
    static constexpr int32_t invalid_idx_class = -1;
```

6. Implement the `TestAndTraceFilter` constructor to initialize the filtering parameters:

```
public:
    TestAndTraceFilter(int32_t n, float thr) {
        _thr = thr;
        _n   = n;
    }
```

7. In the `TestAndTraceFilter` class, implement a `private` method to reset the internal variables (`_counter` and `_last_idx_class`) that will be used to trace the ML predictions:

```
void reset() {
    _counter        = 0;
    _last_idx_class = invalid_idx_class;
}
```

8. In the `TestAndTraceFilter` class, implement a `public` method to update the filtering algorithm with the latest classification result:

```
void update(size_t idx_class, float prob) {
    if(idx_class >= _num_classes || prob < _thr) {
        reset();
    }
    else {
        if(prob > _thr) {
            if(idx_class != _last_idx_class) {
                _last_idx_class = idx_class;
                _counter        = 0;
            }
            _counter += 1;
        }
        else {
            reset();
        }
    }
}
```

The `TestAndTraceFilter` object works in two states – *incremental* and *reset* – as shown in the following diagram:

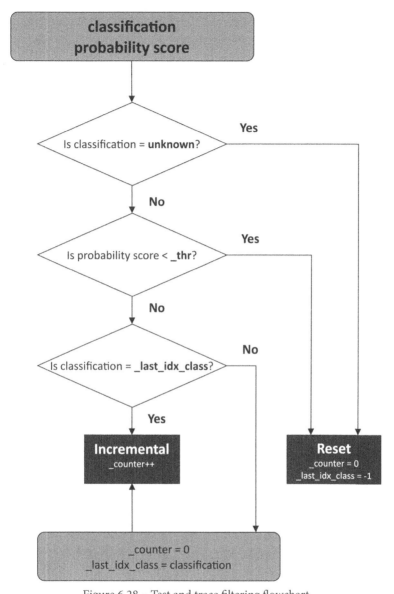

Figure 6.28 – Test and trace filtering flowchart

As you can see, the *incremental* state occurs when the most recent classification is a valid output class and the probability is greater than the minimum probability value. In all the other cases, we enter the *reset* state, where we set `_counter` to `0` and `_last_idx_class` to `-1`.

In the *incremental* state, `_counter` is incremented by one, and `_last_idx_class` keeps the index of the valid output class.

9. In the `TestAndTraceFilter` class, implement a `public` method to return the filter's output:

```
int32_t output() {
    if(_counter >= _n) {
        int32_t out = _last_idx_class;
        reset();
        return out;
    }
    else {
        return invalid_idx_class;
    }
}
```

As you can see, if `_counter` is greater than or equal to `_n`, we return `_last_idx_class` and put the test and trace filter function in the *reset* state.

If `_counter` is smaller than `_n`, we return `invalid_idx_class`.

10. Write a function to run the ML inference (`inference_func`) in an infinite loop (`while(1)`). This function will be executed by the RTOS thread (`inference_thread`). Before you start this inference, wait for the sampling buffer to become full:

```
void inference_func() {
    delay((EI_CLASSIFIER_INTERVAL_MS * EI_CLASSIFIER_RAW_
SAMPLE_COUNT) + 100);
```

Next, initialize the test and trace filter object. Set *N* and *probability threshold* to 4 and `0.7f`, respectively:

```
    TestAndTraceFilter filter(4, 0.7f);
```

After the initialization, run the ML inference in an infinite loop:

```
    while (1) {
        memcpy(buf_inference, buf_sampling,
                INPUT_SIZE * sizeof(float));
        signal_t signal;
        numpy::signal_from_buffer(buf_inference, INPUT_SIZE,
                                  &signal);
        ei_impulse_result_t result = { 0 };
        run_classifier(&signal, &result, false);
```

Before we run the inference, we need to copy the data from `buf_sampling` to `buf_inference` and initialize the Edge Impulse `signal_t` object with the `buf_inference` buffer.

11. Get the output class with the highest probability and update the `TestAndTraceFilter` object with the latest classification result:

```
size_t ix_max = 0; float  pb_max = 0;
#define NUM_OUTPUT_CLASSES EI_CLASSIFIER_LABEL_COUNT
for (size_t ix = 0; ix < NUM_OUTPUT_CLASSES; ix++) {
    if(result.classification[ix].value > pb_max) {
        ix_max = ix;
        pb_max = result.classification[ix].value;
    }
}
filter.update(ix_max, pb_max);
```

12. Read the output of the `TestAndTraceFilter` object. If the output is not `-1` (invalid output), send the label that was assigned to the predicted gesture over the serial:

```
int32_t out = filter.output();
if(out != filter.invalid_idx_class) {
    Serial.println(result.classification[out].label);
}
```

Next, wait for `200` ms (**window increase** set in the Edge Impulse project) before running the subsequent inference:

```
delay(200);
```

> **Note**
>
> `delay()` puts the current thread in a waiting state. As a rule of thumb, we should always put a thread in a waiting state when it does not perform computation for a long time. This approach guarantees that we don't waste computational resources and that other threads can run in the meantime.

13. Start the RTOS inference thread (`inference_thread`) in the `setup()` function:

```
inference_thread.start(mbed::callback(&inference_func));
```

14. In the `loop()` function, replace the prints to the serial port with the code that's required to store the accelerometer measurements in `buf_sampling`:

```
float ax, ay, az;
read_accelerometer(&ax, &ay, &az);
numpy::roll(buf_sampling, INPUT_ SIZE, -3);
buf_sampling[INPUT_SIZE - 3] = ax;
buf_sampling[INPUT_SIZE - 2] = ay;
buf_sampling[INPUT_SIZE - 1] = az;
```

Since the Arduino `loop()` function is an RTOS thread with high priority, we don't need to create an additional thread to sample the accelerometer measurements. Therefore, we can replace the `Serial.print` functions with the code that's required to fill the `buf_sampling` buffer with the accelerometer data.

The buf_sampling buffer is filled as follows:

* First, we shift the data in the `buf_sampling` array by three positions using the `numpy::roll()` function. The `numpy::roll()` function is provided by the Edge Impulse library, and it works similarly to its NumPy counterpart. (`https://numpy.org/doc/stable/reference/generated/numpy.roll.html`).

* Then, we store the three-axis accelerometer measurements (`ax`, `ay`, and `az`) in the last three positions of `buf_sampling`.

This approach will ensure that the latest accelerometer measurements are always in the last three positions of `buf_sampling`. By doing this, the *inference thread* can copy this buffer's content into the `buf_inference` buffer and feed the ML model directly without having to perform data reshuffling.

Compile and upload the sketch on the Raspberry Pi Pico. Now, if you make any of the three movements that the ML model can recognize (*circle*, *cross*, or *pan*), you will see the recognized gestures in the Arduino serial terminal.

Building a gesture-based interface with PyAutoGUI

Now that we can recognize the hand gestures with the Raspberry Pi Pico, we must build a touchless interface for YouTube video playback.

In this recipe, we will implement a Python script to read the recognized motion that's transmitted over the serial and use the `PyAutoGUI` library to build a gesture-based interface to play, pause, mute, unmute, and change YouTube videos.

The following Python script contains the code that's referred to in this recipe:

- `07_gesture_based_ui.py`:

  `https://github.com/PacktPublishing/TinyML-Cookbook/blob/main/Chapter06/PythonScripts/07_gesture_based_ui.py`.

Getting ready

The Python script that we will develop in this recipe will not be implemented in Google Colaboratory because that requires accessing the local serial port, keyboard, and monitor. Therefore, we will write the program in a local Python development environment.

We only need two libraries to build our gesture-based interface: `pySerial` and `PyAutoGUI`.

`PySerial` will be used to grab the predicted gesture that will be transmitted over serial, similar to what we saw in *Chapter 5, Indoor Scene Classification with TensorFlow Lite for Microcontrollers and the Arduino Nano*.

The identified movement, in turn, will perform one of the following three YouTube video playback actions:

Gesture	Circle	Cross	Pan
Function	Mute/Unmute	Play/Pause	Move to the next video

Figure 6.29 – Table reporting the gesture mapping

Since YouTube offers keyboard shortcuts for the preceding actions (`https://support.google.com/youtube/answer/7631406`), we will use `PyAutoGUI` to simulate the keyboard keys (**keystrokes**) that are pressed, as shown in the following table:

Gesture	Playback action	Keyboard shortcut
Circle	Mute/Unmute	m
Cross	Play/Pause	k
Pan	Move to the next video	Shift + N

Figure 6.30 – Keyboard shortcuts for the YouTube playback actions

For example, if the microcontroller returns `circle` over the serial, we will need to simulate the press of the **m** key.

How to do it...

Ensure you have installed `PyAutoGUI` in your local Python development environment (for example, `pip install pyautogui`). After that, create a new Python script and import the following libraries:

```
import serial
import pyautogui
```

Now, follow these steps to build a touchless interface with `PyAutoGUI`:

1. Initialize `pySerial` with the port and baud rate that's used by the Raspberry Pi Pico::

```
port = '/dev/ttyACM0'
baudrate = 115600
ser = serial.Serial()
ser.port     = port
ser.baudrate = baudrate
```

Once initialized, open the serial port and discard the content in the serial input buffer:

```
ser.open()
ser.reset_input_buffer()
```

2. Create a utility function to return a line from the serial port as a string:

```
def serial_readline():
    data = ser.readline
    return data.decode("utf-8").strip()
```

3. Use a `while` loop to read the serial data line by line:

```
while True:
    data_str = serial_readline()
```

For each line, check whether we have a `circle`, `cross`, or `pan` motion.

If we have a `circle` motion, press the *m* key to *mute/unmute*:

```
if str(data_str) == "circle":
    pyautogui.press('m')
```

If we have a `cross` motion, press the *k* key to *play/pause*:

```
if str(data_str) == "cross":
    pyautogui.press('k')
```

If we have a pan motion, press the *Shift + N* hotkey to move to the next video:

```
if str(data_str) == "pan":
    pyautogui.hotkey('shift', 'n')
```

4. Start the Python script while ensuring your Raspberry Pi Pico is running the sketch that we developed in the previous recipe.

Next, open YouTube from your web browser, play a video, and have your Raspberry Pi Pico in front of you. Now, if you make any of the three movements that the ML model can recognize (*circle*, *cross*, or *pan*), you will be able to control the YouTube video playback with gestures!

7

Running a Tiny CIFAR-10 Model on a Virtual Platform with the Zephyr OS

Prototyping a TinyML application directly on a physical device is really fun because we can instantly see our ideas at work in something that looks and feels like the real thing. However, before any application comes to life, we need to ensure that the models work as expected and, possibly, among different devices. Testing and debugging applications directly on microcontroller boards often requires a lot of development time. The main reason for this is the necessity to upload a program into a device for every change in code. However, virtual platforms can come in handy to make testing more straightforward and faster.

In this chapter, we will build an image classification application with **TensorFlow Lite for Microcontrollers** (**TFLu**) for an emulated Arm Cortex-M3 microcontroller. We will start by installing the **Zephyr OS**, the primary framework used in this chapter to accomplish our task. Next, we will design a tiny quantized **CIFAR-10** model with **TensorFlow** (**TF**). This model will be capable of running on a microcontroller with only 256 KB of program memory and 64 KB of RAM. In the end, we will deploy an image classification application on an emulated Arm Cortex-M3 microcontroller through **Quick Emulator** (**QEMU**).

The aim of this chapter is to learn how to build and run a TFLu-based application with the Zephyr OS on a virtual platform and provide practical advice on the design of an image classification model for memory-constrained microcontrollers.

In this chapter, we're going to implement the following recipes:

- Getting started with the Zephyr OS

- Designing and training a tiny CIFAR-10 model

- Evaluating the accuracy of the TFLite model

- Converting a NumPy image to a C-byte array

- Preparing the skeleton of the TFLu project

- Building and running the TFLu application on QEMU

Technical requirements

To complete all the practical recipes of this chapter, we will need the following:

- A laptop/PC with either Ubuntu 18.04+ or later on x86_64

The source code and additional material are available in the Chapter07 file (https://github.com/PacktPublishing/TinyML-Cookbook/tree/main/Chapter07).

Getting started with the Zephyr OS

In this recipe, we will install the Zephyr project, the framework used in this chapter to build and run the TFLu application on the emulated Arm Cortex-M3 microcontroller. At the end of this recipe, we will check whether everything works as expected by running a sample application on the virtual platform considered for our project.

Getting ready

To get started with this first recipe, we need to know what the Zephyr project is about.

Zephyr (https://zephyrproject.org/) is an open source Apache 2.0 project that provides a small-footprint **Real-Time Operating System** (**RTOS**) for various hardware platforms based on multiple architectures, including Arm Cortex-M, Intel x86, ARC, Nios II, and RISC-V. The RTOS has been designed for memory-constrained devices with security in mind.

Zephyr does not provide just an RTOS, though. It also offers a **Software Development Kit (SDK)** with a collection of ready-to-use examples and tools to build Zephyr-based applications for various supported devices, including virtual platforms through QEMU.

QEMU (`https://www.qemu.org/`) is an open source machine emulator that allows us to test programs without using real hardware. The Zephyr SDK supports two QEMU Arm Cortex-M-based microcontrollers, which are as follows:

- *The BBC micro:bit* (`https://microbit.org/`) with the Arm Cortex-M0

- *Texas Instruments' LM3S6965* (`https://www.ti.com/product/LM3S6965`) with the Arm Cortex-M3

From the preceding two QEMU platforms, we will use the **LM3S6965**. Our choice fell to the Texas Instruments board because it has a bigger RAM capacity than the BBC micro:bit. In fact, although the devices have the same program memory size (256 KB), LM3S6965 has 64 KB of RAM. Unfortunately, the BBC micro:bit has only 16 KB of RAM, not enough for running a CIFAR-10 model.

How to do it...

The Zephyr installation consists of the following steps:

1. Installing Zephyr prerequisites

2. Getting Zephyr source code and related Python dependencies

3. Installing the Zephyr SDK

> **Important Note**
> The installation guide reported in this section refers to Zephyr 2.7.0 and the Zephyr SDK 0.13.1.

Before getting started, we recommend you have the Python **Virtual Environment (virtualenv)** tool installed to create an isolated Python environment. If you haven't installed it yet, open your terminal and use the following `pip` command:

```
$ pip install virtualenv
```

To launch the Python virtual environment, create a new directory (for example, `zephyr`):

```
$ mkdir zephyr && cd zephyr
```

Then, create a virtual environment inside the directory just created:

```
$ python -m venv env
```

The preceding command creates the env directory with all the executables and Python packages required for the virtual environment.

To use the virtual environment, you just need to activate it with the following command:

```
$ source env/bin/activate
```

If the virtual environment is activated, the shell will be prefixed with (env):

```
(env) $
```

> **Tip**
>
> You can deactivate the Python virtual environment at any time by typing deactivate in the shell.

The following steps will help you prepare the Zephyr environment and run a simple application on the virtual Arm Cortex-M3-based microcontroller:

1. Follow the instructions reported in the Zephyr *Getting Started Guide* (https:// docs.zephyrproject.org/2.7.0/getting_started/index.html) until the *Install a Toolchain* section. All Zephyr modules will be available in the ~/zephyrproject directory.

2. Navigate into the Zephyr source code directory and enter the samples/ synchronization folder:

```
$ cd ~/zephyrproject/zephyr/samples/synchronization
```

Zephyr provides ready-to-use applications in the samples/ folder to demonstrate the usage of RTOS features. Since our goal is to run an application on a virtual platform, we consider the synchronization sample because it does not require interfacing with external components (for example, LEDs).

3. Build the pre-built synchronization sample for qemu_cortex_m3:

```
$ west build -b qemu_cortex_m3 .
```

The sample test is compiled with the `west` command (`https://docs.zephyrproject.org/latest/guides/west/index.html`). West is a tool developed by Zephyr to manage multiple repositories conveniently with a few command lines. However, West is more than a repository manager. In fact, the tool can also plug additional functionalities through extensions. Zephyr exploits this pluggable mechanism to offer the commands to compile, flash, and debug applications (`https://docs.zephyrproject.org/latest/guides/west/build-flash-debug.html`).

The `west` command used to compile the application has the following syntax:

```
$ west build -b <BOARD> <EXAMPLE-TO-BUILD>
```

Let's break down the preceding command:

- `<BOARD>`: This is the name of the target platform. In our case, it is the QEMU Arm Cortex-M3 platform (`qemu_cortex_m3`).

- `<EXAMPLE-TO-BUILD>`: This is the path to the sample test to compile.

Once we have built the application, we can run it on the target device.

4. Run the `synchronization` example on the LM3S6965 virtual platform:

```
$ west build -t run
```

To run the application, we just need to use the `west build` command, followed by the build system target (`-t`) as a command-line argument. Since we had specified the target platform when we built the application, we can simply pass the `run` option to upload and run the program on the device.

If Zephyr is installed correctly, the `synchronization` sample will run on the virtual Arm Cortex-M3 platform and print the following output:

```
threadA: Hello World from arm!
threadB: Hello World from arm!
threadA: Hello World from arm!
threadB: Hello World from arm!
```

You can now close QEMU by pressing *Ctrl + A*.

Designing and training a tiny CIFAR-10 model

The tight memory constraint on LM3S6965 forces us to design a model with extremely low memory utilization. In fact, the target microcontroller has four times less memory capacity than Arduino Nano.

Despite this challenging constraint, in this recipe, we will be leveraging the following tiny model for the CIFAR-10 image classification, capable of running on LM3S6965:

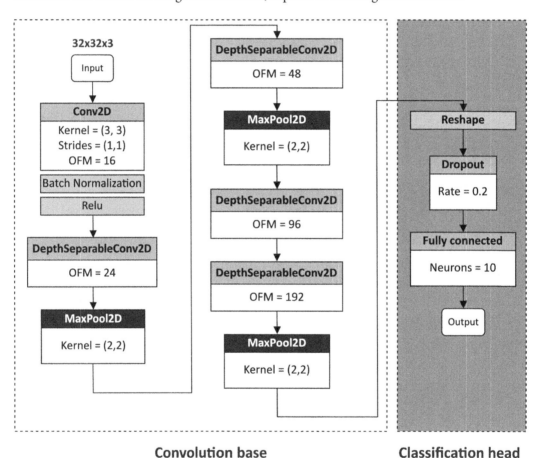

Figure 7.1 – A model tailored for CIFAR-10 dataset image classification

The preceding network will be designed with TF and the Keras API.

The following Colab file (in the *Designing and training a tiny CIFAR-10 model* section) contains the code referred to in this recipe:

- `prepare_model.ipynb`

  (`https://github.com/PacktPublishing/TinyML-Cookbook/blob/ main/Chapter07/ColabNotebooks/prepare_model.ipynb`).

Getting ready

The network tailored in this recipe takes inspiration from the success of the MobileNet V1 on the **ImageNet** dataset classification. Our model aims to classify the 10 classes of the CIFAR-10 dataset: *airplane, automobile, bird, cat, deer, dog, frog, horse, ship,* and *truck*.

The CIFAR-10 dataset is available at `https://www.cs.toronto.edu/~kriz/ cifar.html` and consists of 60,000 RGB images with 32 x 32 resolution.

To understand why the proposed model can run successfully on LM3S6965, we want to outline the architectural design choices that make this network suitable for our target device.

As shown in *Figure 7.1*, the model has a convolution base, which acts as a feature extractor, and a classification head, which takes the learned features to perform the classification.

Early layers have large spatial dimensions and low **Output Feature Maps** (**OFMs**) to learn simple features (for example, simple lines). Deeper layers, instead, have small spatial dimensions and a high OFMs to learn complex features (for example, shapes).

The model uses pooling layers to halve the spatial dimensionality of the tensors and reduce the risk of overfitting when increasing the OFM. Generally, we want several activation maps for deep layers to combine as many complex features as possible. Therefore, the idea is to get smaller spatial dimensions to afford more OFMs.

In the following subsection, we will explain the design choice in using **Depthwise Separable Convolution** (**DWSC**) layers instead of the standard convolution 2D.

Replacing convolution 2D with DWSC

DWSC is the layer that made MobileNet V1 a success on the ImageNet dataset and the heart of our proposed convolution-based architecture. This operator took the lead in MobileNet V1 to produce an accurate model that can also run on a device with limited memory and computational resources.

As seen in *Chapter 5, Indoor Scene Classification with TensorFlow Lite for Microcontrollers and the Arduino Nano*, and shown in the following figure, DWSC is a depthwise convolution followed by a convolution layer with a 1 x 1 kernel size (that is, **pointwise convolution**):

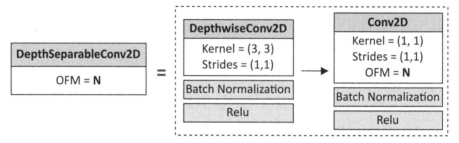

Figure 7.2 – The DWSC

To demonstrate the efficiency of this operator, consider the first DWSC layer in the network presented in *Figure 7.1*. As shown in the following diagram, the input tensor has a 32 x 32 x 16 dimension while the output tensor has a 32 x 32 x 24 dimension:

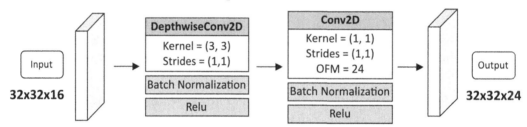

Figure 7.3 – The first DWSC in the CIFAR-10 model

If we replace the DWSC with a regular convolution 2D with a 3 x 3 filter size, we will need 3,480 trainable parameters, of which 3,456 are weights (3 x 3 x 16 x 24), and 24 are biases. The DWSC, instead, just needs 560 trainable parameters, distributed as follows:

- 144 weights and 16 biases for the depthwise convolution layer with a 3 x 3 filter size

- 384 weights and 24 biases for the pointwise convolution

Therefore, in this particular case, the DWSC layer yields roughly six times fewer trainable parameters than a regular convolution 2D layer.

The model size reduction is not the only benefit this layer offers. The other advantage in using the DWSC is given by the reduction of the arithmetic operations. In fact, although both layers are made of several **Multiply-Accumulate (MAC)** operations, the DWSC needs considerably fewer MAC operations than convolution 2D.

This aspect is demonstrated by the following two formulas for the calculation of the total MAC operations for convolution 2D and the DWSC:

$$MACs_{conv2d} = F_{size} \cdot W_{out} \cdot H_{out} \cdot C_{out} \cdot C_{in}$$

$$MACs_{dwsc} = (F_{size} \cdot W_{out} \cdot H_{out} \cdot C_{in}) + (W_{out} \cdot H_{out} \cdot C_{out} \cdot C_{in})$$

The formula is broken down as follows:

- $MACs_{conv2d}$: The total MAC operations for convolution 2D
- $MACs_{dwsc}$: The total MAC operations for the DWSC
- F_{size}: The filter size
- $W_{out} \cdot H_{out}$: The width and height of the output tensor
- $C_{in} \cdot C_{out}$: The number of input and output feature maps

The calculation of the total MAC for the DWSC has two parts. The first part $(F_{size} \cdot W_{out} \cdot H_{out} \cdot C_{in})$ calculates the MAC operations for depthwise convolution, assuming that the input and output tensors have the same feature maps. The second part $(W_{out} \cdot H_{out} \cdot C_{out} \cdot C_{in})$ calculates the MAC operations for the pointwise convolution.

If we use the preceding two formulas for the case reported in *Figure 7.3*, we will discover that convolution 2D needs 3,583,944 operations while DWSC needs only 540,672 operations. Therefore, there is a computational complexity reduction of over six times with DWSC.

Hence, the efficiency of the DWSC layer is double since it decreases the trainable parameters and arithmetic operations involved.

Now that we know the benefits of this layer, let's discover how to design a model that can run on our target device.

Keeping the model memory requirement under control

Our goal is to produce a model that can fit in 256 KB of program memory and run with 64 KB of RAM. The program memory usage can be obtained directly from the .tflite model generated. Alternatively, you can check the **Total params** value returned by the Keras summary() method (https://keras.io/api/models/model/#summary-method) to have an indication of how big the model will be. **Total params** represents the number of trainable parameters, and it is affected mainly by the OFM and layers. In our case, the convolution base has five trainable layers with a maximum of 192 activation maps. This choice will make our model utilize just 30% of the total program memory.

The estimation of the RAM utilization is a bit more complicated and depends upon the model architecture. All the non-constant variables, such as the network input, output, and **intermediate tensors**, stay in RAM. However, although the network may need several tensors, TFLu has a **memory manager** capable of efficiently providing portions of memory at runtime. For a sequential model such as ours, where each layer has one input and one output tensor, a ballpark figure for the RAM utilization is given by the sum of the following:

- The memory required for the model input and output tensors
- The two largest intermediate tensors

In our network, the first DWSC produces the largest intermediate tensor with 24,576 elements (32 x 32 x 24), as shown in the following figure:

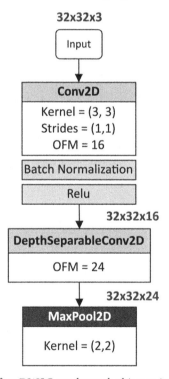

Figure 7.4 – The first DWSC produces the biggest intermediate tensor

As you can see from the preceding diagram, the first DWSC produces a tensor with 24 OFMs, which we found as a good compromise between accuracy and RAM utilization. However, you may consider reducing this further to make the model even smaller and more performant.

How to do it...

Create a new Colab project and follow these steps to design and train a quantized CIFAR-10 model with TFLite:

1. Download the CIFAR-10 dataset:

```
(train_imgs, train_lbls), (test_imgs, test_lbls) =
datasets.cifar10.load_data()
```

2. Normalize the pixel values between 0 and 1:

```
train_imgs = train_imgs / 255.0
test_imgs = test_imgs / 255.0
```

This step ensures that all data is on the same scale.

3. Define a Python function to implement the DWSC:

```
def separable_conv(i, ch):
    x = layers.DepthwiseConv2D((3,3), padding="same")(i)
    x = layers.BatchNormalization()(x)
    x = layers.Activation("relu")(x)
    x = layers.Conv2D(ch, (1,1), padding="same")(x)
    x = layers.BatchNormalization()(x)
    return layers.Activation("relu")(x)
```

The `separable_conv()` function accepts the following input arguments:

- `i`: Input to feed to the depthwise convolution 2D
- `ch`: The number of OFMs to produce

The batch normalization layer standardizes the input to a layer and makes the model training faster and more stable.

4. Design the convolution base, as described in *Figure 7.1*:

```
input = layers.Input((32,32,3))
x = layers.Conv2D(16, (3, 3), padding='same')(input)
x = layers.BatchNormalization()(x)
x = layers.Activation("relu")(x)
x = separable_conv(0, x, 24)
x = layers.MaxPooling2D((2, 2))(x)
x = separable_conv(0, x, 48)
x = layers.MaxPooling2D((2, 2))(x)
```

```
x = separable_conv(0, x, 96)
x = separable_conv(0, x, 192)
x = layers.MaxPooling2D((2, 2))(x)
```

We use pooling layers to reduce the spatial dimensionality of the feature maps through the network. Although we can use DWSC with non-unit strides to accomplish a similar sub-sampling task, we preferred pooling layers to keep the number of trainable parameters low.

5. Design the classification head:

```
x = layers.Flatten()(x)
x = layers.Dropout(0.2)(x)
x = layers.Dense(10)(x)
```

6. Generate the model and print its summary:

```
model = Model(input, x)
model.summary()
```

As shown in the following screenshot, the model summary returns roughly 60,000 parameters:

```
=================================
Total params: 60,194
Trainable params: 59,074
Non-trainable params: 1,120
```

Figure 7.5 – A CIFAR-10 model summary (trainable parameters)

In the case of 8-bit quantization, 60,000 floating-point parameters correspond to 60,000 8-bit integer values. Therefore, the weights contribute to the model size with 60 KB, well away from the 256 KB maximum target. However, we should not consider this number as the model size, since what we deploy on a microcontroller is the TFLite file, which also contains the network architecture and the quantization parameters.

A ballpark figure for the RAM utilization can be estimated from the tensor size of each intermediate tensor in the network. This information can be extrapolated from the output of model.summary(). As anticipated in the previous *Getting ready* section, the intermediate tensors of the first DWSC layer have the largest number of elements. The following screenshot is taken from the output of model.summary() and reports the tensor shapes for these two tensors:

```
act1 (Activation)              (None, 32, 32, 16)        0

dwc0_dwsc2 (DepthwiseConv2D)   (None, 32, 32, 16)      160

bn0_dwsc2 (BatchNormalization) (None, 32, 32, 16)       64

act0_dwsc2 (Activation)        (None, 32, 32, 16)        0

conv0_dwsc2 (Conv2D)           (None, 32, 32, 24)      408

bn1_dwsc2 (BatchNormalization) (None, 32, 32, 24)       96

act1_dwsc2 (Activation)        (None, 32, 32, 24)        0

pool1 (MaxPooling2D)           (None, 16, 16, 24)        0
```

DWSC

Figure 7.6 – A CIFAR-10 model summary (the first DWSC)

As you can see from the **DWSC** area marked in the preceding screenshot, the tensors with the largest number of elements are as follows:

- The output of **act0_dwsc2**: **(None, 32, 32, 16)**

- The output of **conv0_dwsc2**: **(None, 32, 32, 24)**

Therefore, the expected memory utilization for the intermediate tensor should be in the order of 41 KB. To this number, we should add the memory for the input and output nodes to get a more precise ballpark figure of the RAM usage. The input and output tensors need 3,082 bytes, of which 3,072 bytes are for the input and 10 bytes are for the output. In total, we expect to use 44 KB of RAM during the model inference, which is less than the 64 KB target.

> **Note**
>
> In *Figure 7.6*, there are three layers with the **(None, 32, 32, 16)** output shape: **conv0_dwsc2**, **bn1_dwsc2**, and **act1_dwsc2**. However, only the pointwise convolution layer (**conv0_dwsc2**) counts for memory utilization of the intermediate tensors because batch normalization (**bn1_dwsc2**) and activation (**act1_dwsc2**) will be fused into the convolution (**conv0_dwsc2**) by the TFLite converter.

7. Compile and train the model with 10 epochs:

```
model.compile(optimizer='adam',
loss = tf.keras.losses.SparseCategoricalCrossentropy(
from_logits=True), metrics=['accuracy'])


model.fit(train_imgs, train_lbls, epochs=10,
validation_data=(test_imgs, test_lbls))
```

After 10 epochs, the model should obtain an accuracy of 73% on the validation dataset.

8. Save the TF model as `SavedModel`:

```
model.save("cifar10")
```

Our CIFAR-10 model is now ready for being quantized with the TFLite converter.

Evaluating the accuracy of the TFLite model

The tiny model just trained can classify the 10 classes of CIFAR-10 with an accuracy of 73%. However, what is the model's accuracy of the quantized variant generated by the TFLite converter?

In this recipe, we will quantize the model with the TFLite converter and show how to perform this accuracy evaluation on the `test` dataset with the **TFLite Python interpreter**. After the accuracy evaluation, we will convert the TFLite model to a C-byte array.

The following Colab file (the *Evaluating the accuracy of the quantized model* section) contains the code referred to in this recipe:

*   `prepare_model.ipynb`:

    `https://github.com/PacktPublishing/TinyML-Cookbook/blob/main/Chapter07/ColabNotebooks/prepare_model.ipynb`.

Getting ready

In this section, we will explain why the accuracy of the TFLite model may differ from the trained one.

As we know, the trained model needs to be converted to a more compact and lightweight representation before being deployed on a resource-constrained device such as a microcontroller.

Quantization is the essential part of this step to make the model small and improve the inference performance. However, post-training quantization may change the model accuracy because of the arithmetic operations at a lower precision. Therefore, it is crucial to check whether the accuracy of the generated `.tflite` model is within an acceptable range before deploying it into the target device.

Unfortunately, TFLite does not provide a Python tool for the model accuracy evaluation. Hence, we will use the TFLite Python interpreter to accomplish this task. The interpreter will allow us to feed the input data to the network and read the classification result. The accuracy will be reported as the fraction of samples correctly classified from the test dataset.

How to do it...

Follow these steps to evaluate the accuracy of the quantized CIFAR-10 model on the test dataset:

1. Select a few hundred samples from the `train` dataset to calibrate the quantization:

    ```
    cifar_ds = tf.data.Dataset.from_tensor_slices(train_
    images).batch(1)
    def representative_data_gen():
        for i_value in cifar_ds.take(100):
            i_value_f32 = tf.dtypes.cast(
    i_value, tf.float32)
            yield [i_value_f32]
    ```

    The TFLite converter uses the `representative` dataset to estimate the quantization parameters.

2. Initialize the TFLite converter to perform the 8-bit quantization:

    ```
    tflite_conv = tf.lite.TFLiteConverter.from_saved_
    model("cifar10")
    tflite_conv.representative_dataset = tf.lite.
    RepresentativeDataset(representative_data_gen)
    tflite_conv.optimizations = [tf.lite.Optimize.DEFAULT]
    tflite_conv.target_spec.supported_ops = [tf.lite.OpsSet.
    TFLITE_BUILTINS_INT8]
    tflite_conv.inference_input_type = tf.int8
    tflite_conv.inference_output_type = tf.int8
    ```

    For quantizing the TF model to 8-bit, we import the `SavedModel` directory (`cifar10`) into the TFLite converter and enforce full integer quantization.

3. Convert the model to the TFLite file format and save it as `.tflite`:

    ```
    tfl_model = tfl_conv.convert()
    open("cifar10.tflite", "wb").write(tfl_model)
    ```

4. Evaluate the TFLite model size:

```
print(len(tfl_model))
```

The expected model size is 81,304 bytes. As you can see, the model can fit in 256 KB of program memory.

5. Evaluate the accuracy of the quantized model using the test dataset. To do so, start the TFLite interpreter and allocate the tensors:

```
tfl_inter = tf.lite.Interpreter(model_content=tfl_model)
tfl_inter.allocate_tensors()
```

Get the quantization parameters of the input and output nodes:

```
i_details = tfl_inter.get_input_details()[0]
o_details = tfl_inter.get_output_details()[0]
i_quant = i_details["quantization_parameters"]
i_scale      = i_quant['scales'][0]
i_zero_point = i_quant['zero_points'][0]
o_scale      = o_quant['scales'][0]
o_zero_point = o_quant['zero_points'][0]
```

Initialize a variable to zero (num_correct_samples) to keep track of the correct classifications:

```
num_correct_samples = 0
num_total_samples   = len(list(test_imgs))
```

Iterate over the test samples:

```
for i_value, o_value in zip(test_imgs, test_lbls):
    input_data = i_value.reshape((1, 32, 32, 3))
    i_value_f32 = tf.dtypes.cast(input_data, tf.float32)
```

Quantize each test sample:

```
    i_value_f32 = i_value_f32 / i_scale + i_zero_point
    i_value_s8 = tf.cast(i_value_f32, dtype=tf.int8)
```

Initialize the input node with the quantized sample and start the inference:

```
    tfl_conv.set_tensor(i_details["index"], i_value_s8)
    tfl_conv.invoke()
```

Read the classification result and dequantize the output to a floating point:

```
o_pred = tfl_conv.get_tensor(o_details["index"])[0]
o_pred_f32 = (o_pred - o_zero_point) * o_scale
```

Compare the classification result with the expected output class:

```
if np.argmax(o_pred_f32) == o_value:
    num_correct_samples += 1
```

6. Print the accuracy of the quantized TFLite model:

```
print("Accuracy:", num_correct_samples/num_total_samples)
```

After a few minutes, the accuracy result will be printed in the output log. The expected accuracy should still be around 73%.

7. Convert the TFLite model to a C-byte array with xxd:

```
!apt-get update && apt-get -qq install xxd
!xxd -i cifar10.tflite > model.h
```

You can download the model.h and cifar10.tflite files from Colab's left pane.

Converting a NumPy image to a C-byte array

Our application will be running on a virtual platform with no access to a camera module. Therefore, we need to supply a valid test input image into our application to check whether the model works as expected.

In this recipe, we will get an image from the test dataset that must return a correct classification for the ship class. The sample will then be converted to an int8_t C array and saved as an input.h file.

The following Colab file (refer to the *Converting a NumPy image to a C-byte array* section) contains the code referred to in this recipe:

*   prepare_model.ipynb:

    https://github.com/PacktPublishing/TinyML-Cookbook/blob/main/Chapter07/ColabNotebooks/prepare_model.ipynb

Getting ready

To get ready for this recipe, we just need to know how to prepare the C file containing the input test image. The structure of this file is quite simple and reported in the following figure:

```
// Input image
int8_t g_test[] = {
// data
}

// Array size
const int g_test_len = 3072;

// Index label
const int g_test_ilabel = 8;
```

Figure 7.7 – The C header file structure for the input test image

As you can observe from the file structure, we only need an array and two variables to describe our input test sample, which are as follows:

- g_test: An int8_t array containing a ship image with the normalized and quantized pixel values. The pixels stored in the array (// **data**) should be comma-separated integer values.

- g_test_len: An integer variable for the array size. Since the input model is an RGB image with a 32 x 32 resolution, we expect an array with 3,072 int8_t elements.

- g_test_ilabel: An integer variable for the class index of the input test image. Since we have a ship image, the expected class index is eight.

The input image will be obtained from the test dataset. Therefore, we will need to implement a function in Python to convert an image stored in NumPy format to a C array.

How to do it...

Follow the these steps to generate a C header file containing a ship image from the test dataset:

1. Write a function to convert a 1D NumPy array of np.int8 values into a single string of comma-separated integer values:

```
def array_to_str(data):
    NUM_COLS = 12
```

```
        val_string = ''
        for i, val in enumerate(data):
            val_string += str(val)
            if (i + 1) < len(data):
                val_string += ','
            if (i + 1) % NUM_COLS == 0:
                val_string += '\n'
        return val_string
```

In the preceding code, the NUM_COLS variable limits the number of values on a single row. In our case, NUM_COLS is set to 12 so that we can add a newline character after every 12 values.

2. Write a function to generate a C header file containing the input test image stored in an int8_t array. To do so, you can have a template string with the following fields:

- The size of the array (size)

- The values to put in the array (data)

- The index of the class assigned to the input image (ilabel)

```
def gen_h_file(size, data, ilabel):
    str_out = f'int8_t g_test[] = '
    str_out += "\n{\n"
    str_out += f'{data}'
    str_out += '};\n'
    str_out += f"const int g_test_len = {size};\n"
    str_out += f"const int g_test_ilabel = {ilabel};\n"
    return str_out
```

As you can see from the preceding code, the function expects {data} to be a single string of comma-separated integer values.

3. Create a pandas DataFrame from the CIFAR-10 test dataset:

```
imgs = list(zip(test_imgs, test_lbls))
cols = [Image, 'Label']
df = pd.DataFrame(imgs, columns = cols)
```

4. Get only `ship` images from the pandas DataFrame:

```
cond = df['Label'] == 8
ship_samples = df[cond]
```

In the preceding code, 8 is the index for the `ship` class.

5. Iterate over the ship images and run the inference:

```
c_code = ""


for index, row in ship_samples.iterrows():
    i_value = np.asarray(row['Image'].tolist())
    o_value = np.asarray(row['Label'].tolist())
    o_pred_f32 = classify(i_value, o_value)
```

6. Check whether the classification returns a *ship*. If so, convert the input image into a C-byte array and exit the loop:

```
if np.argmax(o_pred_f32) == o_value:
    i_value_f32 = i_value / i_scale + i_zero_point
    i_value_s8  = i_value_f32.astype(dtype=np.uint8)
    i_value_s8  = i_value_s8.ravel()

    # Generate a string from NumPy array
    val_string = array_to_str(i_value_s8)

    # Generate the C header file
    c_code = gen_h_file(
    i_value_s8.size, val_string, "8")
    break
```

7. Save the generated code in the `input.h` file:

```
with open("input.h", 'w') as file:
    file.write(c_code)
```

You can download the `input.h` file containing the input test image from Colab's left pane.

Preparing the skeleton of the TFLu project

Only a few steps are separating us from the completion of this project. Now that we have the input test image, we can leave Colab's environment and focus on the application with the Zephyr OS.

In this recipe, we will prepare the skeleton of the TFLu project from the pre-built TFLu `hello_world` sample available in the Zephyr SDK.

The following C files contain the code referred to in this recipe:

- `main.c`, `main_functions.cc`, and `main_functions.h`:

  `https://github.com/PacktPublishing/TinyML-Cookbook/blob/ main/Chapter07/ZephyrProject/Skeleton`

Getting ready

This section aims to provide the basis for starting a new TFLu project with the Zephyr OS from scratch.

The easiest way to create a project is to copy and edit one of the pre-built samples for TFLu. The samples are available in the `~/zephyrproject/zephyr/samples/ modules/tflite-micro` folder. At the time of writing, there are two ready-to-use examples:

- `hello_world`: A sample showing the basics of TFLu to replicate a `sine` function: `https://docs.zephyrproject.org/latest/samples/modules/ tflite-micro/hello_world/README.html`

- `magic_wand`: A sample showing how to implement a TFLu application to recognize gestures with accelerometer data: `https://docs.zephyrproject. org/latest/samples/modules/tflite-micro/hello_world/ README.html`

In this recipe, we will base our application on the `hello_world` application, and the following screenshot shows what you should find in the sample directory:

Figure 7.8 – The contents of the hello_world sample folder

The `hello_world` folder contains three subfolders, but only `src/` is of interest to us because it contains the source code for the application. However, not all the files in `src/` are essential for our project. For example, `assert.cc`, `constants.h`, `constants.c`, `model.cc`, `model.h`, `output_handler.cc`, and `output_handler.h` are only required for the sine wave sample application. Therefore, the only C files needed for a new TFLu project are as follows:

- `main.c`: This file contains the standard C/C++ `main()` function, responsible for starting and terminating the program execution. The `main()` function consists of a `setup()` function called once and a `loop()` function executed 50 times. Therefore, the main function replicates more or less the behavior of an Arduino program.

- `main_functions.h` and `main_functions.cc`: These files contain the declaration and definition of the `setup()` and `loop()` functions.

In the end, the `CMakeList.txt` and `prj.conf` files in the `hello_world` directory are required for building the application. We will learn more about these files in the last recipe of this chapter.

How to do it...

Open the terminal and follow these steps to create a new TFLu project:

1. Navigate into the `~/zephyrproject/zephyr/samples/modules/tflite-micro/` directory and create a new folder named `cifar10`:

   ```
   $ cd ~/zephyrproject/zephyr/samples/modules/tflite-micro/
   $ mkdir cifar10
   ```

2. Copy the content of the `hello_world` directory to `cifar10`:

   ```
   $ cp -r hello_world/* cifar10
   ```

3. Navigate into the `cifar10` directory and remove the following files from the `src/` directory:

   `constants.h`, `constants.c`, `model.c`, `model.h`, `output_handler.cc`, `output_handler.h`, and `assert.cc`

   These files can be removed because they are only required for the sine wave sample application, as explained in the *Getting ready* section of this recipe.

4. Copy the `model.h` and `input.h` files generated in the previous two recipes into the `cifar10/src` folder.

    Once you have copied the files, the `cifar10/src` folder should contain the following files:

Figure 7.9 – The contents of the hello_word/src folder

Before continuing, ensure you have the files listed in the previous screenshot.

Now, open your default C editor (for example, **Vim**) to make some code changes in the `main.c` and `main_functions.cc` files.

5. Open the `main.c` file and replace `for (int i = 0; i < NUM_LOOPS; i++)` with `while(true)`. The code in the `main.c` file should become the following:

```
int main(int argc, char *argv[]) {
    setup();
    while(true) {
        loop();
    }
    return 0;
}
```

This preceding code replicates exactly the behavior of an Arduino sketch, where `setup()` is called once and `loop()` is repeated indefinitely.

6. Open `main_functions.cc` and remove the following:

    *   `constants.h` and `output_handler.h` from the list of header files.

    *   The `inference_count` variable and all its usages. This variable will not be required in our application.

    *   The code within the `loop()` function.

    Next, replace `g_model` with the name of the array in `model.h`. The `g_model` variable is used when calling `tflite::GetModel()`.

Now that we have the project structure ready, we can finally implement our application.

Building and running the TFLu application on QEMU

The skeleton of our Zephyr project is ready, so we just need to finalize our application to classify our input test image.

In this recipe, we will see how to build the TFLu application and run the program on the emulated Arm Cortex-M3-based microcontroller.

The following C files contain the code referred to in this recipe:

- `main.c`, `main_functions.cc`, and `main_functions.h`:

  `https://github.com/PacktPublishing/TinyML-Cookbook/blob/main/Chapter07/ZephyrProject/CIFAR10`

Getting ready

Most of the ingredients required for developing this recipe are related to TFLu and have already been discussed in earlier chapters, such as *Chapter 3, Building a Weather Station with TensorFlow Lite for Microcontrollers*, or *Chapter 5, Indoor Scene Classification with TensorFlow Lite for Microcontrollers and the Arduino Nano*. However, there is one small detail of TFLu that has a big impact on the program memory usage that we haven't discussed yet.

In this section, we will talk about the `tflite::MicroMutableOpResolver` interface.

As we know from our previous projects, the TFLu interpreter is responsible for preparing the computation for a given model. One of the things that the interpreter needs to know is the function pointer for each operator to run. So far, we have provided this information with `tflite::AllOpsResolver`. However, `tflite::AllOpsResolver` is not recommended because of the heavy program memory usage. For example, this interface will prevent building our application because of the low program memory capacity on the target device. Therefore, TFLu offers `tflite::MicroMutableOpResolver`, an alternative and more efficient interface to load only the operators required by the model. To know which different operators the model needs, you can visualize the TFLite model (`.tflite`) file with the **Netron** web application (`https://netron.app/`).

How to do it...

Let's start this recipe by visualizing the architecture of our TFLite CIFAR-10 model file (`cifar10.tflite`) with Netron.

The following screenshot shows a slice of our model visualized with this tool:

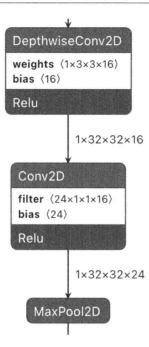

Figure 7.10 – A visualization of a slice of the CIFAR-10 model in Netron (courtesy of netron.app)

Inspecting the model with Netron, we can see that the model only uses five operators: **Conv2D**, **DepthwiseConv2D**, **MaxPool2D**, **Reshape**, and **FullyConnected**. This information will be used to initialize tflite::MicroMutableOpResolver.

Now, open your default C editor and open the main_functions.cc file.

Follow these steps to build the TFLu application:

1. Use the #include directives to add the header file of the input test image (input.h):

    ```
    #include "input.h"
    ```

2. Increase the arena size (tensor_arena_size) to 52,000:

    ```
    constexpr int tensor_arena_size = 52000;
    ```

> **Note**
>
> The original variable name for the tensor arena is kTensorArenaSize. To keep consistency with the lower_case naming convention used in the book, we have renamed this variable to tensor_arena_size.

The TFLu tensor arena is the portion of memory allocated by the user to accommodate the network input, output, intermediate tensors, and other data structures required by TFLu. The arena size should be a multiple of 16 to have a 16-byte data alignment.

As we have seen from the design of the CIFAR-10 model, the expected RAM usage for the model inference is in the order of 44 KB. Therefore, 52,000 bytes is okay for our case because it is greater than 44 KB, a multiple of 16, and less than 64 KB, the maximum RAM capacity.

3. Replace `uint8_t tensor_arena[tensor_arena_size]` with `uint8_t *tensor_arena = nullptr`:

    ```
    uint8_t *tensor_arena = nullptr;
    ```

    The tensor arena is too big for being placed in the stack. Therefore, we should dynamically allocate this memory in the `setup()` function.

4. Declare a global `tflite::MicroMutableOpResolver` object to load only the operations needed for running the CIFAR-10 model:

    ```
    tflite::MicroMutableOpResolver<5> resolver;
    ```

    This object is created by providing the maximum number of different operations that the model requires as a template argument.

5. Declare two global variables for the output quantization parameters:

    ```
    float o_scale = 0.0f;
    int32_t o_zero_point = 0;
    ```

6. In the `setup()` function, remove the instantiation of the `tflite::AllOpsResolver` object. Next, load the operators used by the model into the `tflite::MicroMutableOpResolver` object (`resolver`) before the initialization of the TFLu interpreter:

    ```
    resolver.AddConv2D();
    resolver.AddDepthwiseConv2D();
    resolver.AddMaxPool2D();
    resolver.AddReshape();
    resolver.AddFullyConnected();
    static tflite::MicroInterpreter static_interpreter(
    model, resolver, tensor_arena, tensor_arena_size,
    error_reporter);
    interpreter = &static_interpreter;
    ```

7. In the `setup()` function, get the output quantization parameters from the output tensor:

```
const auto* o_quantization = reinterpret_cast<TfLiteAffin
eQuantization*>(output->quantization.params);
o_scale      = o_quantization->scale->data[0];
o_zero_point = o_quantization->zero_point->data[0];
```

8. In the `loop()` function, initialize the input tensor with the content of the input test image:

```
for(int i = 0; i < g_test_len; i++) {
        input->data.int8[i] = g_test[i];
}
```

Next, run the inference:

```
TfLiteStatus invoke_status = interpreter->Invoke();
```

9. After the model inference, return the output class with the highest score:

```
size_t ix_max = 0;
float  pb_max = 0;
for (size_t ix = 0; ix < 10; ix++) {
   int8_t out_val = output->data.int8[ix];
   float  pb = ((float)out_val - o_zero_point) * o_
scale;
   if(pb > pb_max) {
        ix_max = ix;
        pb_max = pb;
   }
}
```

The preceding code iterates over the quantized output values and returns the class (`ix_max`) with the highest score.

10. In the end, check whether the classification result (`ix_max`) is equal to the label index assigned to the input test image (`g_test_label`):

```
if(ix_max == g_test_ilabel) {
```

If so, print `CORRECT classification!` and return the classification result:

```
    static const char *label[] = {"airplane",
"automobile", "bird", "cat", "deer", "dog", "frog",
"horse", "ship", "truck"};
    printf("CORRECT classification! %s\n",
label[ix_max]);
    while(1);
}
```

Now, open the terminal, and use the following command to build the project for `qemu_cortex_m3`:

```
$ cd ~/zephyrproject/zephyr/samples/modules/tflite-micro/
cifar10
$ west build -b qemu_cortex_m3 .
```

After a few seconds, the `west` tool should display the following output in the terminal, confirming that the program has been successfully compiled:

```
Memory region         Used Size  Region Size  %age Used
           FLASH:      137668 B       256 KB      52.52%
            SRAM:        4536 B        64 KB       6.92%
        IDT_LIST:          0 GB         2 KB       0.00%
```

Figure 7.11 – The memory usage summary

From the summary generated by the `west` tool, you can see that our CIFAR-10-based application uses **52.57%** of program memory (**FLASH**) and **6.92%** of RAM (**SRAM**). However, we should not be misled by RAM usage. In fact, the summary does not consider the memory that we allocate dynamically. Therefore, to the 4,536 bytes statically allocated in RAM, we should add the 52,000 bytes of the tensor arena, which brings us to 88% of RAM utilization.

Now that the application is built, we can run it on the virtual platform with the following command:

```
$ west build -t run
```

The `west` tool will boot the virtual device and return the following output, confirming that the model correctly classified the image as a ship:

```
-- west build: running target run
[1/1] To exit from QEMU enter: 'CTRL+a, x'[QEMU] CPU: cortex-m3
qemu-system-arm: warning: nic stellaris_enet.0 has no peer
Timer with period zero, disabling
*** Booting Zephyr OS build v2.7.99-1639-g73a957e4b316  ***
CORRECT classification!: ship
```

Figure 7.12 – The expected output after the model inference

As you can see from the preceding screenshot, the virtual device outputs the **CORRECT classification** message, confirming the successful execution of our tiny CIFAR-10 model!

8

Toward the Next TinyML Generation with microNPU

Here, we are at the last stop of our journey into the world of TinyML. Although this chapter may look like the end, it is actually the beginning of something new and extraordinary for **Machine Learning** (**ML**) at the very edge. In our journey, we have learned how vital power consumption is for effective and long-lasting TinyML applications. However, computing capacity is the key to unlocking new use cases and making the "things" around us even more intelligent. For this reason, a new, advanced processor has been designed to extend the computational power and energy efficiency of ML workloads. This processor is the **Micro-Neural Processing Unit** (**microNPU**).

In this final chapter, we will discover how to run a quantized **CIFAR-10** model on a virtual **Arm Ethos-U55** microNPU.

We will start this chapter by learning how this processor works and installing the software dependencies to build and run the model on the Arm **Corstone-300 Fixed Virtual Platform** (**Corstone-300 FVP**). Next, we will use the **TVM** compiler to convert the pretrained **TensorFlow Lite** (**TFLite**) model into C/C++ code. In the end, we will show how to compile and deploy the code generated by TVM into Corstone-300 FVP to perform the inference with the Ethos-U55 microNPU.

The purpose of this chapter is to get familiar with the Arm Ethos-U55 microNPU, a new class of processor for ML workloads on microcontrollers.

> **Attention**
>
> Since some of the tools presented in this chapter are still under heavy development, there is the possibility that some instructions and tools may change in the future. Therefore, we recommend checking out the software library repositories using the Git commit hash reported.

In this chapter, we're going to implement the following recipes:

- Setting up Arm Corstone-300 FVP
- Installing TVM with Arm Ethos-U support
- Installing the Arm toolchain and Ethos-U driver stack
- Generating C code with TVM
- Generating C-byte arrays for input, output, and labels
- Building and running the model on Arm Ethos-U55

Technical requirements

To complete all the practical recipes of this chapter, we will need the following:

- Laptop/PC with Ubuntu 18.04+ on x86-64

The source code and additional material are available in `Chapter08` folder (`https://github.com/PacktPublishing/TinyML-Cookbook/tree/main/Chapter08`).

Setting up Arm Corstone-300 FVP

Arm Ethos-U55 is the first microNPU designed by Arm to extend the ML capabilities of Cortex-M-based microcontrollers. Unfortunately, there is no hardware availability with this new processor at the time of writing. However, Arm offers a free **Fixed Virtual Platform** (**FVP**) based on the Arm Corstone-300 system to quickly experiment with ML models on this processor without the need for physical devices.

In this recipe, we will give more details on the computational capabilities of the Arm Ethos-U55 microNPU and install the Corstone-300 FVP.

Getting ready

Let's start this first recipe by introducing Corstone-300 FVP and Ethos-U55 microNPU.

Corstone-300 FVP (`https://developer.arm.com/tools-and-software/open-source-software/arm-platforms-software/arm-ecosystem-fvps`) is a virtual platform based on an Arm Cortex-M55 CPU and Ethos-U55 microNPU.

Arm Ethos-U55 (`https://www.arm.com/products/silicon-ip-cpu/ethos/ethos-u55`) is a processor for ML inference that works alongside a Cortex-M CPU, as shown in the following diagram:

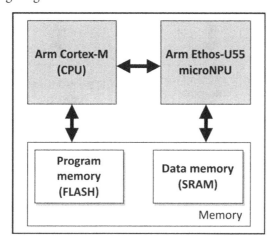

Figure 8.1 – Microcontroller with an Arm Cortex-M CPU and Ethos-U55 microNPU

The role of the CPU is to drive the ML workload on the microNPU, which independently runs the model inference. Arm Ethos-U55 has been designed to efficiently compute most of the elementary operations that we may find in quantized 8-bit/16-bit neural networks, such as the **Multiply and Accumulate** (**MAC**) at the heart of convolution, fully connected, and depthwise convolution layers.

The following table reports some of the operators supported by Arm Ethos-U55:

Convolution 2D	Depthwise convolution 2D	De-convolution	Max pooling
Average pooling	Fully connected	LSTM/GRU	Add/Sub/Mul
Softmax	Relu/Relu6/Tanh/Sigmoid	Reshape	many more...

Figure 8.2 – Table reporting some of the operators supported by the Arm Ethos-U55 microNPU

From a microcontroller programming perspective, we still need to provide the model as a C/C++ program and upload it into the microcontroller. Furthermore, the weights, biases, and quantization parameters can still be stored in program memory, while the input and output tensors are stored in SRAM, as shown in the following figure:

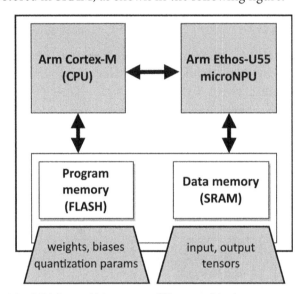

Figure 8.3 – Weights and biases can still be stored in the program memory

Therefore, nothing changes from what we have seen in the previous chapters regarding memory locations for the ML parameters and the input/output tensors. However, what differs from the traditional computation on a Cortex-M CPU is how we program the model inference on Arm Ethos-U55. When running the model inference on a microNPU, the program is a sequence of commands (that is, a **command stream**) to tell the processor the operations to execute and where to read/write data from/to memory.

Once the program has been uploaded into the microcontroller, we can offload the computation on the microNPU by specifying the memory location of the command stream and the region of SRAM dedicated to the input and output tensors. Next, Arm Ethos-U55 runs all commands independently, writing the output in the user-defined data memory region and sending an interrupt on completion. The CPU can use the interrupt to know when to read the output data.

How to do it...

Open the terminal and create a new folder named project_npu in the home directory (~/):

```
$ cd ~/ && mkdir project_npu
```

Enter the `~/project_npu` folder and create three folders named `binaries`, `src`, and `sw_libs`:

```
$ cd ~/project_npu
$ mkdir binaries
$ mkdir src
$ mkdir sw_libs
```

These three folders will contain the following:

- The binaries to build and run the application on Arm Corstone-300 FVP (`binaries/`)
- The application source code (`src/`)
- The software library dependencies for our project (`sw_libs/`)

Now, take the following steps to install Arm Corstone-300 on an Ubuntu/Linux machine:

1. Open the web browser and go to **Arm Ecosystem FVPs** (`https://developer.arm.com/tools-and-software/open-source-software/arm-platforms-software/arm-ecosystem-fvps`).

2. Click on **Corstone-300 Ecosystem FVPs** and then click on the **Download Linux** button, as shown in the following screenshot:

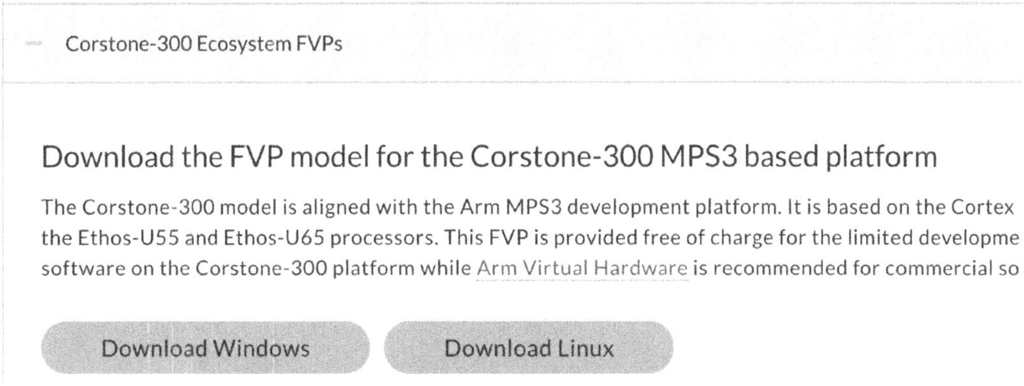

Corstone-300 Ecosystem FVPs

Download the FVP model for the Corstone-300 MPS3 based platform

The Corstone-300 model is aligned with the Arm MPS3 development platform. It is based on the Cortex the Ethos-U55 and Ethos-U65 processors. This FVP is provided free of charge for the limited developme software on the Corstone-300 platform while Arm Virtual Hardware is recommended for commercial so

Download Windows   Download Linux

Figure 8.4 – Download Linux button for Corstone-300 FVP

Download the `.tgz` file and extract the `FVP_Corstone_SSE-300.sh` script.

3. Open Terminal again and make the `FVP_Corstone_SSE-300.sh` executable:

```
$ chmod +x FVP_Corstone_SSE-300.sh
```

4. Execute the `FVP_Corstone_SSE-300.sh` script:

```
$ ./FVP_Corstone_SSE-300.sh
```

Follow the instructions on Terminal to install the binaries for Corstone-300 FVP under the `~/project_npu/binaries` folder. To do so, enter `~/project_npu/binaries/FVP_Corstone_SSE-300` when the **Where would you like to install to?** question is prompted.

5. Update the `$PATH` environment variable to store the path of the Corstone-300 binaries. To do so, open the `.bashrc` file with any text editor (for example, **gedit**):

```
$ gedit ~/.bashrc
```

Then, add the following line at the bottom of the file:

```
export PATH=~/project_npu/binaries/FVP_Corstone_SSE-300/
models/Linux64_GCC-6.4:$PATH
```

The preceding line updates the `$PATH` environment variable with the location of the Corstone-300 binaries.

Now, save and close the file.

6. Reload the `.bashrc` file in Terminal:

```
$ source ~/.bashrc
```

Alternatively to using the `source` command, you can simply close and re-open the terminal.

7. Check whether the Corstone-300 binaries are installed by printing the version info of `FVP_Corstone_SSE_Ethos-U55`:

```
$ FVP_Corstone_SSE_Ethos-U55 --version
```

If the `$PATH` environment variable has been updated successfully, the preceding command should return the Corstone-300 version in Terminal, as shown in the following figure:

```
~ $FVP_Corstone_SSE-300_Ethos-U55 --version

Fast Models [11.15.24 (Aug 17 2021)]
Copyright 2000-2021 ARM Limited.
All Rights Reserved.
```

Figure 8.5 – Output message displayed after the command

As shown in the previous figure, the command returns the version of the Corstone-300 executable.

The virtual hardware with Arm Cortex-M55 and Ethos-U55 is now installed and ready to be used.

Installing TVM with Arm Ethos-U support

In the previous recipe, we briefly talked about the Ethos-U55 program, a command stream used to instruct the operations to execute on the microNPU. However, how is the command stream generated? In this chapter, we will be using TVM, a **Deep Learning (DL)** compiler technology that aims to generate C code from an ML model for a specific target device.

In this recipe, we will learn what TVM is by preparing the development environment that we will use later on in the chapter.

Getting ready

The goal of this recipe is to install the TVM compiler from the source. The installation needs the following prerequisites:

- CMake 3.5.0 or later

- C++ compiler with C++14 support (for example, g++ 5 or later)

- LLVM 4.0 or later

- Python 3.7 or Python 3.8

Before getting started, we recommend that you have the Python **virtual environment (virtualenv)** tool installed to create an isolated Python environment. You can refer to *Chapter 7, Running a Tiny CIFAR-10 Model on a Virtual Platform with the Zephyr OS*, to learn how to install and activate the virtual environment.

However, before showing how to install TVM straight away, we want to give you an overview of the main characteristics of this technology since you may not have prior knowledge about this tool and DL compiler stacks.

Learning the motivation behind TVM

TensorFlow Lite for Microcontrollers (TFLu) is the software library that made the creation of our DL applications possible in the previous chapters. TFLu takes advantage of vendor-specific optimized operator libraries (**performance libraries**) to execute the model on the target device efficiently. For example, TFLu can delegate the computation to the **CMSIS-NN** library, which yields superior performance and low memory usage on Arm Cortex-M-based microcontrollers.

Generally, these performance libraries provide a collection of handwritten operators optimized per processor architecture (for example, Arm Cortex-M0 or Cortex-M4) and underlying hardware capabilities. With the need to bring DL to a wide range of devices and the numerous functions to optimize, the significant engineering effort required to develop these libraries becomes clear. Therefore, driven by the necessity to bring efficient DL accelerations on various platforms, a research team at the University of Washington developed TVM, a compiler stack to generate optimized code from DL models.

Learning how TVM optimizes the model inference

Apache TVM (`https://tvm.apache.org/`) is a full-fledged open source compiler that aims to translate DL models (for example, TFLite models) to optimized code for any processor types:

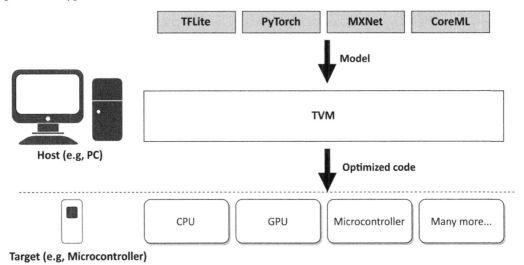

Figure 8.6 – TVM generates optimized code from a pretrained model

The significant benefit of having a compiler stack is getting efficient code automatically for new DL accelerators without being an expert on performance optimizations.

As shown in the previous diagram, TVM accepts a pretrained model in various formats (for example, TFLite and PyTorch) and performs the code optimizations in two main steps, as shown in the following diagram:

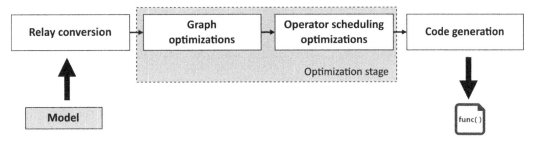

Figure 8.7 – Main optimization stages in TVM

The previous diagram shows that TVM first converts the input model into an internal high-level neural network language (**relay**). Next, the compiler does the first optimization step at the model level (**graph optimizations**). **Fusion** is the common optimization technique applied at the graph level, which aims to join two or more operators together to improve computational efficiency. When TVM spots fusion patterns, it transforms the model by replacing the original operators with the new fused one, as shown in the following example:

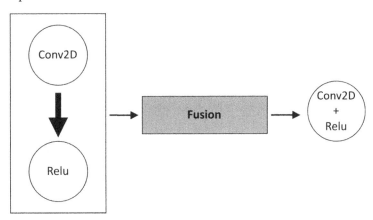

Figure 8.8 – Conv2D + ReLU fusion

In the preceding example, fusion aims to create a single operator for **Convolution 2D** (**Conv2D**) and **ReLU** activation instead of having two separate ones as in the original model.

When fusion happens, generally, the computation time decreases because the code has fewer arithmetic instructions and memory transfers from/to main memory.

The second optimization step performed by TVM is at the operator level (**operator scheduling**), which aims to find the most efficient way to execute each operator on the target device. This optimization is at the code level and affects the adoption of computing strategies such as tiling, unrolling, and vectorization. As we can imagine, the best compute method will depend on the target platform.

> **Note**
>
> What we have just described are just the main points to give you the big picture of how this compiler technology works. For more information about TVM architecture, please refer to the TVM introduction guide, which provides a step-by-step explanation of the model optimizations: `https://tvm.apache.org/docs/tutorial/introduction.html#sphx-glr-tutorial-introduction-py`.

How to do it...

The installation of TVM is made up of three parts:

1. Installing TVM prerequisites
2. Building the TVM C++ library from source
3. Setting up the Python environment

With the following steps, we will explain how to install TVM:

1. Use the Ubuntu **Advanced Packaging Tool** (**APT**) to install the required TVM dependencies:

   ```
   $ sudo apt-get install -y python3 python3-dev python3-
   setuptools gcc libtinfo-dev zlib1g-dev build-essential
   cmake libedit-dev libxml2-dev llvm-dev
   ```

   Verify the Python, CMake, g++, and `llvm-config` versions:

   ```
   $ python --version && cmake --version && g++ --version &&
   llvm-config --version
   ```

   Check whether the versions satisfy the minimum required version for TVM, reported in the *Getting ready* section. If not, you can refer to the following links to update their versions manually:

   - CMake: `https://cmake.org/download/`
   - LLVM: `https://apt.llvm.org/`
   - g++: `https://gcc.gnu.org/`
   - Python: `https://www.python.org/downloads/`

2. Enter the ~/project_npu folder and clone the TVM source code from the GitHub repository:

   ```
   $ git clone --recursive https://github.com/apache/tvm tvm
   ```

3. Enter the tvm/ folder and make TVM point to the dbfbd164c3 commit:

```
$ cd ~/project_npu/tvm
$ git checkout dbfbd164c3
```

4. Create a new directory named build inside the tvm/ folder:

```
$ mkdir build
```

5. Copy the cmake/config.cmake file to the build/ directory:

```
$ cp cmake/config.cmake build
```

6. Edit the build/config.cmake file to enable **microTVM**, **Ethos-U support**, and **LLVM**. To do so, you must have set(USE_MICRO ON), set(USE_LLVM ON), and set(USE_ETHOSU ON) in build/config.cmake. As we will see later in this chapter, microTVM is an extension of TVM for microcontroller platforms.

7. Build the TVM C++ library from the source:

```
$ cd build
$ cmake ..
$ make -j8
```

We recommend specifying the -j flag to run the building process simultaneously on different jobs. The number of jobs should be set accordingly with the number of cores available in the system, for example, 8 for a system with eight cores.

8. Update the $PYTHONPATH environment variable to tell Python where to locate the library built in the previous step. To do so, open the .bashrc file with any text editor (for example, gedit):

```
$ gedit ~/.bashrc
```

9. Add the following line at the bottom of the file:

```
export PYTHONPATH=~/project_npu/tvm/python:${PYTHONPATH}
```

Save and close the file once you have updated the $PATH environment variable.

10. Reload the .bashrc file:

```
$ source ~/.bashrc
```

If you had virtualenv activated in the same shell, start the Python virtual environment again.

11. Check whether Python is correctly locating the TVM Python library in the ~/ project_npu/tvm/python directory:

```
$ python -c "import sys; print(sys.path)"
```

The preceding code prints the list of directories that the Python interpreter inspects to search modules. Since sys.path is initialized from PYTHONPATH, you should see the ~/project_npu/tvm/python path from the list of directories printed in the console.

12. Install the necessary Python dependencies for TVM:

```
$ pip3 install --user numpy decorator attrs scipy
```

13. Check whether TVM is correctly installed:

```
$ python -c "import tvm; print('HELLO WORLD,')"
```

The preceding code should print HELLO WORLD in the output terminal.

14. Install the Python dependencies listed in ~/project_npu/tvm/apps/ microtvm/ethosu/requirements.txt:

```
$ cd ~/project_npu/tvm/apps/microtvm/ethosu
$ pip3 install -r requirements.txt
```

TVM requires some of the dependencies installed with this step to generate code for the Ethos-U55 microNPU.

TVM can now generate C code for Cortex-M CPUs with an Ethos-U microNPU.

Installing the Arm toolchain and Ethos-U driver stack

TVM generates C code for the target device provided using the TFLite model as input. However, the generated source code needs to be compiled manually to run it on Corstone-300 FVP. Furthermore, the Cortex-M55 CPU needs additional software libraries to drive the computation on the Ethos-U55 microNPU.

In this recipe, we will install the Arm GCC toolchain to **cross-compile** the code for Arm Cortex-M55 and the remaining software libraries' dependencies required for our application.

Getting ready

In this section, we will give you an overview of the three remaining dependencies for our application: the **Arm GCC toolchain**, the **Ethos-U core driver**, and the **Ethos-U core platforms**.

Corstone-300 FVP is a virtual platform based on Arm Cortex-M55 and needs a dedicated compiler to build the application for this target device. The compiler is commonly called a cross-compiler because the target CPU (for example, Arm Cortex-M55) is different from the CPU of the computer building the application (for example, x86-64). To cross-compile for Arm Cortex-M55, we need the **GNU Arm Embedded toolchain** (`https://developer.arm.com/tools-and-software/open-source-software/developer-tools/gnu-toolchain/gnu-rm/downloads/product-release`), which offers a free collection of programming tools that includes the compiler, linker, debugger, and software libraries. The toolchain is available for various **Operating Systems** (**OSs**), such as Linux, Windows, and macOS.

The toolchain is not the only thing required, though. The Cortex-M55 CPU needs the **Arm Ethos-U core driver** (`https://review.mlplatform.org/plugins/gitiles/ml/ethos-u/ethos-u-core-driver/`) to offload the ML workload on Arm Ethos-U55. The Arm Ethos-U core driver offers an interface to execute command streams on the Ethos-U microNPU. The driver is OS-agnostic, which means that it does not use any OS primitives, such as queues or mutexes. Therefore, it can be cross-compiled for any supported Cortex-M CPU and work with any **Real-Time Operating System** (**RTOS**).

The last remaining library required for our application is the **Arm Ethos-U core platform** (`https://review.mlplatform.org/plugins/gitiles/ml/ethos-u/ethos-u-core-platform/`). This project primarily contains demonstrations to run ML workloads on Arm Ethos-U platforms, including Corstone-300 FVP. From this project, we will use the Makefile to build the application.

How to do it...

Open the terminal and take the following steps to install the GNU Arm Embedded toolchain and get the remaining software dependencies for our application:

1. Enter the `~/project_npu/binaries` folder and install the GNU Arm Embedded toolchain for Linux x86-64. To do so, create a new folder named `toolchain` in the `~/project_npu/binaries` directory:

    ```
    $ cd ~/project_npu/binaries
    $ mkdir toolchain
    ```

2. Download the GNU Arm Embedded toolchain. You can conveniently use the `curl`
    tool and uncompress the downloaded file into the `toolchain` folder:

```
$ gcc_arm='https://developer.arm.com/-/media/Files/
downloads/gnu-rm/10-2020q4/gcc-arm-none-eabi-10-2020-q4-
major-x86_64-linux.tar.bz2?revision=ca0cbf9c-9de2-491c-
ac48-898b5bbc0443&la=en&hash=68760A8AE66026BCF99F05AC017A
6A50C6FD832A'
```

```
$ curl --retry 64 -sSL ${gcc_arm} | \
tar -C toolchain --strip-components=1 -jx
```

> **Note**
>
> This operation can take some minutes, depending on the internet connection
> speed.

3. Open the `.bashrc` file with any text editor (for example, gedit):

```
$ gedit ~/.bashrc
```

4. Add the following line at the bottom of the file to include the toolchain path to the
    `$PATH` environment variable:

```
export PATH=~/project_npu/binaries/toolchain/gcc-arm-
none-eabi-10.3-2021.10/bin:$PATH
```

After updating the `$PATH` environment variable, save and close the file.

5. Reload the `.bashrc` file:

```
$ source ~/.bashrc
```

6. Check whether the GNU Arm Embedded toolchain is installed correctly by printing
    the list of supported CPUs:

```
$ arm-none-eabi-gcc -mcpu=.
```

The returned list of supported CPUs should include the Cortex-M55 CPU, as shown
in the following screenshot:

```
arm-none-eabi-gcc: note: valid arguments are: arm8 arm810 strongarm strongarm110 fa526
fa626 arm7tdmi arm7tdmi-s arm710t arm720t arm740t arm9 arm9tdmi arm920t arm920 arm922t
arm940t ep9312 arm10tdmi arm1020t arm9e arm946e-s arm966e-s arm968e-s arm10e arm1020e a
rm1022e xscale iwmmxt iwmmxt2 fa606te fa626te fmp626 fa726te arm926ej-s arm1026ej-s arm
1136j-s arm1136jf-s arm1176jz-s arm1176jzf-s mpcorenovfp mpcore arm1156t2-s arm1156t2f-
s cortex-m1 cortex-m0 cortex-m0plus cortex-m1.small-multiply cortex-m0.small-multiply c
ortex-m0plus.small-multiply generic-armv7-a cortex-a5 cortex-a7 cortex-a8 cortex-a9 cor
tex-a12 cortex-a15 cortex-a17 cortex-r4 cortex-r4f cortex-r5 cortex-r7 cortex-r8 cortex
-m7 cortex-m4 cortex-m3 marvell-pj4 cortex-a15.cortex-a7 cortex-a17.cortex-a7 cortex-a3
2 cortex-a35 cortex-a53 cortex-a57 cortex-a72 cortex-a73 exynos-m1 xgene1 cortex-a57.co
rtex-a53 cortex-a72.cortex-a53 cortex-a73.cortex-a35 cortex-a73.cortex-a53 cortex-a55 c
ortex-a75 cortex-a76 cortex-a76ae cortex-a77 neoverse-n1 cortex-a75.cortex-a55 cortex-a
76.cortex-a55 neoverse-v1 neoverse-n2 cortex-m23 cortex-m33 cortex-m35p cortex-m55 cort
ex-r52
```

Figure 8.9 – The list of supported CPUs should include cortex-m55

7. Enter the `~/project_npu/sw_libs` folder and clone the CMSIS library:

```
$ cd ~/project_npu/sw_libs
$ git clone "https://github.com/ARM-software/CMSIS_5.git"
cmsis
```

Next, check out the `5.8.0` release:

```
$ cd cmsis
$ git checkout -f tags/5.8.0
$ cd ..
```

8. Enter the `~/project_npu/sw_libs` folder and clone the Arm Ethos-U core driver:

```
$ cd ~/project_npu/sw_libs
$ git clone "https://review.mlplatform.org/ml/ethos-u/
ethos-u-core-driver" core_driver
```

Next, check out the `21.11` release:

```
$ cd core_driver
$ git checkout tags/21.11
$ cd ..
```

9. Clone the Arm Ethos-U core platform:

```
$ git clone "https://review.mlplatform.org/ml/ethos-u/
ethos-u-core-platform" core_platform
$ cd core_platform
```

Next, check out the `21.11` release:

```
$ git checkout tags/21.11
$ cd ..
```

Now, we are definitely ready to prepare our application and run it on Corstone-300 FVP!

Generating C code with TVM

Compiling the TFLite model to C code is straightforward with TVM. TVM only needs an input model, a target device, and a single command line to generate a TAR package with the generated C code.

In this recipe, we will show how to convert a pretrained CIFAR-10 model into C code with **microTVM**, an extension of TVM for microcontroller deployment.

The following Bash script contains the commands referred to in this recipe:

- `compile_model_microtvm.sh`:

  https://github.com/PacktPublishing/TinyML-Cookbook/blob/
  main/Chapter08/BashScripts/compile_model_microtvm.sh

Getting ready

In this section, we will examine how TVM can generate C code and explain what microTVM is.

TVM is a DL compiler technology that we can use in Python and in the same environment where we build, train, and quantize the model with TFLite. Although TVM natively offers a Python API, there is an alternative and more straightforward API that is based on a command-line interface: **TVMC**.

TVMC is a command-line driver that exposes the same features that TVM offers with the Python API but with the advantage of reducing the number of lines of code. Only a single command line will be required to compile the TFLite model to C code in our specific case.

At this point, you may wonder: where can we find the TVMC tool?

TVMC is part of TVM Python installation, and you will just need to execute `python -m tvm.driver.tvmc compile <options>` in your terminal to compile the TFLite model. The options required by the `compile` command will be presented in the *How to do it...* section.

> **Tip**
>
> To discover more about TVMC, we recommend reading the following documentation: `https://tvm.apache.org/docs/tutorial/tvmc_command_line_driver`.

Although we have said that we will generate C code from the model, traditionally, TVM produces the following output files:

- `.so`: A C++ library containing the optimized operators to execute the model. The TVM C++ runtime will be responsible for loading this library and running the inference on the target device.

- `.json`: A JSON file containing the computation graph and weights.

- `.params`: A file containing the parameters of the pretrained model.

Unfortunately, the preceding three files are not suitable for microcontroller deployment for the following reasons:

- Microcontrollers do not have the **Memory Management Unit** (**MMU**), so we cannot load dynamic libraries at runtime.

- The weights are stored in an external file (`.json`), which is not ideal on microcontrollers for two reasons: the former is that we may not have an OS that provides an API to read external files. The latter is that weights loaded from an external file go into SRAM, which is generally smaller than the program memory.

For the preceding reasons, an extension to TVM was proposed to produce a suitable output for microcontrollers: **microTVM**.

Running TVM on microcontrollers with microTVM

microTVM (`https://tvm.apache.org/docs/topic/microtvm/index.html`) is an extension of TVM, which provides an alternative output format that does not require an OS and dynamic memory allocation.

> **Note**
>
> Devices without an OS are commonly called **bare-metal** devices.

The output format we refer to is **Model Library Format** (**MLF**), a TAR package containing C code. Therefore, the code generated by TVM/microTVM will need to be integrated into the application and compiled for the specific target platform.

How to do it...

The following steps will show how to convert a pretrained CIFAR-10 quantized model into C code with TVM/microTVM:

1. Create a new folder named `build/` in the `~/project_npu/src` directory:

   ```
   $ cd ~/project_npu/src
   $ mkdir build
   ```

2. Download the pretrained CIFAR-10 quantized model from the *TinyML-Cookbook* GitHub repository: `https://github.com/PacktPublishing/TinyML-Cookbook/blob/main/Chapter08/cifar10_int8.tflite`.

   Alternatively, you can reuse the CIFAR-10 model you generated in *Chapter 7, Running a Tiny CIFAR-10 Model on a Virtual Platform with the Zephyr OS*.

   Save the model in the `~/project_npu/src/` folder.

3. Enter the `~/project_npu/src/` folder and compile the CIFAR-10 model into MLF with TVMC:

   ```
   $ cd ~/project_npu/src/
   $ python3 -m tvm.driver.tvmc compile \
   --target="ethos-u -accelerator_config=ethos-u55-256, c" \
   --target-c-mcpu=cortex-m55 \
   --runtime=crt \
   --executor=aot \
   --executor-aot-interface-api=c \
   --executor-aot-unpacked-api=1 \
   --pass-config tir.disable_vectorize=1 \
   --output-format=mlf \
   cifar10_int8.tflite
   ```

In the preceding code, we pass several arguments to TVMC's `compile` subcommand. Let's unpack the most important ones:

- `--target="ethos-u -accelerator_config=ethos-u55-256, c"`: This option specifies the target processors for the ML inference. In our case, we have two target processors: Arm Ethos-U55 and Cortex-M CPU. The primary target is the Ethos-U55 microNPU. As we know, the Ethos-U microNPU is a processor capable of performing MAC operations very efficiently. When passing `ethos-u55-256`, we tell TVM that the Ethos-U55 compute engine has 256 MACs. This value is not programmable by the user but fixed in hardware. Therefore, Corstone-300 FVP must use the same Ethos-U55 configuration to run the application properly. The other processor specified in the `-target` argument is the Cortex-M CPU through the c option. The CPU executes only the layers that cannot be offloaded on the microNPU.

- `--target-c-mcpu=cortex-m55`: This option tells the target CPU to execute the unsupported layers on the microNPU.

- `--runtime=crt`: This option specifies the runtime type. In this case, we must specify the C runtime (`crt`) since we will run the application on a bare-metal platform.

- `--executor=aot`: This option instructs microTVM to build the model graph **Ahead of Time (AoT)** rather than at **runtime**. In other words, it means that the application does not need to load the model during the program execution because the graph is already generated and known beforehand. This executor allows reducing SRAM usage.

- `--executor-aot-interface-api=c`: This option specifies the interface type for the AoT executor. We pass the c option because we generate C code.

- `--pass-config tir.disable_vectorize=1`: This option tells TVM to disable the code vectorization since C has no native vectorized types.

- `--output-format=mlf`: This option specifies the output generated by TVM. Since we want an MLF output, we must pass `mlf`.

- `cifar10_int8.tflite`: This is the input model to compile to C code.

After a few seconds, TVM will generate a TAR package file named `module.tar` and print the following output on the console:

```
./
./codegen/
./codegen/host/
./codegen/host/include/
./codegen/host/include/tvmgen_default.h
./codegen/host/src/
./codegen/host/src/default_lib2.c
./codegen/host/src/default_lib0.c
./codegen/host/src/default_lib1.c
./metadata.json
./parameters/
./parameters/default.params
./src/
./src/relay.txt
```

Figure 8.10 – TVM output after the code generation

The files and directories printed by TVM on the console are included in the `module.tar` file.

4. Untar the generated `module.tar` file into the `~/project_npu/src/build` folder:

```
$ tar -C build -xvf module.tar
```

Now, you should have the same files and directories listed by TVM in *Figure 8.10* in the `~/project_npu/src/build` directory.

Generating C-byte arrays for input, output, and labels

The C code produced by TVM does not include the input and output tensors because they need to be allocated explicitly by the user.

In this recipe, we will develop a Python script to generate three C-byte arrays containing the input and output tensors and labels required to report the classification result in the application. The input tensor will also be filled with a valid image to test the inference on a microNPU.

The following Python script contains the code referred to in this recipe:

- `prepare_assets.py`:

  `https://github.com/PacktPublishing/TinyML-Cookbook/blob/main/Chapter08/PythonScripts/prepare_assets.py`

Getting ready

To get ready with this recipe, we need to know how to structure the Python script for the C-byte array generation.

The Python script should produce a C header file for each C-byte array. The generated files must be saved in the `~/project_npu/src/include` folder and named as follows:

- `inputs.h`: Input tensor
- `outputs.h`: Output tensor
- `labels.h`: Labels

> **Important Note**
> The C header files must use the preceding filenames because our application will be based on a prebuilt example that expects these files.

To create the C-byte array for the input tensor, the script should accept the path to an image file as a command-line argument to fill the array with a valid image.

However, we cannot directly add the raw input image. As we know from *Chapter 7, Running a Tiny CIFAR-10 Model on a Virtual Platform with the Zephyr OS*, the CIFAR-10 model needs an RGB input image with 32x32 resolution with normalized and quantized pixel values. Therefore, the image needs to be preprocessed before storing it in the array.

The generation of the C-byte arrays for the output and labels is easier than the input one because of the following:

- The output array has 10 values of the `int8_t` type and can be initialized with all zeros.
- The labels array has 10 strings reporting the name of each class (`airplane`, `automobile`, `bird`, `cat`, `deer`, `dog`, `frog`, `horse`, `ship`, and `truck`).

As we mentioned in the first recipe of this chapter, the Cortex-M CPU needs to inform the Ethos-U55 microNPU of the location of the input and output tensors. However, not all parts of the memory system are accessible for reading and writing by the microNPU. Therefore, we need to pay attention to where we store these arrays. The following table gives us an overview of what memory Corstone-300 FVP has and which can be accessed by Arm Ethos-U55:

Memory	Size	microNPU access
ITCM	512KB	No
DTCM	512KB	No
SSE-300 SRAM	2MB	Yes
Data SRAM	2MB	Yes
DDR	32MB	Yes

Figure 8.11 – System memory on Corstone-300 FVP

As you can see from the preceding table, Ethos-U55 cannot access **Instruction Tightly Coupled Memory (ITCM)** and **Data Tightly Coupled Memory (DTCM)**, which are the program and data memory for the Cortex-M CPU.

If we do not explicitly define the memory storage for the input and output arrays, their contents could be placed in ITCM or DTCM. For example, if we initialize the input array with fixed values, the compiler may assume that it is constant data storage that can be placed in program memory. To ensure that the input and output tensors are in memory spaces accessible by the Ethos-U55 microNPU, we need to specify the **memory section attribute** when declaring the arrays. In this project, we will store the input and output tensors in DDR.

The following code shows how to place an $int8\_t$ array named K in the DDR storage with a 16-byte alignment on Corstone-300 FVP:

```
int8_t K[4] __attribute__((section("ethosu_scratch"),
aligned(16)));
```

The name passed into the __attribute__ section specification (ethosu_scratch) and the alignment (16) must match what is reported in the Linker script used to compile our application. In our case, we will be using the Linker file available at the following link: https://github.com/apache/tvm/blob/main/apps/microtvm/ethosu/corstone300.ld.

How to do it...

Before developing the Python script, let's extract the input quantization parameters from the CIFAR-10 model. You can simply use the **Netron** web application (`https://netron.app/`) for this purpose. On Netron, click on the **Open Model...** button and read the quantization parameters displayed for the first layer of the network, as shown in the following screenshot:

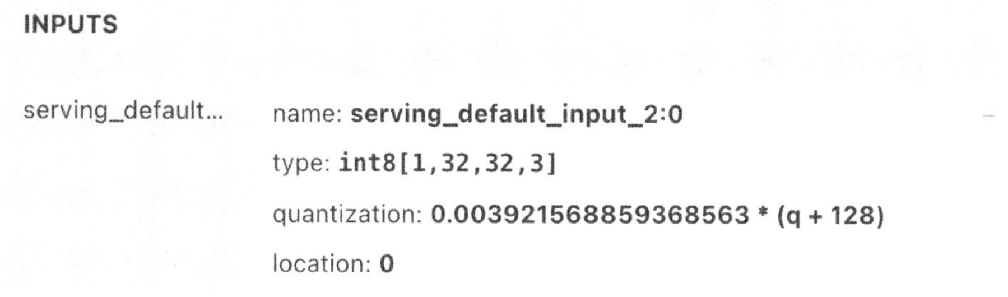

INPUTS

serving_default...   name: **serving_default_input_2:0**

type: **int8[1,32,32,3]**

quantization: **0.003921568859368563 * (q + 128)**

location: **0**

Figure 8.12 – Netron output for the first layer

The **quantization** field reports the formula to convert the 8-bit quantized value into a floating point, also described in *Chapter 3*, *Building a Weather Station with TensorFlow Lite for Microcontrollers*. Therefore, the scale parameter is **0.0039215688...** while the zero point is **-128**.

> **Attention**
>
> Pay attention to the zero point value. This parameter is not +128 because the 8-bit quantization formula subtracts the zero point from the integer 8-bit value.

Now, open your preferred Python editor and create a new file named `prepare_assets.py` in the `~/project_npu/src` folder.

Open the `prepare_assets.py` file and take the following steps to generate the C-byte arrays for the input, output, and labels:

1. Use two variables to keep the input quantization parameters of the CIFAR-10 model:

    ```
    input_quant_offset = -128
    input_quant_scale = 0.003921568859368563
    ```

2. Write a function to generate the content of the input and output C header files:

    ```
    def gen_c_array(name, size, data):
        str_out = "#include <tvmgen_default.h>\n"
    ```

```
    str_out += f"const unsigned int {name}_len = {size};\n"
    str_out += f'int8_t {name}[] __attribute__
((section("ethosu_scratch"), aligned(16))) = '
    str_out += "\n{\n"
    str_out += f'{data}'
    str_out += '\n};'
    return str_out
```

Since the format, type, and data storage are the same for the input and output tensors, we can have a template string to replace only the different parts, which are as follows:

- The name of the array (`name`)

- The size of the array (`size`)

- The values to store in the array (`data`)

As you can see from the preceding code, the function expects `{data}` to be a single string of integer values that are comma-separated.

3. Write a function to convert a 1D NumPy array of `np.int8` values into a single string of integer values that are comma-separated:

```
def array_to_str(data):
    NUM_COLS = 12
    val_string = ''
    for i, val in enumerate(data):
        val_string += str(val)
        if (i + 1) < len(data):
            val_string += ','
        if (i + 1) % NUM_COLS == 0:
            val_string += '\n'
    return val_string
```

In the preceding code, the `NUM_COLS` variable limits the number of values on a single row. In our case, `NUM_COLS` is set to `12` to add a new-line character after every 12 values.

4. Define the function for generating the input C-byte array:

```
def gen_input(img_file):
    img_path    = os.path.join(f"{img_file}")
    img_resized = Image.open(img_path).resize((32, 32))
```

In the previous code, the `gen_input()` function takes the path to the image file (`image_name`) as an argument. The image is then loaded and resized to 32x32 using the Python **Pillow** library.

5. Convert the resized image into a NumPy array of floating-point values:

```
img_data = np.asarray(img_resized).astype("float32")
```

Next, normalize and quantize the pixel values:

```
img_data /= 255.0
img_data /= input_quant_scale
img_data += input_quant_offset
```

6. Cast the quantized image to `np.int8` and convert it into a single string of integer values:

```
input_data = img_data.astype(np.int8)
input_data = input_data.ravel()
val_string = array_to_str(input_data)
```

In the previous code, we used the NumPy `ravel()` function to return a contiguous flatten array since the `array_to_str()` function only accepts the input array as a 1D object.

7. Generate the input C-byte array as a string and save it as the C header file (`inputs.h`) in the `include/` folder:

```
c_code = gen_c_array("input", input_data.size,
  val_string)
with open("include/inputs.h", 'w') as file:
    file.write(c_code)
```

8. Write a function to generate the C header file of the output tensor (`outputs.h`) in the `include/` folder:

```
def gen_output():
    output_data = np.zeros([10], np.int8)
    val_string = array_to_str(output_data)
    c_code = gen_c_array("output", output_data.size,
  val_string)
    with open("include/outputs.h", 'w') as file:
        file.write(c_code)
```

9. Write a function to generate the C header file of the labels (`labels.h`) in the `include/` folder:

```
def gen_labels():
  val_string = "char* labels[] = "
  val_string += '{"airplane", "automobile", "bird", '
  val_string += '"cat", "deer", "dog", '
  val_string += '"frog", "horse", "ship", "truck"};'
  with open("include/labels.h", 'w') as file:
    file.write(val_string)
```

10. Execute the `gen_input()`, `gen_output()`, and `gen_labels()` functions:

```
if __name__ == "__main__":
  gen_input(sys.argv[1])
  gen_output()
  gen_labels()
```

As you can see from the preceding code, we pass the first command-line argument to `gen_input()` to provide the path of the image file supplied by the user.

At this point, the Python script is ready, and we just need to finalize the application to run the CIFAR-10 model on the Ethos-U55 microNPU.

Building and running the model on Ethos-U55

Here we are. Just this recipe keeps us from completing this book. All the tools are installed, and the TFLite model is converted to C code, so where does that leave us? We still need to build an application to recognize images with the CIFAR-10 model. Once the application is ready, we need to compile it and run it on Corstone-300 FVP.

Although it seems there is still a lot to do, in this recipe, we will modify a prebuilt sample for the Ethos-U microNPU to simplify all the remaining technicalities.

In this recipe, we will show you how to modify the Ethos-U example available in TVM to run the CIFAR-10 inference. The application will then be compiled with the Makefile and Linker scripts provided in the prebuilt sample and finally executed on Corstone-300 FVP.

The following Bash script contains the commands referred to in this recipe:

- `build_and_run.sh`:

  https://github.com/PacktPublishing/TinyML-Cookbook/blob/main/Chapter08/BashScripts/build_and_run.sh

Getting ready

The prebuilt example considered in this recipe is available in the TVM source code within the `tvm/apps/microtvm/ethosu` folder. The sample is a demo to perform a single image classification inference with MobileNet V1 on Ethos-U55. Inside the sample folder, you'll find the following:

- Application source code in the `include/` and `src/` subdirectories

- Scripts to build the demo for Corstone-300 FVP (`Makefile`, `arm-none-eabi-gcc.cmake`, and `corstone300.ld`)

- Python scripts to generate the input, output, and label C header files (`convert_image.py` and `convert_labels.py`)

- Script to run the demo on Corstone-300 FVP (`run_demo.sh`)

From the preceding files, we just need the application source code and the scripts to build the demo.

How to do it...

Open the terminal and take the following steps to build and run the CIFAR-10 inference on Ethos-U55:

1. Copy the application source code from the `~/project_npu/tvm/apps/microtvm/ethosu/` sample folder to the `~/project_npu/src` directory:

   ```
   $ cp -r ~/project_npu/tvm/apps/microtvm/ethosu/include ~/project_npu/src/
   $ cp -r ~/project_npu/tvm/apps/microtvm/ethosu/src ~/project_npu/src/
   ```

2. Copy the build scripts (`Makefile`, `arm-none-eabi-gcc.cmake`, and `corstone300.ld`) from the `~/project_npu/tvm/apps/microtvm/ethosu/` sample folder to the `~/project_npu/src` directory:

   ```
   $ cp -r ~/project_npu/tvm/apps/microtvm/ethosu/Makefile ~/project_npu/src/
   $ cp -r ~/project_npu/tvm/apps/microtvm/ethosu/arm-none-eabi-gcc.cmake ~/project_npu/src/
   $ cp -r ~/project_npu/tvm/apps/microtvm/ethosu/corstone300.ld ~/project_npu/src/
   ```

3. Download the `ship.jpg` image from the *TinyML-Cookbook* GitHub repository: `https://github.com/PacktPublishing/TinyML-Cookbook/blob/main/Chapter08/ship.jpg` (source: Pixabay). Save the file in the `~/project_npu/src` folder.

4. Show the list of directories and files in the `~/project_npu/src` folder:

```
$ sudo apt-get install tree
$ cd ~/project_npu/src/
$ tree
```

The expected output in the terminal is shown in the following figure:

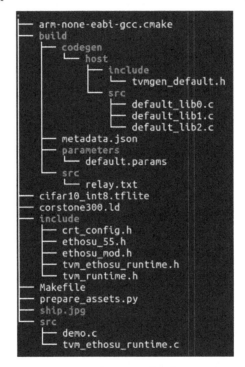

Figure 8.13 – Expected output after the tree command

Before continuing with the next step, check whether you have all the files and directories listed in the previous figure.

5. Use the `prepare_assets.py` Python script to generate the C header files for the input, output, and labels:

```
$ cd ~/project_npu/src
$ python3 prepare_assets.py ship.jpg
```

In the preceding code, we pass the `ship.jpg` file as a command-line argument to initialize the input tensor with the content of a ship image.

The Python script will save the C header files in the `~/project_npu/src/include` folder.

6. Open the `demo.c` file in the `~/project_npu/src/src` directory and go to line **46**. Replace the `.input` field's name with the name used by TVM in the `tvmgen_default_inputs` struct. The `tvmgen_default_inputs` struct is declared in the `~/project_npu/src/build/codegen/host/include/tvmgen_default.h` file. If you have downloaded the pretrained CIFAR-10 model from the *TinyML-Cookbook* GitHub repository, the name should be `serving_default_input_2_0`. Therefore, the `demo.c` file should have the following edit:

```
.serving_default_input_2_0 = input;
```

7. Open the `Makefile` script in the `~/project_npu/src` directory with any text editor. Go to line **25** and replace the `/opt/arm/ethosu` path with `${HOME}/project_npu/sw_libs`:

```
ETHOSU_PATH=${HOME}/project_npu/sw_libs
```

The preceding change is required to inform the `Makefile` script on the location of the software libraries installed in the *Installing the Arm toolchain and Ethos-U driver stack* recipe. Next, save and close the file.

8. Build the application using the `make` command:

```
$ make
```

The `Makefile` script will generate a binary named `demo` in the `~/project_npu/src/build` folder.

9. Run the `demo` executable on the Corstone-300 FVP:

```
$ FVP_Corstone_SSE-300_Ethos-U55 -C cpu0.CFGDTCMSZ=15 \
 -C cpu0.CFGITCMSZ=15 -C mps3_board.uart0.out_file=\"-\" \
 -C mps3_board.uart0.shutdown_tag=\"EXITTHESIM\" \
 -C mps3_board.visualisation.disable-visualisation=1 \
 -C mps3_board.telnetterminal0.start_telnet=0 \
 -C mps3_board.telnetterminal1.start_telnet=0 \
 -C mps3_board.telnetterminal2.start_telnet=0 \
 -C mps3_board.telnetterminal5.start_telnet=0 \
 -C ethosu.extra_args="--fast" \
 -C ethosu.num_macs=256 ./build/demo
```

From the previous command, pay attention to the `ethosu.num_macs=256` argument. This option refers to the number of MACs in the compute engine of the Ethos-U55 microNPU and must match what is specified in TVM when compiling the TFLite model.

Once you have launched the Corstone-300 command, you should see the following output in the console:

```
ethosu_invoke COMMAND_STREAM
handle_command_stream: cmd_stream=0x6100fc60, cms_length 534
QBASE=0x000000006100fc60, QSIZE=2136, base_pointer_offset=0x00000000
BASEP0=0x00000000610104c0
BASEP1=0x0000000060003010
BASEP2=0x0000000060003010
BASEP3=0x0000000060000010
BASEP4=0x0000000060000c10
CMD=0x00000005Interrupt. status=0xffff0022, qread=2136
CMD=0x00000006

CMD=0x0000000c
ethosu_release_driver - Driver 0x20000a18 released
10
The image has been classified as 'ship'
```

Figure 8.14 – Expected output after the CIFAR-10 inference

As reported at the bottom of the previous screenshot, the image is correctly classified as a ship.

And…that's it! With this last recipe but first application on Arm Ethos-U55, you are definitely ready to make even smarter TinyML solutions on Cortex-M-based microcontrollers!

Index

E

F

G

V

W

Y

Z

Packt.com

Subscribe to our online digital library for full access to over 7,000 books and videos, as well as industry leading tools to help you plan your personal development and advance your career. For more information, please visit our website.

Why subscribe?

- Spend less time learning and more time coding with practical eBooks and Videos from over 4,000 industry professionals

- Improve your learning with Skill Plans built especially for you

- Get a free eBook or video every month

- Fully searchable for easy access to vital information

- Copy and paste, print, and bookmark content

Did you know that Packt offers eBook versions of every book published, with PDF and ePub files available? You can upgrade to the eBook version at packt.com and as a print book customer, you are entitled to a discount on the eBook copy. Get in touch with us at customercare@packtpub.com for more details.

At www.packt.com, you can also read a collection of free technical articles, sign up for a range of free newsletters, and receive exclusive discounts and offers on Packt books and eBooks.

Other Books You May Enjoy

If you enjoyed this book, you may be interested in these other books by Packt:

Intelligent Workloads at the Edge

Indraneel Mitra, Ryan Burke

ISBN: 9781801811781

- Build an end-to-end IoT solution from the edge to the cloud
- Design and deploy multi-faceted intelligent solutions on the edge
- Process data at the edge through analytics and ML
- Package and optimize models for the edge using Amazon SageMaker
- Implement MLOps and DevOps for operating an edge-based solution
- Onboard and manage fleets of edge devices at scale
- Review edge-based workloads against industry best practices

Artificial Intelligence for IoT Cookbook

Michael Roshak

ISBN: 9781838981983

- Explore various AI techniques to build smart IoT solutions from scratch
- Use machine learning and deep learning techniques to build smart voice recognition and facial detection systems
- Gain insights into IoT data using algorithms and implement them in projects
- Perform anomaly detection for time series data and other types of IoT data
- Implement embedded systems learning techniques for machine learning on small devices
- Apply pre-trained machine learning models to an edge device
- Deploy machine learning models to web apps and mobile using TensorFlow.js
- and Java

Packt is searching for authors like you

If you're interested in becoming an author for Packt, please visit `authors.packtpub.com` and apply today. We have worked with thousands of developers and tech professionals, just like you, to help them share their insight with the global tech community. You can make a general application, apply for a specific hot topic that we are recruiting an author for, or submit your own idea.

Share Your Thoughts

Now you've finished *TinyML Cookbook*, we'd love to hear your thoughts! If you purchased the book from Amazon, please click here to go straight to the Amazon review page for this book and share your feedback or leave a review on the site that you purchased it from.

Your review is important to us and the tech community and will help us make sure we're delivering excellent quality content.

Made in United States
North Haven, CT
25 March 2022